In Her Words

PATRICIA ST JOHN'S STORY

In Her Words

PATRICIA ST JOHN'S STORY

10 Publishing
a division of 10 of those.com

First published in Great Britain in 1995 by OM Publishing, an imprint of Send
the Light Ltd, under the title of *Patricia St John tells her own story*.

British Library Cataloguing in Publication Data
A record for this book is available from the British Library

ISBN: 978-1-912373-90-1

Designed and typeset by Pete Barnsley (CreativeHoot)

Printed in Denmark by Nørhaven

10Publishing, a division of 10ofthose.com
Unit C, Tomlinson Road, Leyland, Lancashire, PR25 2DY, England

Email: info@10ofthose.com
Website: www.10ofthose.com

Contents

Foreword 1

1   Family Background 9

2   Early Years at Malvern 21

3   Swiss Interlude 33

4   School Days 43

5   War Time Experiences 55

6   Arrival in Tangier 77

7   Family Joys and Sorrows 87

8   Up to the Mountains 97

9   First Contacts 107

10 Fatima and her Friends 115

11 The Children Come 127

12 Out to the Villages 141

13 Endings and Beginnings 151

14 The Hospital at Tangier 161

15 My Life at the Hospital 181

16   Nephews and Nieces 189

17   Questions People Ask 199

18   A Tribute to my Father 209

19   Rwanda.. 223

20   In the Steps of St Paul 239

21   The Grannies 259

22   Lebanon 269

23   Settling Down in England.................................. 279

24   The Refugee Camp 289

25   Global Care 301

26   Home on the Estate 311

Epilogue 325

The Pace Setter 329

Foreword

Patricia St John was one of those very rare people whose writings, life and being all make the same impact. Not only was she what one might call a poet of forgiveness, someone in the great tradition of St Luke and of all those whose stories are interwoven with the one great story of Christ himself, as in St Luke's Gospel the great parables of Jesus are. She was also, as this lovely autobiography dearly demonstrates, what I can only call a redemptive person.

Indeed, I can testify to this, since I first encountered her years ago, when someone gave one of my children a copy of *Treasures of the Snow*. At a moment when I was meant to be doing something else, and with the excuse that I might read it aloud to the children, I took the book up. I can remember now, being moved to tears by the vividness, directness and clarity of the story.

Perhaps the very heart of it comes at the moment where Annette, sitting on one side of the stove in the house in Switzerland with her grandmother on the other, asks, 'If you *hated* someone you could not ask Jesus to come in (to your life), could you?'

1

'If you hate someone,' said Grandmother, 'it just shows how badly you need to ask Him to come in. The darker the room, the more it needs the light.'

'But I couldn't stop hating Lucien,' said Annette softly, fingering her long plaits thoughtfully.

'No,' said Grandmother. 'You're quite right. None of us can stop ourselves thinking wrong thoughts, and it isn't much good trying. But Annette – when you come down in the morning and find this room dark with the shutters closed, do you say to yourself, "I must chase away the darkness and the shadows first, and then I will open the shutters and let in the sun?" Do you waste time trying to get rid of the dark?'

'Of course not!'

'Then how do you get rid of the dark?'

'Well, I pull back the shutters, of course, and then the light comes in!'

'But what happens to the dark?'

'I don't know; it just goes when the light comes!'

'That is just what happens when you ask the Lord Jesus to come in,' said Grandmother. 'He is love and when love comes in, hatred and selfishness and unkindness will give way to it, just as the darkness gives way when you let in the sunshine. But to try to chase it out alone would be like trying to chase the shadows out of a dark room. It would be a waste of time.'

It was the reality of the way in which the love of Jesus casts out all distorted feelings including fear itself, in the end, and heals relationships which the story went on so powerfully to describe. It has had the same effect that it had at that moment on me on countless readers.

But when I met personally with Patricia St John, here in Coventry, I found myself responding even more deeply to the same vivid energy and vitality, the same sense of a creative, and indeed redemptive acceptance and challenge which I had met with in the story. As one of her nephews was to say of her at her memorial service, 'A cup of tea and a sandwich with Auntie could be a celebration.'

It is for this reason that I could say to all those who have valued her stories and to many who have not yet read them, that this Autobiography will hold them and move them as much as the stories have or more, and will give them, in a new way, a sense of the same source out of which the stories well up and from which Patricia so obviously drew her own inspiration, the living grace of God in Christ.

Here is the rich soil from which her own writings sprang, including a vivid description of the time spent in Switzerland which provided the setting for *Treasures of the Snow*, itself.

From the moment when, as a twelve-year-old, Patricia, with her brother, organized a kind of 'Sunday School' in a garage for children from a nearby estate, an experience which some of them, as one testified, never forgot, through the days when as a young nurse in war-time London, she comforted air-raid victims and somehow by her touch drew back into life a young boy who was dying of meningitis, talking him through until his pulse grew stronger, as a housemother at her aunt's school, later as a missionary nurse alongside her remarkable brother in his hospital and then on her own in a little town in the mountains, she lived and communicated the forgiving and healing power of God in such an utterly human way. People always responded to her vivid sympathy and sparkle of humour, and, without at first recognizing it, to the depths of her own growing and deepening relationship with God. The stories of that response amongst ordinary village people and children in the midst of North Africa comes through the pages of this book so grippingly, as through it all Patricia and the startlingly real and endearing characters amongst whom she finds herself seem to grow together into a fuller realization of the amazing truth of forgiveness.

Here, too, is a marvellous evocation of the engaging personality of her brother and his wife and their children and of their extraordinary household and family life ('I have never been in a house where so many people of so many types and nationalities came in and out. Yet all the time I was there I never heard an irritable or impatient word. If that is Christianity, then I want it.') Patricia saw this as 'the heart and crux of all our work', the crucial quality of which was indeed forgiveness. She gives a portrait of a loving, forgiving community of people of all ages and backgrounds, of which she herself was clearly an essential part. Her parents and her wider family come to life so wonderfully through this story and she enables us to see the forces which shaped her own extraordinary personality. We recognize in them and in her grandparents some of the characters reflected in her own stories. There, too, the redemptive theme is finally worked out. The other impressive variations on that theme emerge in her descriptions of her visit to Uganda and Rwanda tracing the central experiences of the East African revival with its profound expression of repentance and grace for the account of it which she later wrote. We see also, later in her life after she had moved to Coventry, the ways in which her continuing identification with the world mission scene through the Coventry charity 'Global Care' led to her visits to the Ethiopian Refugee Camps in the Sudan as well as to Romania. Earlier, her remarkable sister, Hazel, in Beirut in the Lebanon and on a journey back from Beirut to North Africa gave her the material for other stories.

Strangely and characteristically I believe that the supreme expression of her lifelong theme was worked out in her time of, physically, greater weakness, though undiminished vitality, in the final phase of her mission in a housing estate in Coventry.

There, as she mourned the loss of her brothers and looked back at times over her life and missionary experiences with what seems to us a surprising sense of regret and sorrow, with which nonetheless many active people of that kind could surely in their later years identify, she seems to arrive at the deepest core of her message.

We saw the influence of that delightful household in Canley on fellow Christians, on visiting family, and more especially on the young children and teenagers who poured in and out from the housing estate round about and who responded to that magic touch of Patricia's as the young of all ages had always responded, all her life.

But she found herself, as she calls it, 'standing alone' and seeing 'the failures, the mistakes, the might-have-beens' and asking what had been achieved. It is there that she describes Christ coming and standing beside us and saying, 'Look with me', and reminding us of the words in Joel, 'I will restore the years that the locust has eaten' out of his ultimate redemptive power. So this astonishing record has its climax in the quite extraordinary poem which brings it to its close. This is a poem which speaks of that 'power in weakness' that final transfiguring, which we find in the gospel and experience of Christ as nowhere else.

She writes of the one who:

'Stooping very low engraves with care
His Name indelible upon our dust;
And from the ashes of our self-despair.
Kindles a flame of love and humble trust.
He seeks no second site on which to build,
But on the old foundation, stone by stone,
Cementing sad experience with grace,
Fashions a stronger temple of His own.'

Here the theme rises to a fitting greatness at the climax,

which expresses, the greatest surprise of all to me, the very same image of forgiveness as the cathedral of the city in which she had come to end her life: the image of a movement *through* the fragments and ruins of ourselves, our church and our society, *towards* that wholeness into which Christ draws us on.

This is surely the most essential message for people of our own time. It is what the gospel supremely has to offer to the world at this moment. It is the forgiveness which is all that we have. And it finds in this autobiography an expression which is all of a piece with Patricia's life and writings and person in a way which becomes a lasting testimony for us all.

Simon Barrington-Ward,
Bishop of Coventry

1

Family Background

No two love stories are ever quite the same, but I doubt if there has ever been a more unusual courtship than that of my parents. When Harry, my father, was fifteen he attended a church service. Mr Swain was also there with his curly-haired daughter of three. Mr Swain got up to speak and Ella fell off her chair and made a considerable noise about it. It was disturbing to her father's sermon, to say the least of it, and Harry, who knew the family, offered to carry her home. On the way something happened to him; he left his small charge with her mother but he did not forget her. He determined there and then that little Ella Swain was the girl for him and he would wait for her.

He waited a long time. On his father's sudden death he was forced to leave school, turn his back on the academic career he had hoped for and look for work. He became a junior bank clerk in the Westminster Bank with good prospects of advancement, and remained there for twenty years, helping to support his widowed mother.

But again, when he was nineteen, something happened. The details are not clear for he never talked about that night except to say that he met with God; but that meeting transformed him from a rather rebellious lad, thoroughly disappointed with life, into a man with a passionate purpose: to know Christ, to study his Bible and to tell others of what he had found. From then on, every spare moment was spent in learning, studying or preaching and gradually his life's ambition became to go and preach the gospel where it had never been heard before. South America was the place laid on his heart.

Meanwhile little Ella Swain was also growing and as Harry's older sister became her governess for a time, he often saw her. Her healthy, normal appearance, her quick intelligence and tremendous enjoyment of life rested and refreshed him. Unlike him, she was no ascetic; everything from the black gentleman singing love songs on the beach to the poems she learned at school, was delightful and golden. Her father, Mr Swain, was a Board of Education Inspector and believed in a broad, careful education for girls. He was also a scientist and he loved to introduce his small daughter to the wonders and beauties of the universe and she responded with eager enthusiasm – and not only to science; history and poetry captivated her, and while her future husband experienced spiritual raptures at the Communion service, she would sit entranced, reciting Tennyson's poems to herself.

Her father's work meant constant change of home so he asked Mrs St John if she would take Ella as a weekly boarder for a few months in order to enable her to finish her school year in London.

She was then twelve years old and her greatest delight was to play football in the square with the St John boys and their friends. Harry was then twenty-four years old and he loved to tease her. He would pull her plaits and nicknamed her Piglet. Four years later, owing to schooling problems she came back again to stay with the St Johns and it was then that the sixteen-year-old schoolgirl happened to attend some Bible readings intended primarily for young men, where Harry lectured on the book of Amos.

Those lectures opened her eyes. Up to that time she had revered the Bible and respected and believed her parents' teachings, but compared with botany and poetry she had found Scripture a dull subject; and as for St Paul's missionary journeys and the kings of Israel, she considered them the depths of boredom! But through Harry's exposition of the minor prophets, the Book suddenly came alive. Here, in this deep, mystic yet practical teaching, was the bread her eager, growing spirit craved for – literary beauty and strength, scholarly truth, burning challenge and devotion. She responded from the depth of her soul and night by night she would sit absorbed in the church with the young men, and whenever there was opportunity, she would accompany Harry to the different places where he lectured.

She was thrilled and fascinated and began to study her Bible, finding in it the answers to her youthful problems and a Book to live by. During the next two years Harry spent many weekends taking services in Godalming and he always stayed at her home, but although they were close friends, their relationship was quite devoid of romance. To her, he was a revered teacher, twelve years her senior, and in all their conversations they seemed to have kept strictly to the point. He never failed to record them in his diary:

'Travelled down in the train with Piglet. Much enjoyed Joshua 4 and 5 together on the journey.' 'Wrote a long letter to Piglet on Matthew 13. A very dear child, God bless her and keep her amid the vainglories of life.'

But in his heart there was growing a quiet, steady love, along with a fatherly interest in her spiritual growth. In September 1906 he and another man interviewed her as she had asked to become a communicant.

Again the old diary records his thoughts:

'Saw P. as to the Lord's Table. A tender flower. Who will shelter her through life? Never met anyone like her. God will give her a great future.'

And a little later on:

'A long think over future life; I feel drawn to Piglet if it's God's will. I think it would be truly happy.'

But he said nothing for she, as yet, had no such ideas. She had gained a scholarship to read history at Westfield College and was, as usual, throwing herself into her plans and studies with heart and soul.

He knew that this would mean a delay of at least three years; with his constant regard for her highest welfare, he did not attempt to dissuade her. He was thirty-one and longing to settle with a family.

'Great wave of homesickness and longing for a home of my own', he wrote. 'Loneliness grows as I get spiritually separated from those around me. They don't understand me or I them. Thank God there will be children left here as long as I am; my heart goes out to them – a man alone is a poor prospect. I long for a yoke-fellow to be out and out for Christ.'

So he waited patiently while she enjoyed college life to the full. She became Senior Student, and President of the Debating Society, and Miss Maynard, the Principal, planned a glorious academic career for her student when, in her third year, she was offered an assistant lectureship at Holloway. The future stretched bright before her and then, quite suddenly, Harold St John proposed to her while crossing the road in Brighton, dodging the traffic. It was a complete surprise to her, but, because for years he had been 'the best and most saintly man I knew', she accepted immediately and they announced their engagement that night at the supper table.

She had expected to become a housewife in Bayswater with a husband rising to prosperity but this too had to be abandoned. A few months later Harry astonished all who knew him by deciding to resign from the bank and go abroad as a foreign missionary. This was no sudden impulse; years before he had seen the vision but it had seemed impractical then for family reasons and he had resigned himself rather sadly to London life. The land that filled his thoughts was Mexico where his father had died. 'Mexico looms before me', he had written some five years previously. 'Go ye', Christ said, and I can do it in His Name ... but what of Mother?'

'It is easy to put Mexico away and settle in ease and comfort, but I am hungry to find myself without a plank between me and Christ ... I dare not move until I am clearer about my motives.' Then, later on, 'Mexico must go; I must settle to a London life. A bitter, bitter prospect.'

But the seed of desire had lain latent through the years and at thirty-six he was free to go, not to Mexico, but to South America. The sudden knowledge had come to him in the night and he came down in the morning absolutely certain of his call. The only words he could find to explain this revelation were the words of the hymn:

Christ the Son of God has led me
To the midnight lands;
Mine the mighty ordination
Of the pierced hands.

To the sorrow and indignation of his employers he resigned his excellent prospects and proceeded to prepare himself for the mission field. He spent a year studying homeopathic medicine and First Aid while Ella did a special nursing training at the Mildmay Mission Hospital. She and Harry were now in London together and although the off-duty hours of a nurse were few and short he managed to take her out once a fortnight. Miss Cattell, the saintly old matron, disapproved of this. She considered it fast behaviour and requested that another nurse should go with them as chaperone. Ella said she would discuss it with her fiancé which she did, but he cut the discussion short: 'Tell old Muscatels and raisins I'm not having any!', he remarked, and they set out unaccompanied to walk through the park.

They were happy days and glimpses of that courtship are preserved in old, faded letters written by Ella to her parents: 'I am working in Outpatients now. I am living with the St Johns for a few weeks and Harry is madly happy that I have come. I hid behind the chair on Wednesday night when he came home and listened to him talking. When he discovered me, he thought I had just come for the evening so I said, "I've come to stay", and he shouted, "PIGLET, will you marry me tonight?"

He is so mad! Can't eat his meals sensibly or anything but dances round me and keeps kissing me. It is very wonderful that he loves me so! "Little Heaven" is his favourite name for me at present and I do hope I shall always be it for him, but he is so much gooder than I am and so oblivious to cold and hunger and sleep.'

She was always his 'Little Heaven'. They were married in London in 1914 and a special reception had to be given afterwards for her patients and mothers and babies she had delivered during her Midwifery course. Thus, after twelve years of patient waiting, Harry was given his heart's desire:

the wife who was, in every way, the perfect complement of himself.

Together they decided quite simply that with him, the Lord's work would always come first and she never forgot that promise or questioned his long absences from home. Her practicality balanced his mysticism, for she was a born home-maker; and whether in the wilds of Brazil, or their verminous lodgings in Buenos Aires, or later in England where the old red-brick house swarmed with children, there was always a place of peace for him to return to; where he could rest from the heavy strain of the ministry or study undisturbed. She asked very little of him apart from his love, for she was essentially a giver, but for over forty years the calm, deep, selfless quality of their relationship impressed even casual visitors. No child of theirs can remember one sharp or irritable word between them and the atmosphere of that home inspired many young people to whom they opened it so freely.

But this was all far ahead; when they first arrived in Buenos Aires the man who was to meet them and make arrangements had been called up for military service and their first temporary home was one room in a house in Buenos Aires where black beetles swarmed up walls at night and they stood the legs of their camp beds in kerosene. Here, until they moved, Ella learned to housekeep in a kitchen which they shared with four Spanish families and it was a hard struggle from the beginning, but fortunately they were both endowed with a keen sense of humour and she was his sunshine and laughter. 'She's like a humming bird chained to a tortoise', he once wrote rather wistfully, but she was a practical, down-to-earth humming bird. In the next two and a half years she made friends with her neighbours, learned the language thoroughly and bore two babies, Hazel and Farnham.

Harry, in the meantime, had joined up with a group of missionaries and was preaching, teaching and riding on horseback over the mountains to visit small, scattered, sometimes almost illiterate groups of Christians; and everywhere he went he was smitten with the need for Bible-taught pastors and evangelists who would teach and build up these spiritually hungry little churches.

He and his fellow-missionary, Stewart McNair, decided to open a Bible School in the rural area of Carangola in Brazil. So Harry and Ella packed their meagre belongings and started off, with their two-year-old daughter and seven-week-old-son, on what even the optimistic Harry described as 'the most difficult journey they had ever undertaken'. They travelled for 3,500 km by boat and mule back; it was very rough and the boat was extremely crowded. Wherever they stayed they were plagued by insects. They carried their worldly possessions with them, which caused the Customs Official to remark that times had changed since the days of the early apostles who went out without purse or scrip. Harry replied patiently that the apostles did not have to travel with babies and sought to turn the conversation to higher things.

But they arrived at last and settled down into their new home, which Ella dubbed 'the House of a Thousand Fleas'.

The previous owner had kept pigs in the basement and rats visited them freely. Also, in the wet weather, the roof leaked and Hazel and Farnham slept under the kitchen table when it rained. Nevertheless it was roomy and airy and perhaps no little home has ever been more beloved or held dearer memories. Harry taught at the Bible School opposite while a crowd of eager young students worked in the fields for their keep during part of the day and studied during the rest. As for Ella, the coming of this friendly young mother into their midst was a never-ending source of interest and delight to her Brazilian sisters, as were also her few simple belongings; she unconsciously solved the problem of suitable headgear for the morning service by sending out washing to an old woman, and was mildly surprised to recognize her towels adorning the heads of the congregation. However, as the articles were all returned later in the week in clean condition, no questions were asked and the custom persisted.

They were a loving, simple, truly Christian congregation and they loved their new missionaries who quickly learned to live and speak as they did. Harry wrote of them, 'They use the Lord's name on every occasion, with great reverence, and one was not surprised to hear a voice from the kitchen saying "Here is some maize left over from dinner, Cecilia. If God so pleases you must fry it tomorrow", and the answer – "If it is the Lord's will, I will do so."'

Little Palcita, as they called Hazel, played barefoot with her Brazilian friends and spoke their language and became almost as brown as they were, but baby 'Nana' did not thrive. He became ill with a lingering dysentery, complicated by abscesses in his ears. He lay very quiet in his cot, too weak to move except to raise one skinny hand and blow small, pitiful kisses.

Careful feeding and nursing seemed of no avail and the nearest doctor was miles away and refused to come for any money. So with the simple medical knowledge they possessed the parents did what they could and prayed almost unceasingly beside the cot and the crisis passed. But he remained weak and did not seem to thrive and a third child was expected in mid-April. Gradually and reluctantly the parents were beginning to realize that the conditions in which they lived were unsuitable for delicate or new-born babies.

There was another reason too for uprooting; during the two years they had been there, Harry had been deeply impressed by the eager thirst of Christians for able, Spirit-filled teaching. There was everything to hold them in Carangola: the love of the local Christians and students, the friendship of the McNairs, the encouraging results of the work and, most of all, the company of his wife and children. But the Bible School was established and prospering under McNair's able guidance and there were other districts, other countries where no such effort had been made. Already pleading letters were reaching him to come and hold Bible Schools in British Guyana, the West Indies, and other parts of South America.

The final decision must have cost them both much. They returned to England in 1919 and Harry went back to

Brazil alone. In 1921 he left that first dear Bible School and embarked on a life of constant travel in which his wife and babies could no longer join him. Ella longed to go back to Carangola but never once did she attempt to influence him. The choice was made before God alone.

But with regard to the journey to England, there is one event that needs to be mentioned. They left in February and the storms at sea were terrible. The expected new baby nearly arrived in the Bay of Biscay, but Ella survived and reached Southampton. Lodgings for the night had been arranged at the nearby town of St Leonards. From there they planned to travel to Mrs Swain's home in Malvern where arrangements had been made for the birth, which was due in about a month's time.

But Ella had reckoned without her husband; spring was in the air and he was exuberant at being safe home in England with his family. They borrowed a large, top-heavy pram for the two older children and went for a family walk. But Harry was not used to prams, the roads around Carangola having been unsuitable for such vehicles, and at the top of a steep slope he lost control. He clung on as the pram careered to the bottom but he could not stop it capsizing and pitching his babies out onto the grass. They were shaken, but quite unhurt, but the shock had been too much for the mother at the top. She went straight back home and, somewhat to her kind landlady's confusion and astonishment, Patricia Mary was born a few hours later.

2

Early Years
at Malvern

Holmesdale, in Malvern, was a solid, three-storeyed, brick building and it housed four generations. Great Granny was bedridden but continued to exert quite an influence in the family. She was a real stickler for propriety and some of my earliest memories are of turning somersaults on the lowest bough of the apple tree, aged about five, and of hearing a sharp rat-tat on the bedroom window above. Great Granny's voice rang out loud and clear, 'Patricia, I can see your knickers.'

Granny, recently widowed at that time, was one of the great loves of my life. She was an amazingly hard worker and everyone who came in contact with her, became, for a time, the same. The second coming of the Lord was an ever-present reality to her and she lived in a constant state of readiness for departure. No letter was ever left unanswered overnight and she would sometimes exasperate us by keeping us all waiting to start on some expedition while she re-tidied her drawers. 'He may come while we are out,' she would say sweetly, 'and I wouldn't like those left behind to think that Christians had untidy drawers.'

The arrival of my mother, the most hospitable, outgoing person imaginable plus two small children and a new baby, must have upset their quiet world considerably, but Granny rose to the challenge and Great Granny loved us from her bed; and I believe we were, like most little ones, a lovable crowd. Hazel, dark and curly, was a born leader. She would sit Farnham and me down in front of her and tell us hair-raising stories. My mother once happened to overhear the dramatic ending of one of them, recounted with bated breath:

They took her to a hopsy. Nuffin' could be done.
They took her to a norsing home. Nuffin' could be done.
They took her to a convalescin'. Nuffin' could be done.

She also sang songs to us and, fascinated by the local music teacher, Miss Mary Flint, she would sit at the piano, legs dangling, and touch the keys gently. 'I'm Miss Mary Flint,' she would announce grandly and start off accompanying her own impromptu compositions.

Farnham was gentle and very loving. He would stare into space through soft brown eyes and utter deep thoughts, 'Could you put a net over me, Mummy?' he murmured dreamily as she was tucking him up one night.

'Why?' she asked.

'Because then I couldn't get any bigger. I should always

stay little and then I should never have to go away from you.' He also loved numbers. 'One, two, three, four,' he would whisper in his cot. 'And then there's nought. Isn't nought a beautiful and useful number?'

He loved to plan surprises and my mother remembers him rushing excitedly into the house after seeing a hearse, 'Mummy, Mummy!' he shouted. 'Could we get a black cab and fill it with flowers like the one in the road and all go to the station in it and meet Granny when she comes home?'

I was fat and curly and seemed to have a retentive memory, absorbing phrases and reproducing them in surprising contexts. When I was about two, my mother found me holding the rail of my cot and bouncing up and down. When asked what I thought I was doing I replied cheerfully, 'I'se always aboundin' in de work of de Lord.'

My cot stood in Granny's bedroom and early in the morning I would creep into Granny's big double bed and share her early cup of tea. She would improve the happy hour by teaching me hymns from an ancient black book and I, fascinated by the strange, picturesque vocabulary, would lap them up. There was one I specially liked about the archangel summoning the ransomed hosts. When some visitor innocently asked where Granny would be on some future date, I looked up and remarked brightly, 'She may be with the handsome hosts.'

Oliver, two and a half years younger than me, was the strong-minded, inventive member of the family and had a strange power of involving everyone in the vicinity in his projects. He was Great Granny's favourite and she loved to have him sit beside her on the bed. One day my mother left him with her looking at a picture book, but Oliver's interest at that time was focused on trains and he had other plans. My mother came back to find three bedroom chairs arranged one in front of the other with Oliver sitting on the first and Great Granny in her nightgown astride the second. Both were jigging earnestly up and down and saying 'Puff ... puff ... puff.'

He was always carried in, warm and pink from his bath, to say goodnight and he would get in beside her while she drank her nightly cup of hot milk laced with a teaspoonful of whisky. Oliver missed nothing.

One day my mother was invited to tea with a neighbour, a little old lady who was an ardent teetotaller. The tiny sandwiches and fairy cakes were brought in by a maid; tea was poured from a silver teapot. She turned to Oliver, aged two, sitting solidly on my mother's knee. 'And what would you like, my little dear? A glass of milk?'

There was something familiar about the white hair, the lace cap and the gentle voice. It brought back pleasant memories; Oliver jigged up and down. 'Whisky, whisky, whisky!' he shouted.

I was five when John was born and in keeping with the usual custom of those days, we were told nothing.

Granny never allowed anything to be mentioned before it was born and we never seemed to notice my mother's size. Farnham and I thought babies were left by God in the cistern at the top of the house and we sometimes went to look. On this occasion I was sent to stay with Great-Aunt

Emmie and I was told only that there was a toy and it was alive. I anticipated a puppy or a kitten and ran all the way home from the railway station. I burst through the door shouting, 'Where's the kitten?'

'It's not a kitten,' someone said. 'It's a baby brother.' He was lying upstairs in a basket cradle trimmed with lace. I touched the down on his head and sat down on the stairs and wept for joy. He was my baby and wherever he had come from, I adored him.

But my mother had no intention of letting us grow up as ignorant of the facts of life as she had been. We acquired a cat who, to my extreme delight, had kittens in my armpit one night as I lay asleep, and from the mess they made, there was no doubt at all where they had come from. She also bought us a couple of rabbits who had frequent babies and I remember my Grandmother's horror and outrage when I burst into the room where she was entertaining visitors and announced excitedly, 'Come quick and look! The rabbits are mating.'

And in this rather complicated household my mother brought us up to love God and to love all things beautiful and to laugh. The population of Malvern was an elderly one and, as far as I remember, we were the only children in Alexandra Road. But my mother survived and as we grew, the old neighbours came to love her and to tolerate us.

There was a kind of cold war with the Miss Wheelers next door because the rabbits, in spite of all our efforts, would sometimes nip through the railings into their garden and, on the other side were the Miss Heathcotes, and Farnham and I loved to creep up under their kitchen window in the dark and frighten their cook with our brilliant, life-like personification of tom-cats fighting. Once, to our rapture, she threw water over us, but our peals of laughter gave us away.

Elsie, our dear Elsie, reigned supreme in the kitchen. She lived in 'the Cottages at the Back' and came to us as a teenager and I think it must have been Granny who trained her to such a degree of perfection, my mother being more happy-go-lucky about domestic matters. She was a beautiful girl, artistic, creative and very clever, and she came into her own during the Second World War when she rose to a highly responsible position in the W.V.S. But for love of my mother she stayed with us for many years.

To us she was a wonderful person and we still visit her, bed-ridden in a nursing home, and she still loves to reminisce about the old days of our childhood. She remembers how Hazel, passing the kitchen on her way home from school, would always call out, 'Are you there, Elsie?' and, on being reassured, would go on upstairs. On being questioned why she did this, she replied, 'Because I'm so afraid that one day you might not be.'

But Elsie was always there and one of our greatest treats was to be invited to tea in the kitchen, when Elsie taught us songs that our parents would not have taught us:

'His mother was an earwig and his father was a whale, And I'm goin' to put a little bit of salt upon his tail,' we would trill happily, while imbibing slice after slice of hot buttered toast.

Sundays were unforgettable. In an age when many children brought up in Christian homes were put off religion for ever by the gloomy, boring Sundays, my mother made them exciting, colourful days; she needed to, because the little Brethren church where we worshipped was a bleak building furnished with rows of wooden benches and dark, chocolate coloured walls. It was devoid of flowers or instrumental music and the services, from a small child's point of view, were long and wearisome. We were led in week by week, wriggling in the unaccustomed stiffness of Sunday clothes and all sharply on the look-out for anything that might prove the least bit amusing.

How the old bench creaked under our silent mirth when a stray cat wandered down the aisle and the old man with the shaky hand tried to catch it, or when 'the cock began to crow' was accidentally rendered as 'the crow began to cock'; or when five-year-old Oliver shook with ill-concealed giggles over a reading in Colossians. 'I never knew there was a book in the Bible called Goloshes,' he whispered. Otherwise we settled down to entertain ourselves with Daniel's beasts or the last chapters of Job, which dealt with the homely subject of birds' eggs, or the less suitable stories in Judges and we probably learned more than we thought we did. From a very early age I conceived a love of those old, stately Brethren hymns, packed with such a wealth of poetry, doctrine and adoration, that has lasted for the rest of my life.

We were the only children in the congregation apart from four picturesque little sisters who appeared in the holidays in straw hats and ringlets and sat through the service like statues. We considered such virtue an insult to childhood and on Sundays we despised them and called them the 'Stayputs'; but on weekdays, without their hats, they turned out to be good sports and we welcomed their company. One grew up, many years later, to become one of my closest friends and her beautiful Cotswold home is a refuge where I often retreat.

The result of belonging to this childless congregation was that we were cherished and spoiled, especially at Christmas, far beyond our deserts. The members loved my mother, too, although she caused them some anxiety at times; they were never quite sure what she might do next: as on the day of my brother's baptism when she pranced into the sombre church like a breath of spring, her arms full of almond blossom, and insisted on decorating the baptistry. Some shook their heads at this display of worldliness, but most secretly smiled, and as we grew older we too learned to love these grave, kind old men and women and because we had comparatively few friends outside the circle of our church, their deep piety and single-minded devotion to God became our unconsciously accepted standard of adult Christianity, and for this I have often thanked God.

But, the service being over, we belted for home in high spirits, for the rest of Sunday was the most exciting day of the week. There was a special pudding and sweets after lunch and, for the little ones, tiny biscuits shaped like letters (being Sunday, you had to make a text with them) and special bricks and plasticine (being Sunday, you had to build a recognizable Bible story with them).

For the older ones there were missionary books, and how my mother, in her busy life, managed to write to so many missionaries and persuade them to produce letters, postcards, photographs, etc, is still a mystery to me; but there was always a pile of material for our fascinating scrap books and I still have mine with pictures carefully pasted and painstaking accounts of our tiny collections. The evenings were spent round the piano singing those old hymns then beloved of little children, with their bright imagery of blue skies, shepherd and lambs, or marching round the table with a percussion band to the strains of 'Onward Christian Soldiers' or some such military theme. In winter we gathered round the fire and my mother would read us a Sunday book, and Sunday books in those days were not very cheerful. They were nearly all about poor little orphans who lived in slums and died making beautiful speeches pages long. My mother would cry and we would shout with laughter at her (we were not nice children) and we would all enjoy ourselves immensely.

It was during one of those fireside readings that I had my first distinct experience of God. The story was called 'Pearl's Secret' and, as usual, it was about a little girl who died. It was a true story set in China and the child had copied out the first verse of Isaiah 43 just before she was taken ill and that night we learned the verse by heart. 'Thus saith the Lord, fear not; I have redeemed thee, I have called thee by thy name; thou art mine.'

I, probably aged about six, did not understand the word 'redeemed' but the last two phrases seemed clear and simple. I went straight up to the room where we slept and I knelt down. 'My name is Patricia,' I said, 'and if you are really calling me I want to come and be yours.'

I cannot remember any clear result except that, next morning I ran out into the garden and looked up into the hollyhocks, which were much taller than I was, and thought how exquisitely beautiful they were. It is my first memory of consciously noticing beauty and surely this was to have been expected. I had, in a new way, became God's child; I had been accepted into the realm of beauty.

When a little child turns to God in sincerity, how much does he really understand? Probably not very much; just a sense of security and belonging; probably not much more than those children understood who ran to Christ on earth and felt his hands laid on their heads. He may even forget the experience and, in later years, imagine that nothing happened.

The importance of it lies in the strength and faithfulness of the love that received him and that will be for ever drawing him back to his first resting-place. My mother believed strongly in early conversions and, like those mothers of long ago she 'brought her little children to Jesus'. In the busy home and far away in strange lands, my parents prayed for us and one of my very earliest memories is of waking up late one night and seeing my mother kneeling in the dark beside Hazel's bed. I watched surprised, for she had already prayed with us before tucking us up, but after a time she rose and knelt again by Farnham's bed. It seemed a long time before she came and knelt by me and I pretended to be asleep because I wanted to see this through. Surely she would not bother about the baby; he was far too little to understand. Yet, sure enough she moved on to the cot. I never forgot that night but I cannot explain why; perhaps I drifted off to sleep with an added sense of security; perhaps I glimpsed dimly that night the truth of the words that I discovered years later – that the angels of God's little ones do always behold the face of the Father in Heaven.

3

Swiss Interlude

People who have read *Treasures of the Snow* often ask me whether I ever actually lived in Switzerland. The answer is Yes. When I was seven years old, my mother took the unusual step in those days of transplanting us all for a year to a tiny village in the Montreux Oberland and sending us to the village school to learn French.

Great Granny died when I was five and my father, after spending some time in England, left for a year to lead Bible Schools abroad. In her childhood my mother had had a dearly-loved Swiss Nanny called Elise and over the years they had kept in touch. Elise lived in the village square at Rossinière and rented chalets. Life and chalets were cheap, the exchange was good and schooling was free. My mother decided to take the plunge and Granny came along too. It was a difficult journey; we were mostly sea-sick and at Dieppe Oliver, aged five, disappeared. His frantic mother finally located him on the roof of a very dirty train, smeared with black grease, eagerly inspecting the little lights through holes in the roof along with an equally black and greasy French porter. Oliver had seen an irresistible little ladder and followed him up and the porter was delighted to welcome him.

However, we arrived on a glorious autumn day. The chalet stood at the top of a steep hill above the river valley. Through the open window we looked across the mountainside opposite where beech trees flamed like bright torches amid the dark pines and away to the left rose higher mountains with their early sprinkling of snow. The air smelt of freshly dug earth and cows and pine sap and Elise received us like long-lost grandchildren, squeezing us lovingly against her voluminous grey apron. It was a blissful beginning to a golden year.

I had never been to school before and I was unfortunate in my teacher. Hazel and Farnham, aged nine and ten, were put in the second class with a stern, but reasonable master, but the woman who taught the first class of seven and eight-year-olds was a terror. Soon after we left, she developed serious mental illness and died in a psychiatric hospital, so she was probably severely disturbed during my year in school. She would beat screaming children unmercifully and drag them to the front of the room by the lobes of their ears (the little girl who sat next to me was permanently blue around the ears), but as far as I know, no one complained. I cannot remember whether I told my mother about these goings on or not, or whether she believed that when in Rome you did as Rome did, but in my case she left me to it.

However, I was the only foreign child in the class and, to begin with, I knew not a word of French and Mademoiselle knew not a word of English, so we held each other in slight awe. I never dared to misbehave in class and she never got further than flicking her cane in my direction and looking longingly at my ears.

Only once was there any real protest. The children would bury their heads in their arms as she went by, but one boy accidentally looked up and caught the cane full across his cheek and had to have two stitches at the local hospital. As far as I know, the parents did not object to the cut, but they objected to the hospital bill.

To our intense excitement, the police arrived in class and Mademoiselle had to pay five francs.

Being the first foreigners ever to reside in the village, we were bullied to begin with, and I remember being stoned in the ravine where I was playing and going home covered with bruises. But we gave as good as we got and it was Oliver, aged five, who finally routed the arch-bully, aged about ten. He sauntered into the chalet one afternoon and stood rather uncertainly on the threshold. After a pause he remarked, 'Mummy, I think you had better go and look at Ami. I've just killed him.'

Ami recovered, but he never attacked again. In a short time we were all good friends and chattered as easily in French as in English.

But it was the sheer beauty of the place and our freedom to enjoy it that made that year so memorable. Almost as soon as we arrived the children were given a week's holiday to collect firewood and we spent hours in the dim, pine-scented forests collecting cones and branches for the stove in the front room which would be our only source of heat during the winter. Here crimson brambles lit up the gloom and scarlet toadstools grew in clumps in gardens of emerald moss and busy squirrels leaped in the boughs overhead. To me it was a new magic world and I never wanted to go indoors ... and then the snow fell.

School started at 7 am and our chalet was much further up the hill. We would set out half asleep, Hazel and Farnham on rough wooden skis constructed from the slats of a barrel and I, muffled up to the eyes, on a tiny sledge. I suppose there were dark, rainy mornings, but in memory the moon was always shining, casting blue shadows on the snow, and the stars were always blazing. My mother would give me a kiss and a push and away I would go, steering skilfully through the great frosty silence, with an icy nose, until I met up with other little sledges and the spell was broken.

And then Christmas! Unlike our Christmas in England, this was chiefly a religious festival and presents were not a great feature. But Christmas Eve made up for everything when the whole village and those from outlying districts would arrive by the dozen on great family sleighs straight from the milking, and we would surge into the warm brightness of the church, enjoying the smell of polished wood, cowboots and pine sap, the Christmas tree having been brought straight from the forest. The school children sang their carols, the old pastor preached his sermon, and I sat and gazed at the picture above the pulpit of the Good Samaritan, kneeling on a very Swiss road beside the wounded man and a large, sympathetic St Bernard dog all ready to assist. Then, the sermon over, all the children hurried forward to receive an orange and a gingerbread bear with white icing paws and eyes. I thought mine was exquisite and decided to keep it for ever.

And then the south winds blew up the valley from the lake, the cows grew restive in the stalls and the snow began to melt. We were not allowed to climb at this time of year because of the real danger of avalanches, but we went far enough to find the soldanellas pushing through the drifts, their triumphant purple heads melting the ice by the warmth of their germination. Then came sheets of pink primulas and yellow oxlips on the bare yellow patches beside the swollen streams and then, that glorious day when parents were warned to keep small children indoors because the cows were to be let out. Through the open doors they galloped, half blind with months of dim captivity; drunk, crazy with liberty and sunshine; they leaped and cavorted and mated and tossed their tails and back legs in the air. Spring had arrived.

School holidays were unpredictable; they depended entirely on the weather. We would all arrive in the classroom one morning and the teacher would look out of the window: 'It's a good day,' she would announce. 'Go home for a week and dig potatoes; or for three days to take the cows up the mountain; or for six weeks to make the hay ... or to collect firewood.' And off we would all scamper as wild and liberated as the cows.

On long summer evenings or on Saturdays we would wander at will, sometimes as a family, sometimes on our own. We climbed the mountains that framed the valley, sometimes spending the night in the hayloft of a high chalet and tackling the final crest just before dawn. Rare Alpine flowers grew on these crests in early summer – bell gentians, sulphur or Alpine anemones, vanilla orchids and, occasionally, edelweiss. After the steep scramble we would fling ourselves down on the summit and watch snowy peak after snowy peak catch fire as the sunrise caught them. We were on top of the world and the whole of Switzerland, range upon range, seemed to lie below us.

There was just one mountain we never attempted. Mt Corjon rose up across the valley, a great rocky bastion where climbers were known to have fallen to their deaths. Farnham and I were never tired of making up stories about it: tales of frozen corpses, bottomless abysses, and haunted crevasses and nothing would have persuaded us to go further than the lower slopes. But Farnham's two best friends were sons of a mountain guide and they rushed excitedly into our house one day.

'Papa is taking us up Corjon tomorrow,' they shouted. 'He says you can come too.'

Their father was just behind them and he addressed my mother. 'We shall be roped,' he explained. 'And we shall start at 4 am. Would you like Farnham to come?'

Our mother was delighted, she knew Farnham would be perfectly safe with a mountain guide and she thought it would be a wonderful introduction to real mountaineering, but she missed the flicker of fear in the little boy's eyes. He was two years younger than his friends and Corjon was an object of terror to him. But he was a brave child and he said nothing; he went off to bed early, his rucksack packed and his nailed boots laid out ready.

But he could not sleep. Lying there in the dark, death seemed very near. He would slip and fall and then ... He wasn't quite sure. He just felt desperately lonely and afraid.

And then the patient teaching he had received all his life came alive; the forgiveness of sin, the certainty of Heaven, and everlasting life suddenly became very real, and with this reality, common sense prevailed. The One who had died to open Heaven was alive and very near to keep him safe. He slipped out of bed, knelt down and gave himself into those keeping hands and slept soundly.

I was asleep when he left but I have never forgotten his return. Late in the afternoon he burst into the house dropping with tiredness but his brown eyes were alight with happiness and his arms full of edelweiss. His joy was contagious and overflowing and I thought it was because he had climbed Corjon and I burned with envy. Not until many years later did he tell anyone that there was much more to it than that.

It was a slightly hazardous existence but my mother accepted hazards as part of our growing up process and I only once ever saw her really nervous. A little girl named Norah was staying with us while her parents were abroad and we were all shinning delightedly up a high beech tree.

I came slithering down and landed beside my mother with a bump. She was sitting with closed eyes and folded hands.

'What are you doing, Mummy?' I asked curiously. 'I'm just praying that if one of you falls it won't be Norah,' she said calmly.

Yet when the real hazards came, the angels were at hand; it was a particularly cold winter that year, and the steep slope outside our chalet, leading straight into the main road was a sheet of ice. It was so dangerous that it had been railed off by the local policeman just above our front door and we all had to go out of the back and use the gentler slope to the village.

It was very quiet in the house; we older ones were at school, my mother was in the kitchen and John, aged three, was playing happily with his toys in the front room. There was nothing outwardly to account for that urgent prompting – 'Go and see what John is doing.'

Quite silently he had opened the front door and managed to dislodge the big sledge. Just as she ran out after him, it started down the piste with John sitting astride. It was far too slippery to get any purchase with her feet so she did the only thing possible. She flung herself across the road and seized his legs. He tumbled off onto the ice and the empty sledge went over her and careered on its way. She was terribly bruised but her adventurous little son was safe.

This glorious year came to an end all too soon, though two years later we returned to the same chalet from

April till September. But that September we had to back to dull old England, to streets and houses and shoes and stockings and to schools comparatively devoid of drama and sensation, yet the memories remained; my best friend, called Annette, the little boy who broke his leg, called Dani, the unutterable beauty of the seasons and my adored white kitten called Klaus. I never quite got it all out of my system until, years later, I wrote *Treasures of the Snow*.

And there was a happy sequel, when much later on still, International Films decided to film the book. They wrote to the mayor of the town and asked if they could shoot it in its authentic surroundings. The first answer was 'No' ; a previous film crew had visited the village and done a lot of damage, trampling the hay and leaving the gates open to roaming cows.

But when they were told the name of the book and the author, the atmosphere changed. The grannies of the village remembered the laughing young mother who loved all children and had made them a Christmas party, and everyone rose to the occasion. Old costumes were produced, electrical apparatus was set up, chalets were opened up for interior scenes. Their kindness and helpfulness exceeded all expectations and the reason was made quite clear:

'We didn't want another film crew in the village,' they explained. *'Mais pour Madame St Jean – eh bien – cela c'est different!'*

4
School Days

Once we got used to it, dull old England turned out to be less dull than expected, and in any case, we were quite capable of providing our own drama. Looking back, those Malvern years seem so packed with interest and discovery that it is difficult to write about them. Memories came vividly alive when, years later, I wrote *The Tanglewoods' Secret*, *Rainbow Garden* and *The Mystery of Pheasant Cottage*: the wigwam in the woods, slow, sunny carefree hours when we wandered timelessly searching for nests, the lambing, the hop fields, the natural history museum, the animal cemetery; swimming in the river or cycling joyfully off to the other end of nowhere – these memories came tumbling out on top of each other; happy, funny, occasionally sad, and the problem was, what to discard.

My mother's sister was at this time teaching English in a small private school in Malvern and on her very meagre salary, she arranged for Hazel and me to attend as day girls, and later, as boarders. We both quickly came to love school; in those days the emotional strain of boyfriends did not start till our later teens but we compensated by hating or adoring our teachers. At ten, I adored my history mistress, the local vicar's daughter, Winifred Chapman, and she proved worthy of it. She was the perfect friend and teacher of young children and she made history a fascinating subject. But she was caught in a serious train accident and she and a young Roman Catholic priest lay trapped in the wreckage all night while others in the carriage died one by one. Boiling oil dripped on their legs, but they prayed together and talked about the Lord. He died early in the morning but she was rescued. Both her legs had to be amputated but her cheerfulness and courage were legendary. She became a pioneer in the planning of camps for disabled Girl Guides and worked tirelessly for missions until her death in 1987.

At thirteen, I adored my English teacher, Evelyn Pike, and that love endured. Her influence on me as a teenager (her love of all that was strong and beautiful in literature and nature, her hatred of all affectation and hypocrisy) was incalculable. Hundreds who were schoolgirls during the forty years she taught at Clarendon School would say the same. Retired in Bournemouth, and now in her eighties, they write to her from all over the world and visit her by the dozen. No Old Girls' Reunion was ever quite the same without her, and when I am in England I always visit her once or twice a year.

School in those early days was definitely fun. There was an intrepid elderly matron called Miss Annie who supervised our health and cured all ills with homeopathic pills. She taught us to be tough; once a week she took us to play hockey in a tufted field where we jumped over the cow pats and when the River Severn flooded she took the seniors swimming in the meadows and encouraged them to dive off a five-bar gate. Sun on snow was irresistible to her; at the first tempting gleam she would cancel lessons at once in the cause of health and climb the Beacon with us and we would arrive rosy and breathless and cluster around the toposcope, north, south, east, and west from which, in the days of the Spanish Armada, 'Twelve fair counties saw the blaze on the Malvern's lonely height.' Then, screaming with life and laughter, we would prance or roll home down the steep slopes, throwing snowballs, pushing each other over, expressing our joy as we pleased with Miss Annie, foursquare and unconcerned, puffing in the rear.

But apart from these unpredictable excitements, there were very few organized activities outside our lessons and we did not need them. Long afternoons were spent roaming the woods and fields with our special friends and talking, talking, talking, laying the foundations for those strong, steady friendships that have lasted through life. There was Marian with her tight dark plaits and sparkling brown eyes, my joyful companion in all mischief; Joan, with her long golden hair and wonderful imagination; Irene, a little older than me, who simply and gently helped me to be good. There were others too, and though separated far and wide through life, from time to time we manage to find each other again. Then the years roll away and it is as though we had never been apart; at once, we are all twelve years old again.

When I was eleven, my aunt became headmistress and Miss Annie retired and things became a little less rollicking. My aunt was an astonishing person. She became deaf in her early twenties and when told that nothing could be done to cure the condition she had, at first, panicked. But the consultant did not beat about the bush: 'You will never be any better,' he told her, 'So you can either conquer it, or let it conquer you.' Walking home that day, she decided to conquer; she acquired a hearing aid in the shape of a quite large black box and proceeded to live a normal life and to rise to the rank of a headmistress. Then stone deaf and frail in her health, she could reduce the whole school to silence with a quirk of her eyebrow. We loved and respected her at a distance and her moral and spiritual influence was strong and abiding. Her standards of education were high and the teachers she gathered round her were not only very proficient in their subjects, they were also women of like faith.

Four times a week my aunt taught Scripture to her seniors; she taught us the Bible as I have seldom heard it taught since.

I was a naughty child with a monkey-like instinct for climbing. I once climbed out of the skylight of the four-storey school building and sat triumphantly astride the roof, doing my homework. The teachers turned out in force to gaze at me and I watched them out of the corner of my eye, pretending not to see them, revelling in the fact that none of them dared call out for fear of startling me and causing me to fall. Finally, there was a calm command. 'Patricia, come down.' I slid down the tiles and in at the skylight. On another occasion when a new member of staff was taking our names I suggested that we all give ourselves flower names: May Winter, Pansy Alexander, Lily Campion were accepted, but when I stood and announced myself as 'Rhododendron St John', the game was up.

There was also the teacher who found it difficult to keep order and who would spend quite a long time standing with her back to us, writing on the board. Our classroom was on the first floor and my desk by the window. I would slip out, shin down the drainpipe and re-enter the class room with noisy, voluble apologies for being late. The poor lady was completely bewildered. Surely she had seen me in class? – then how had I got out? Or was she making a mistake? The class was delighted with these antics, but I must have been an embarrassment to Hazel, who was sensible and responsible. But the sense of family in us all was unusually strong and she stood by me loyally. When, on one occasion, I was considered too wicked to go on the school picnic, she stayed behind with me and no reproach was uttered.

But in spite of these interests and friendships, school was not the most important part of my life, for in the evening I went home, and home was a cheerful, exciting place. My mother was the most hospitable person in the world and although there was so little to share (I don't know what my father's income was, but it must have been minimal), she entertained travelling preachers, missionaries, children and anyone in distress – also any of our friends we cared to bring along were always welcome; and this more than made up for the simple meals and the second-hand clothes. One of our most frequent visitors was Maurice Wood, Farnham's friend and later Bishop of Norwich. He was a charming fellow but he had an enormous appetite. We remember him bouncing up to my mother one evening with shining eyes.

'They've opened a fish and chip shop at the Link,' he announced eagerly. 'Could we buy some?'

'Why yes,' replied my mother. 'You can go and get some for supper.'

His face fell. 'I didn't mean FOR supper,' he burst out. 'I meant AFTER supper.'

There were other friends who frequently dropped in for a meal or chat; one of the regulars was Amy of the tousled hair and smutty face and the kindest heart imaginable. Her stories held us spellbound, especially the one about her mother who suffered with the haricot veins but went with the Mothers' Union on a cherrybang trip to Weston.

'Did she enjoy herself?' asked my mother.

'Not so splendid as it might 'ave been,' answered Amy, 'seeing as how they spent five hours in a hedge, it being that damp underfoot.'

'How was that?' asked my mother.

It appeared that a neighbour, Mrs Smith, had a wig that tended to lift in a high wind. Warned to sit at the back of the coach, she refused.

'"I've paid me money and I'll sit where I like," sez she. Twenty mile out of Weston, off goes her hat and, sure enough, the wig lifted and flewed to the side of the charry. Everybody screamed right loud and the driver, seeing what he took to be a head of human hair flying under his wheel, pulled on the brakes so hard as they never got started again; sat in the ditch for five hours, they did, and another cherrybang brought them home. Not much of a trip it wasn't.'

But Amy's love of trips was by no means quenched and she longed to go abroad. She saved, coin by coin, from her tiny earnings and signed on with the Women's Institute for a day trip to Rouen in France.

'How did it go?' asked my mother eagerly next day. She had no doubt greatly aided and abetted with the preparations.

'Not much of a trip it wasn't,' replied Amy shortly. 'Went to Ruin in an 'igh wind and was sick in a basin all the way.'

Gilson was a real gentleman of the road. Quiet and courteous, he would often turn up for his lunch carrying all his worldly possessions in a small sack. We never knew where he came from or where he was going but he always gave as good as he got. He would collect the family's muddy boots and clean them or weed the garden bed and, if no job presented itself he would return later, usually after dark, with some strange gift. He once nearly startled my mother out of her wits by creeping up to her in the dusk when she was bringing in some washing from the garden, and saying in a hoarse whisper, 'Would you like a nice sheep's head or a bit of London Pride?'

And then there was Mrs Biggs who could never claim her Old Age Pension, then £2.00 a week, because she had no fixed address and could not sign her name. All she needed, she told my mother rather pitifully, was someone to 'hintercede' for her, and my mother took up the crusade with energy and determination. They would go off together in the bus, Mrs Biggs looking like an old rusty black bundle of rags, and spend hours in social service centres and lawyers' offices. In the absence of any birth certificate, fixed address or final decision as to whether her name was Hannah or Anna, the fact that they succeeded seemed miraculous. I think my mother simply wore them down. Mrs Biggs went off triumphantly to claim her first pension and spent it all on presents for us.

'All I needed,' she kept saying, 'was someone to hintercede for me.'

These and many others like them we numbered among our friends; they were part of home along with the preachers and missionaries and Granny's many relatives who came to stay. It was a busy, interesting world we lived in, but for me there was that third, almost secret world, which was perhaps the most important of all: the world of the hills and woods and changing seasons. I was a little ashamed of this because in some ways it made me different from my peers. Apart from running, athletics and swimming, I had never cared much for sport. When chosen to play in the first hockey eleven I pretended to be wildly excited but inwardly I was dismayed! Fancy wasting an autumn Saturday afternoon chasing a little ball up and down a muddy field when I could have been out in the woods where the hawthorns were turning crimson or up on the windy hills where the bracken was turning gold!

For something happened in my early teens that somehow changed the face of nature. I was at that stage a headstrong child, prone at times to tempers and sulks and I hated myself. I loved my home and my family and no child could have longed more to be helpful and admired. I remember waking, morning after morning, resolving that today at least, I would be that little ray of sunshine – only to fail miserably the first time my will was crossed. I told no one but I was gradually sinking into mystified despair; why, oh why, could I not be what I longed to be?

Then one day after some angry outburst, I went to my room and picked up that old Bible that I had almost ceased to read and I opened it at Revelation 3:20 which I must have known by heart for many years. But that day I seemed to understand the words for the first time: 'Behold, I stand at the door and knock; if any man hear my voice and open the door, I will come in.' I seemed to see, not a closed door, but a little ship, tossed out of course by winds and waves, with no hope of ever reaching the harbour. And I seemed to see Jesus standing in the storm and saying, 'If you will ask me in I will take you where you want to go.' I think I cried out aloud, 'Oh please, please come in.'

Since that first, long-ago child's grasp of Isaiah 43:1, I had never doubted that I belonged to the Lord, and this in no way negated that experience. To receive is simply a further step to belonging. It just confirmed what was once said by a well-known children's evangelist, 'A little child needs a little child's Saviour. A growing child needs a growing child's Saviour.' Over and over, in each stage of our growth he reveals himself in the very way that we need him.

I don't think there was any great outward difference. I was still prone, at times, to the traumas of a self-willed, emotional teenager, but inwardly something had changed. I knew he was there, part of me, and I knew that there was hope, and that if I remembered to call out to him, he could control me. But more than that, the world had changed. I had always loved growing things, but now it was his life springing up; I had always loved light – sunrise, clouds and sunset, but now he was that light. I was sometimes desperately miserable, yearning for some Holy Grail I had not yet glimpsed, and sometimes I was wildly, almost painfully happy. If sometimes I was difficult to live with, mine was a patient family. Their general attitude was live and let live.

For Malvern was such a beautiful place; in those good old days we were free to wander as we pleased, and I doubt if either I or my parents had ever heard the word 'rapist', so there was no fear in those quiet woods, fields and hills.

Sometimes with the whole family, sometimes with Farnham or little John, but very often alone, I would go where I longed to be. There was that thrilling moment in late February, usually early in the morning (I still recognize it) when, through the breath of a south wind, or the solitary song of a bird, you suddenly knew for certain that spring was on the way. And then – the finding of the first primrose, the cry of the first lamb, the waking early to the rapture of the dawn chorus, and spring was there at flood tide. Then the Easter holidays came and we spent long days in the Cowleigh Woods searching for nests, building wigwams, damming streams or climbing trees while the bluebells sprouted knee-deep around us and the meadows grew golden with buttercups.

Memories of early summer are linked with early mornings and late evenings, I suppose, because we were at school most of the day. We would lie in the bracken on the North Hill and watch the first larks rise or cycle joyfully down the Birchwood Road where foxgloves were springing up on the banks and wild roses jewelled the hedges and the sunset smelled of honeysuckle. In the summer holidays we would set out early and walk the whole length of the hills to Hollybush Hill and back (about sixteen miles) or swim in a muddy river, or ride the donkeys on the hills. Hungry and happy we would return with the dusk; mother was glad to see us and asked no questions. Best of all, she sometimes came with us. She could coax a bonfire into flame even in the snow and no sausages, before or since, have ever tasted so good as those she would toast over smoky wood ash.

But perhaps I loved the autumn best of all; harebells on the high chalk turf, the last glory of the trees, more beautiful in their dying than in their living; the freshness of the wind on the slopes of the Beacon, laden with the scent of russet bracken and then the cold loneliness of snow. These things were the most important part of my life, the book from which I learned the deepest lessons, and I dreaded a future that would take them from me.

So while Hazel grew naturally into young adulthood, I clung almost obsessively to my childhood. Already the questions loomed ahead. What did I intend to do when I left school? It was certainly a surprise when on reaching the Upper VI as a boarder, I found myself appointed Head Girl.

REBUKE

I have been very sinful, Lord, to-day;
Undisciplined, I walked my self-willed way.

Unloving, I had given Thee no thought,
And all day long Thy Face I had not sought.

Yet though my hardened heart would not repent,
Thou didst not strike nor threaten punishment.

But when the wasted day was nearly over
Thou led'st me to a twi-lit field of clover.

I saw the hawthorn, white as souls forgiven,
And all the sunset colours of Thy heaven.

There was no other person there to see
And so I knew that it was all for me.

He Whom I had neglected all the day,
And from whose loving Voice had turned away,

Had borne with all my failure and defeat And then had
cast His beauty at my feet!

5

War Time Experiences

By 1938 my aunt's school was increasing its numbers by leaps and bounds and she was buying up house after house in the neighbourhood for dormitory space. Each house needed a house mother so during my last year at school we moved to Applegarth, a beautiful house on the hillside overlooking the eastern plain and all the glory of sunrise. I was sad to leave the old red-brick home, but we went to see Applegarth in April; the orchard grass under the blossom was thick with cowslips and my heart was won. We kept ducks down at the end of the orchard but they became overfamiliar (my mother was never a strong disciplinarian). They were always arriving at the front door, quacking their way in single file through the house and out at the back. It wasn't very good for the carpets but I don't think anyone minded.

One has to grow up! Hazel went to Westfield College, London to study French and Farnham went to Queens' College, Cambridge for a degree in Modern Languages and after Cambridge he did his medical studies at the London Hospital. John followed him into medicine at Barts,

London. Oliver read Engineering at Cambridge and in the war was involved in aviation research, mainly on Blind Landing, and was awarded the Queen's Commendation for Valuable Services in the Air. He then did a second, external London degree in Maths. I had also decided to do medicine and I and two other girls from Clarendon had been accepted at the Royal Free Hospital to start our courses in September. But, strangely enough when the time came, the hospital said that only two entrance papers had been received. Whether the mistake lay with the hospital, the school, or the post was never discovered but I lost my place for that year. I was bitterly disappointed and was left wondering what to do.

But just at this point the war started and Clarendon (that safe little school squatting under the shelter of those great hills) was inundated with applications from anxious parents wanting to get their daughters away from the cities. Had anyone known that that most decisive weapon of the war, Radar, was being perfected at an unsuspicious-looking farmhouse, less than a mile away, they might have thought differently. But nobody did know till it was all over.

My aunt immediately bought up two new houses and started a junior school and I stayed to help, teaching seven to eleven-year-olds under the guidance of a Froebel-trained teacher who was a genius with children. I lived at home with my mother and she needed me.

The two younger boys were at boarding school but she was house mother to seven of the Clarendon girls and we had three evacuees, a little girl and her nanny and an elderly Cockney lady from the East End of London, called Rose. We were responsible for getting the whole household down into the cellar when the German planes zoomed over, wave upon wave, to the destruction of Birmingham and Coventry, but Rose would never hurry.

She would put on her dressing gown and black hat, pack her possessions and her rations, which she kept under the bed, and appear in her own time, moaning and muttering. This annoyed Granny who felt she was letting the side down, and the ensuing conversation would go something like this:

Granny (in her briskest voice): 'Rose, stop grumbling like that. Remember, the Lord is looking after us.'

Rose: 'Yes, yes, the Almighty, 'e'll do what 'e can, but that 'Itler, 'e's that artful!'

In spite of the anxiety and the news of deaths, the time at Clarendon was a happy interlude. I loved those children and would gladly have trained as a Froebel teacher, but it was not the time for ordinary training. Girls were being called up right and left. Farnham had taken his modern language degree and changed course to medicine, and John had also become a medical student. I applied to nurse at St Thomas's Hospital, London and started my training in January 1943.

The three months' theoretical training at an old manor house in Surrey went well. I made friends quickly and found the exams fairly easy and it was here away from home for the first time, that the beauty and value of what I had left behind dawned on me with a sense of shock and disbelief: a happy harmonious home, a loving, united family, a strong, consistent Christian heritage. I'd known vaguely that I was fortunate but I had accepted them as my normal, natural birthright . . . until one afternoon when my mother travelled down from Malvern to spend my half-day off with me. We walked out to a little village and had tea in a café and walked back the three or four miles to the Nurses' Home. It was a quiet day in early spring; on the folded Surrey hillsides sheep and lambs bleated to each other and in the hedges birds trilled over their nest-building, and, as on that old walk to Emmaus, when 'their eyes were opened' I suddenly recognized the depth of my parents' self-giving over the years, the daily cost of that small Paradise my mother had created for us and which I had always taken for granted. I did not try to tell her; there was no need.

We were so close on that March evening that words seemed unnecessary. Her hairstyle and clothes were plain in the extreme, her manner simple and kindly, but I remember the glowing pride with which I introduced her to my new friends and even the most sophisticated were drawn to her ('What a nice Mum you've got, Singer').

I remember, too, the sense of desolation when her taxi drove off into the dusk. On that day I think I finally grew up.

But the three months drew to a close and nothing had prepared me for the crises of the war-time wards or the speed at which we were expected to work. I was geared to the country, the seasons and the slow pace of little children and I was terrified. I seemed to run all day with a racing pulse nor was I in the least used to the fierceness of those war-time Sisters. I started with a notorious old Battle-Axe who was shortly after transferred to the Navy, when the Hon. Somebody or Other had a serious nervous breakdown under her, and her exalted parents complained. A number of my friends dropped out (only thirteen survived of the original set of twenty-four), but I galloped on, more afraid of failure or of making a mistake than I was of any Sister.

I started developing septic toes and fingers and then boils; it was almost a relief to be sent off duty, but it happened too often. Every hand was needed and the last straw was when I left a door open and a stray cat wandered in (we were working in temporary army huts) and sat on a sterile trolley.

Matron was one of England's great ladies. She had just been awarded the OBE for the evacuation of most of St Thomas's Hospital in the space of twelve hours during the Battle of Britain and she was in no mood for dealing with inefficient probationers. She had a habit of addressing the ceiling when dealing with such, which made them feel that they were not there. She glanced first at my reports and then on high. 'You've been off almost as much as on,' she remarked. 'Perhaps you are not cut out for practical nursing. You did well in your exams. Why don't you go and do something with your brains?'

It was over; I could go without any further fuss and yet, I had failed and perhaps things would never be the same again. I decided to go for a walk and think things out. I walked a long way and came to a railway station and there at the entrance in huge black letters:

Jesus said, 'Do you believe that I am able to do this?'

I stood in front of that hoarding for a very long time for I knew I was facing one of the biggest, most far-reaching decisions of my life. If I said, 'Yes, I do believe,' then I must go back to the fear and possibility of further failure and sickness.

But, if I said, 'No, I don't believe,' I was free to start a different kind of life – and yet, would I ever be able to believe in him again? I thought, probably not, and I realized very clearly that to face life without him was an impossibility; he had been there too long.

'I believe that you are able.' I accepted the offer of another chance and proved that he was able. I had no further sickness, and somehow the work seemed different. I was always anxious but no longer afraid, embracing each new experience, stretched and growing with the joy and the heartbreak: the first death of a child, the thrill of an unexpected recovery, the courage and humour of war casualties and bomb victims maimed for life, the anguished confidences whispered in the quiet night hours; the birth of a baby in a bombed tenement when I was spending my day off at the London hospital with Farnham, who was now a medical student. He was on night call and the sirens had sounded and the raid had started, but we climbed over the rubble and broken glass and arrived just in time. Never shall I forget the feeling of peace and achievement as we sat, with the world apparently exploding around us, and drank hot sweet cups of tea around the bed with that tiny new morsel of humanity cradled in his mother's arms.

And there was so much laughter too; and perhaps we would not have been able to face the tragedies around us without it. We sometimes worked in the blacked-out skeleton of the London building where a few wards had been left open for emergencies, and sometimes we were sent out to military hospitals in safer areas. Our Thomas's Sisters were fierce to such as us but they were marvellous nurses and we respected them. As we grew more responsible we often grew to love them. But when we came under the rule of less dedicated Sisters we despised them. We had become nursing snobs.

There was a night Sister at the military hospital whom we called the Purple Python (I've no idea why!). She was young and pretty and spent a major part of her off and on duty in the Officers' ward and had several times been caught behind a hut with an officer behaving in a way that our Thomas's Sisters would never have behaved, even had they had the chance! We, who were in charge of thirty-six privates each, gave her scant respect. I remember listening for her footsteps on the ramp, night after night, while my friend, Cherry, consorted with her boyfriend in the laundry.

The moment I heard her I raised the alarm; Michael shot into the ward, intent on a patient and Cherry, who was fat, doubled herself into a laundry basket and I slammed the lid down. The Purple Python never seemed very interested in the night report and I was always in a hurry to get rid of her lest Cherry should die of asphyxiation.

I displeased her once because on a quiet night, I wrote a long letter to my mother describing these carryings on and illustrated it with a rather uncomplimentary sketch of the lady. I was tired in the morning and accidentally handed it in with the night report. She returned it to me the next evening with something like a snarl, holding it at arm's length between her finger and thumb, as though it might explode.

But once, quite unintentionally, I got my own back. My only help during those rather hectic nights when the convoys of wounded were flying in, bringing the invasion casualties by the dozen, was an elderly V.A.D.

She did her routine work well till about 2 am and then she would collect spare pillows and settle down to sleep in the bath till 5 am. I was often tempted to turn the taps on but I never did. She was old and weary and much more experienced than I was, and very pleasant; and one day she really saved me.

Our ward lay directly opposite the army hut where Night Sister ate her midnight meal so it was my job to serve up her tray on the dot of twelve. Men might be dying or haemorrhaging but that tray must never be late. So my world caved in one night when I rushed into the kitchen at eleven fifty-eight and saw a black cat streaking out of the window with the Purple Python's chicken leg in its mouth.

Food was severely rationed. Even if I gave her mine, it would have to be cooked. 'Whatever shall I do?' I wailed.

'Leave it to me, ducks,' said the V.A.D. 'Just go and see what that chap wants and come back here.'

I answered the call and came hurrying back. The tray was ready with cold meat and salad tastefully arranged. I picked it up and charged for the hut opposite.

'Wherever did you get that from?' I asked gratefully on my return. 'From the pig bucket, ducks,' replied my V.A.D., 'and it's all the old cat deserves.'

So I let her sleep; I loved that ward and seldom wanted to be out of it. I had just heard that the only man I had ever wanted to marry had been killed in Crete.

There had been other possibilities but my ideal of manhood was a high one. Farnham, in my mind, stood on a shining pedestal and somehow, in my eyes, all but that one had fallen short. In none other, save in that one, had I ever sensed quite that same simple compassionate integrity and cleanness of life. But some of these casualties had worse troubles than I had.

There were those still young and strong, facing the future minus an arm or a leg with amazing courage and humour. Others had come home wounded to find another man installed in their place and sometimes that outward courage crumbled in the small hours of the night. In a very real way, their wounds healed mine.

Letters from hospital preserved by my mother bring back many memories, some funny, some sad or joyful. I am reminded of porter who lost his leg in a bomb raid.

'He got his crutches today and is leaping around the ward making vulgar jokes about everything you don't joke about in hospital, but so brave and funny. You should have seen him lying on his bed waving his stump in the air and singing at the top of his voice, "Half a leg, half a leg, half a leg onward!"'

The air-raid casualties amazed us with their resilience and resourcefulness. There was Smith, with his plans for the future: 'I was sitting by a man's bed specialling the other night. There is very little room between the beds in the army huts and if you are sitting on the locker you are almost touching the next bed. I was just separated by a screen from an old sailor and suddenly something breathed one inch from my ear and a voice whispered, "Hello, me little darlin'!" I nearly jumped out of my skin but recovered and we whispered sweet nothings through a hole in the screen. When he had told me all about the raid, I said, "Where are you going to live when you leave here?"

Smith: "In the Anderson Shelter with our Mum."

Me: "Can't you get a room anywhere?"

Smith: " 'tain't no good. Can't live away from our Mum."

Me: "Wouldn't she go with you?"

Smith: "Won't leave the rabbits; so me and our Mum we'll stop in the Anderson Shelter along of 'em."'

There was Bing whose arm had been blown off in the Blitz ... 'I wash what he can't wash himself every morning and he sits up and roars directions. " 'Ullo, me li'l lollipop! Mind 'ow yer scrub me stump! Don't yer go makin' me jump or I'll slap yer faice and yer'll fink as a big elephant 'as kicked yer ... WO HO!"'

Their attitude to raids was, on the whole, philosophic. A letter told (I read) of one summer night when a German plane full of bombs crashed quite close.

'The noise was simply terrific and all the women woke up. In I went trotting round to see if anyone was considering having hysterics and then went to fetch the beds in from the garden. The first patient I came to turned on me with genuine disappointment and indignation and wailed out, "WOT! yer ain't coming' ter fetch me in just when all the fun's startin'?"'

Another favourite was a little Cockney fellow who was desperately ill. 'He lies in bed with a drip feed and I creep round his bed dusting very softly. He suddenly opens his eyes and bellows out, in a voice that can be heard all down the ward:

"Winkles and oysters! That's what I'd like for me tea – ate a dozen oysters the day before I came in here ..." But he hates being disturbed and when I take his temperature, he roars out, "I shall tell me wife of you when she comes Sunday and I a'vise you to 'ide. My wife, she's twenty-two stone and if she starts chasing you over them beds, you won't stand a chance ..."'

It was all the sadder when the brave voice sank to a whisper and the fight to be cheerful was over. So many died as an indirect result of the bombing and blasting. Yet there was also the joy of unexpected healings ... I shall never forget Reggie, aged twelve:

'I was suddenly told to drop all, the other night, and go to another ward to special a boy who was dying of meningitis. He was absolutely worn out and cried in a weak, hopeless sort of way when they shoved needles into him. He soon became delirious and then sunk into a coma. The staff nurse tried to rouse him to take his medicine, but he just moaned and sunk back into coma. The doctor more or less said he was dying and his pulse went down to 42 with pauses when there was no pulse at all. Then he began to get cold and I felt sure it was the end; but I went on applying heat and praying and praying and I thought of Jairus's daughter (twelve years old). Staff nurse came and said I must try and rouse him and get him to drink, so I tried for about seven minutes but it seemed as though he was too far gone. Then suddenly a sort of miracle happened. Most of the night his eyes had been rolled right back and quite glazed, but just then a sort of light dawned in them and he smiled and drank his milk. It was just morning and they had drawn the blackout and all the sweet air and early morning light was stealing in. It was just as the Bible story described it, "And the spirit of the child came again to him."

'He was a bit worried by the saline apparatus at the bottom of the bed, so I talked a bit and said something about getting better and going up Hydon Fall to see the squirrels and he said in a very weak voice, "I've got a book all about birds and flowers and animals and I collect birds' eggs but I only take one when there's more than *four." So in order to keep him quiet, I talked and while the ward raged without (it was rush hour!) I sat behind the curtains and we talked about all the nests we had ever found and his pulse grew stronger and he asked for a cup of tea. Sister thinks there is no doubt that he will recover, but I suppose I shan't see him again. Mustn't it be wonderful to be a Private Nurse, and see a patient all the way through?'*

So time flew and I was working in the theatre at Chertsey when peace in Europe was announced on the radio. We were sent off early and a group of us tore to the station and caught a train to Waterloo. We pushed our way through the cheering crowds to Buckingham Palace and by an amazing feat of determination two of us climbed onto the backs of the lions on the Victoria and Albert Monument and cheered ourselves hoarse as the royal family made its last appearance of the day on the balcony of Buckingham Palace. Then by common consent we were almost carried by the crowd to Downing Street where we just happened to collide with a car driven slowly through the cheering multitude with Mr Churchill sitting cross-legged on the roof smoking a cigar – and, for me, came the unsurpassed thrill of running beside, actually touching the hem of his trousers. Then the last burst of praise to God that day in Westminster Abbey and the last late train back to Chertsey. The war in Europe was over and the boys were coming home. It was a wonderful era in which to be young and alive.

Our training time drew to a close; and as I received my coveted Nightingale Badge I acknowledged with wonder and thanksgiving that God had been abundantly able and I had been right to believe. Several ways were open to me but my beloved Granny was rapidly growing frailer and I longed to be near her. Rightly or wrongly (I have never been sure which) I decided to go home and worked for a time as a private nurse with the local GP. A little later I became house mother to the thirty youngest boarders in my aunt's school. When Granny developed pneumonia, I was able to nurse her on the premises.

The children were aged seven to eleven and I have many happy memories of those years: of supper picnics in the bluebell woods, of running under the hose in the back garden on hot summer evenings, of riotous games with the four kittens. But the first winter was the winter of deep snow and the flu epidemic and several of the children became quite ill.

There was a night of terrible gales when a ceiling came down in the middle of the night and the heating was cut off and the water in the pipes froze. Half the children in my care had parents abroad; their health and welfare was a great responsibility and the verse about the angels of young children became real and precious; and there was one night when those angels positively spread out their wings and made an impassible barrier.

We had been warned that there was a dangerous sex maniac loose in the town. He had attacked one or two girls and had even entered a nursing home disguised as a doctor and raped a girl in her bed ... he was not caught but the weeks passed, the rumours died down and were forgotten until one night at 10 pm when I was sitting in the house room, next to the front door waiting for Ruth, my assistant, to come back from a meeting at the big school. She was due any moment.

I heard the door open and called to her. Instead of a reply, I heard footsteps going upstairs. 'She'll be down in a minute,' I thought and went to put the kettle on. While I was in the kitchen I heard footsteps descending and then, to my surprise, I heard the front door close. A moment later Ruth arrived.

'Why are you going in and out?' I asked.

'I'm not,' she replied. 'I've only just arrived.'

Next morning we were bombarded by questions from children interested but not alarmed.

'Who was that man who came and stood by our beds and looked at us all in turns?' they asked.

'I thought it was Doctor Maclean,' said one. (During the epidemic our doctor often came to see a child late at night.)

'I thought it was Farnham,' said another. (Farnham was a popular and frequent visitor.)

'He had big feet,' remarked a third pointing to an enormous muddy footprint on the beige mat.

No one seemed scared and they quickly forgot, until about ten days later. One night, when the door was firmly locked, a group of children came calling to the top of the stairs.

'There's a man climbing the creeper,' they said. 'He's coming to our window.'

Ruth and I ran out. The man jumped to the ground and made off, but we pursued and caught him and a passer-by phoned the police. He was a half-witted lad and, apart from pleading for mercy, he offered little resistance. He quickly confessed to the other crimes and was imprisoned. But who had restrained him as he stood looking down on those drowsy children in the dark? Who had guarded them that night not only from harm but from fear? 'Their angels do always behold the face of my Father in Heaven.'

It was during those two years that I started to write. There were no cheap flights and easy furloughs in those days and most of the children I was looking after had said goodbye to their parents for four years. They were happy during the day but I often found a child homesick and crying at night. I wanted to make bedtime very happy, so in the winter term I would light a fire and the children would come down in their dressing gowns clasping their teddies and relax on the carpet. Ruth would serve cocoa and biscuits and I would read aloud to them.

But what to read? I longed for something comforting and reassuring but there seemed to be nothing of that kind of any literary merit. Books with a Christian message for children still dealt mostly with slums and dying orphans who made beautiful death-bed speeches which seemed anything but cheerful, so I decided to write one myself and I studied the possible ingredients. These children lacked a mother. They needed to belong and to feel special, for however much you may love thirty children, the thing you cannot easily do is to make one feel loved and special above all the others; but what was more special than that lost sheep? The shepherd left the ninety-nine and went after one. Malvern is sheep country so I set the story in our own fields and woods and hills and the characters were two children whose parents were abroad. Night after night, I worked on *The Tanglewoods' Secret*, re-living those days when Farnham and I roamed the Cowleigh woods. And I only had one idea in writing it; to read it to those children round the fire at night ...

But Hazel was home just then and her ideas have always been much wider than mine. She happened to notice a small advertisement in a Scripture Union magazine, offering a prize of a hundred pounds for the best story with a Christian message by a new writer and she gave me no peace. I objected; I could not bear the thought of my little story, so personal in many ways, being dragged into the light of publicity. I said I could not get it finished by the closing date but she overruled every objection. I finished up confined to my room, writing furiously, while Hazel brought me my meals on a tray.

She sent it off triumphantly by the last post before the deadline, and although it was not considered worth the promised hundred pounds, it came first and they paid me fifty.

I was pleased, surprised and embarrassed, but I supposed that, like most books, it would soon be forgotten and I had no thought of writing another. But then the letters began to come. The first was from a granny, telling how Robin, aged seven, had found the Good Shepherd, and then a little note from Rosemary, also seven. The letters went on coming and it slowly dawned on me that here was something that I could do for God and the thought thrilled me, because I had always been such an ordinary sort of girl. I had never really excelled at anything except swimming and high jump.

I needed a theme; my first book had been born out of my children's obvious need for security, but what next? The world was settling down after the war but, as the atrocities came to light there was so much anger and hatred. I remembered the boys coming back from the war to wives who had proved unfaithful. I remembered the faces of those who had seen the first photographic exhibition of the horrors of Belsen and the state of the bombed cities of Europe; the resentment of those who could not forgive others, the remorse of those who could not forgive themselves, and I knew that this generation of children needed, above all things, to learn the meaning of forgiveness. I went back in memory to the year we had spent in Switzerland: my little school friend, Annette; Dani, the charming five-year old who had broken his leg; my adored white kitten, and all the drama of cows and seasons and school days, and I started to write *Treasures of the Snow*.

But I accidentally left the half-finished manuscript in a public phone box and when I went back to search for it, it had gone. I was not unduly upset. I had reached that point in the story, probably well-known to all authors, when one wonders if what one is writing is really worth it; and anyhow, hasn't it all been said before? I decided that I was probably not meant to be a writer, and turned my attention to other things. But my mother was quite upset and started to pray about it, and not long after the manuscript was returned to me.

'TO WHAT PURPOSE?'
'Military Block' – 1944 (Matthew 26.8)

The body that my body made

Lies dead, and trodden in the mud, For even so hath God repaid

My tears, my travail and my blood. On alien ground they left my son,

The life I breathed, the child I bore, And men applaud a victory won,

And shout the triumphs of the war.

I hold an inquest for my son

Who fell unheeded in the strife;

His manhood's prime had scarce begun

He hardly knew the taste of life.

That energy of limb and brain,

That brave young beauty now defaced –

I question – was he born in vain?

To what strange purpose was this waste?

Straight as a sapling tree he grew

And loved the land that gave him birth; He traced her wandering streams, he knew The tender secrets of her earth.

He loved her hills, her woods, her skies,

Her changing seasons brought him joy, And thus he grew and learned to prize

The birthright of an English boy.

The thrushes called him forth at dawn

To roam some hidden forest track;

No hindering swamp or tangled thorn

Could turn that gay adventurer back.

He knew where first wild flowers were found,

Unchecked his footsteps wandered free,

An English lad, on English ground

Till twilight brought him home to me.

And so that other sons might stand

Set free, beneath an English sky, And learn to love their native land,

He thought it meet and right to die. And since all things we cherish most

Are bought and held by sacrifice, Our sons have counted not the cost,

Our sons have paid the utmost price.

So shall it be in future years

When time has swallowed up our pain, And God has wiped away our tears,

And we have found our sons again, That other little feet shall roam

Her ways, and far across the sea Young lips shall speak of her as home, Rejoicing in their liberty.

The south shall wake anew to Spring,

O'er Surrey hills the sun will rise, On Sussex downs the larks will sing

And peewits call from windy skies; The heather bells on Devon moors

Shall scent the salt Atlantic gales And tides will beat upon the shores

And echo round the coasts of Wales.

The beeches on the Cotswold Hills

Will break in tender green again, In Midland shires the daffodils

Will rustle under April rain.

By lock and willow tree and weir,

Unruffled will the Severn glide, From harvest fields shall listeners hear

The reapers sing at eventide.

And sheep will graze on pasture ground,

And cottage windows beam with light,

Where little children gather round,

And ploughmen seek their homes at night. Unguarded shall

our cities stand,

Their walls and towers of ancient stone,
And men will look upon the land
And joy to call it all their own.
Yea, all ,their own – their heritage –
Their birthright – so the charter runs;
Well ratified in every age
And sealed with blood of England's sons.
The body that my body made
Lies dead, and beaten by the rain;
This was the price that must be paid,
The sacrifice was not in vain.

6
Arrival in Tangier

From our very earliest years I think there were unseen, unrecognized forces at work in our young lives. We had arrived in England just after the end of the First World War, at a time when interest in missionary work had suddenly revived; the large well-known societies such as China Inland Mission and the Japan Evangelistic Band were in urgent need of funds to support new work and well-to-do Christian ladies would hold meetings in their spacious drawing rooms. It was quite the fashion for those gathered to come forward at the end, deeply moved by the appeal, and drop their pearl necklaces and valuable jewellery into the collecting plate.

I have no idea how my mother ever got into such a gathering for she told me about it only many years later when I myself was grown up. The details were forgotten and I only know that she sat, rather miserable, at the back and realized that she was out of place. She had nothing to give. Then almost like a voice came the thought, 'What is the most precious thing that you possess?'

'My three children,' she replied. Her heart lifted and she walked boldly to the front and offered her three babies to

God for the mission field (Oliver and John were not yet born). And that, in those days, was no small sacrifice. There were no short-termers, no easy furloughs and so many died. Yet she secretly held to her resolve. In the margin of her Bible, opposite Psalm 84, verse 3 ('Yea the sparrow hath found a house and the swallow a nest where she may lay her young, even thine altars, oh Lord of Hosts'), she had written. 'Only yielded up in the place of sacrifice are they perfectly safe.'

It must have been hard for her sometimes to believe that her gift had been accepted, for we were anything but holy children. But sometimes at school, in the evenings, my aunt read aloud from the great missionary biographies of that time – of Hudson Taylor, Miss Carmichael, the Misses Cable and French, and my father often brought lesser lights to stay. Something must have rubbed off on us for I remember a day when Farnham and I, aged about twelve and thirteen, sat dangling our legs from the top boughs of a beech tree, swaying happily in the wind, and we decided that when we grew up we would be missionaries, provided we could go together. We envisaged enormous hardships (we were probably right in those days), and thought we'd better prepare, so the Hotspot Club came into being with six members.

It was a sort of Get-together for training in athletics, and desperate deeds of courage arid self-denial, such as swimming a mile, sleeping on the floor under the bed with no bedclothes, balance walking along the high gable roof of the outside toilet, or scratching our arms and signing our names in blood.

The meetings took place behind a screen in my bedroom; it was a great squash with Joan and Peter, whose parents lived in Egypt and who spent much of the holidays with us, and we needed refreshments. We found a recipe for dandelion wine which appeared economical (dandelions were plentiful in the churchyard) and we followed it to the letter. My mother did not take it seriously and mercifully the bottles burst loudly all over the room in the middle of the night. According to my uncle, who lapped up the few drops left, we should all have been roaring drunk had we attempted a glassful each.

We also did some other practical work of our own devising. Farnham and I would go down of an evening to the local lodging house with an old violin, to sing some of our favourite hymns to the tramps and others sitting around. At other times we would go to the hop fields and gather up the children, and another 'Sunday School' took place one day each week after school in our garage for children from a nearby council estate, some of them arriving in prams.

I was thrilled a year or two ago when I went to speak at a women's meeting in the neighbourhood and an older woman came up to me and said, 'My brothers and I used to come to your garage Sunday School, and we've always remembered what you said.'

We grew up but the vision never quite faded. Hazel went to Westfield College in London and gained a degree in French and Latin. It was almost taken for granted that she would come back and work with our aunt at

Clarendon, but while doing a year of teaching training at Cambridge, she decided she would first like to teach abroad for two years. There were three possibilities but she chose Lebanon because, as a child, the words from Isaiah, 'The glory of Lebanon' had fascinated her and appealed to her imagination.

She joined the staff of the British Syrian Training College for Girls in Beirut, but after one year, the war broke out and she stayed on for another five years. She came home to teach at Clarendon from 1944–48 but then returned, and in 1950 became headmistress of the Training College, with the school attached.

She remained in Lebanon until she retired in 1981 with intervals at home; and in 1971 was awarded the MBE for her services to education in the Middle East and decorated by the President of Lebanon.

Farnham did a degree in Modern Languages at Cambridge and then felt the call of God strongly and clearly to switch over to medicine. Through a friend, he had become interested in a small Mission Hospital in Tangier, Morocco, but the war had put an end to his hopes of joining that team in the foreseeable future.

He trained at the London Hospital, surviving the Blitz, and on qualifying he was called up and expected to be sent overseas. He went for his interview.

'What had you planned to do if the war had not interrupted you?' he was asked.

'I was planning to work in a Mission Hospital in Tangier,' he replied.

He was told to leave the room. After a short time he was called back. 'We want you to go out to Tangier immediately,' said the officer in charge, 'and try to improve relationships between England and Morocco.' Farnham left as soon as possible on a convoy to Gibraltar and crossed to Tangier. He remained there for over thirty years. At the end of his time of service he was awarded the OBE for 'Improving relationships between Britain and Morocco', though actually his own overriding concern was the relationship between God and the men and women around him.

After four years of working under an older doctor, a staff crisis developed and Farnham was asked to become Medical Director and one year later in 1949, I decided to join him.

He needed me at that point. The valiant old missionary who was housekeeping for him was becoming very tired. Farnham, loving, outgoing, and friendly to all was beginning to long for a wife and too many single ladies would have been glad to have filled the role. He wrote urging me to come, my parents were willing, so, oblivious of formalities, I packed and went. It did not seem to have occurred to either of us that that was not the way to join a mission and I received a rather surprised letter from Headquarters shortly after my arrival. But I was there and there was no turning back; I remained an Associate of the mission through all my years of service.

The Nurses' Home, set high on a cliff overlooking the Straits of Gibraltar and the clean white hospital buildings seemed a Paradise on first arrival. The mimosa trees foamed golden in the garden and my bedroom seemed full of sunshine and oranges. But as far as I remember, I was sent into Outpatients next morning, which was quite an eye-opener. There always seemed to be a preponderance of cheerful, grubby little boys with a lot to say and I tried to communicate with my hands and eyebrows, there being no immediate, organized language study for hospital workers in those days; nor had the term 'culture shock' been invented, but no doubt we suffered from it. Sometimes, at the end of a hot, exhausting day, I would go up to the flat roof and gaze out over the dark Mediterranean to the far lights of Spain and wonder!

I had not been prepared for the waves of homesickness, nor for the discovery that missionaries (myself included) and converts were not always as saintly as I had naively imagined. There were times when I was tempted to question whether it was all worth it.

I vividly remember one incident that steadied my sense of values at a time when I needed the reminder. It was a stifling afternoon and in two small single wards downstairs, two expatriate men were dying. I was specialling them, going from one to another.

In one room lay an Englishman and his wife sat beside him; in a quiet dispassionate voice she told me what had happened. Her husband was a trainer of Arab racing steeds and they lived in a palatial house up the mountain surrounded by beauty and luxury. Cocktail parties were held in his house night after night and the wealthy, expatriate population flocked to his home. All was going well, until, one day, he complained of a violent headache and went to see his doctor. He was warned that his blood pressure was exceedingly high and told, among other things, to stop drinking alcohol.

A few nights later he woke in a panic. 'I can't lie here thinking about death,' he said to his wife. 'I must take something to help me forget.' He went downstairs, drank heavily, and had a stroke. That afternoon he died without regaining consciousness, and as I stood looking down on him, I felt acutely sad and depressed; so much in the years behind – all that life could give of riches and pleasure; but for the future he had felt only fear and hopelessness, so what had it all amounted to?

But one stride across the passage in another small room lay Don Samuel from Spain. We were still in that era of history when a Protestant could be imprisoned for his faith, and Don Samuel had spent months in a cell. On his release he had joined his wife and children in Tangier and it had been a joyful reunion with the hope of a happy united family life. But within a few weeks it became clear that the poor diet and harsh conditions had taken their toll; he was already suffering from advanced cancer of the stomach and that afternoon he too lay dying, with his wife and family sitting beside him.

But just as he seemed to be drawing his last breath, a look of incredible joy dawned on his face. 'Fetch the doctor,' he whispered, 'I want him to see what I see!' I ran to Outpatients and Farnham ran back with me. We were just in time; Don Samuel was pointing to the ceiling. 'Look! Look!' he was saying in Spanish. 'You must see it! To the light, to the light! I'm going to Jesus – oh, can't you see?' ... he was gone, and we were left staring at the whitewashed ceiling, but some glory lingered in the quiet room and the message hung in the air: so little in the years behind; so much of hardship and persecution and pain, but ahead, a beauty and fulfilment that we could not even begin to imagine, and wasn't that really what life was all about?

Yet in my own mind I was still unsure; I had read many missionary biographies and their heroes and heroines always seemed to have a 'call' – some special verse, some definite word from God or some clear light, whereas, as far as I could see, I had simply done the obvious next thing. I had prayed about it and truly desired to do God's will, but there had been no special confirmation and the thought nagged me. Had God really called me and sent me or had it just been a case of doing my own thing?

And then something happened. Almost a year previously a young man had been carried down from a little town in the mountains with acute osteomyelitis and at first Farnham had thought that the leg must be amputated. But after four operations Mohamed was recovering and now it was almost time to go home. We were free in those days to hold ward services and Mohamed had understood a great deal. His home was in a small town in the mountains some two hours away by car, and it was agreed that we should take him home.

It was June and very hot. We set out at about five am, and were soon bumping along the winding mountain road with a deep valley on our left and great rocky peaks rising ahead. Poppies flamed along the road side and the air smelt of camphor bushes. We stopped high in the hills and breakfasted in the shade of an olive tree and here Mohamed began to talk.

'Why do we have to come all that way,' he said suddenly, 'for healing and to hear this message? Why doesn't one of you come up and live amongst us? There are houses to be had in our town.'

Farnham and Mohamed opened the New Testament and were soon absorbed in that same message but I sat a little apart and turned to my normal daily reading. I was studying the book of Ezekiel and I happened to have reached chapter 34: 'My sheep wandered on the mountains on every high hill and none did search or seek after them.'

I looked round at the landscape; sun-kissed hill beyond hill, misty valley beyond valley still bathed in the shadows of early morning, and nestled in the folds I could see the blue-green of the prickly pear enclosures each guarding a tiny village – and none did search or seek after them. Suddenly, undramatically, but very surely I knew that this was what I had been waiting for – the unexpected turning in the path and the promised voice, 'This is the way, walk ye in it.'

He never promised us a voice when the path lay clear and straight ahead. He gives us common sense and normal human indications and the quiet sense of his guidance. But when we come to the fork in the road then the promise rings true: 'Thine ears shall hear a voice behind thee saying, "This is the way, walk ye in it, when ye turn to the right hand or to the left."' At the turning he will speak so clear and we wonder and hesitate. Then surely it is safe to go ahead with the prayer of faith: 'I want to do your will and I think that this is right. If I'm making a mistake, please put out your hand and stop me.'

And is it possible that he will not answer that prayer? If we were leading a loved child along a road – a child who wanted to stay close to us and had mistakenly turned aside, is it conceivable that we would not call to him or reach out and draw him back? And surely he, who is the Father of fatherhood and the source of motherhood, will do no less?

I did not say anything at the time for there were problems. The hospital was short of nurses and I was housekeeping for Farnham, and housekeeping for Farnham meant coping with a never-ending stream of visitors: tribal patients from the mountains vaguely needing accommodation, mothers with sick babies who could not wait till next day, bright lads who came for teaching, missionaries travelling to the south, just calling in for a chat or leisurely tourists who wanted to look round the hospital. Sometimes a number would converge at once, producing what a young Swiss helper once described as *'une rude salade'*. But Farnham, however weary, was always welcoming, always apparently pleased to see them – the only problem being that he was so often not there . . .

7

Family Joys and Sorrows

There was no doubt that Farnham needed a wife; we prayed about it as we travelled home in the summer of 1950 to be present at John's wedding. He had got engaged while doing a house job at the Mildmay Mission Hospital to Gwynne Morton who was a nurse there. She became my much loved sister-in-law here in Coventry where John was later in practice, the very successful mother of seven children, their home a lovely welcoming base to which we could always return from overseas.

Oliver was the first to be married in 1945 to Eileen Morris, also a wonderful life-long companion who, along with Oliver and their three boys was soon to join enthusiastically in work with a live Church Youth Group in the early days of the Duke of Edinburgh's Scheme which made full use of their interest in climbing, skiing and mountaineering.

But all that was far ahead as we arrived back joyfully for a month at home.

Clarendon, my aunt's school, had moved to North Wales, to a most impressive building called Kinmel Hall, bought by Sir John Laing and rented for the purposes of a Christian School. My parents had moved with the school and lived in a large flat overlooking the Venetian gardens with their shaped trees, rosebeds and water lily pond. Seven little girls slept in the flat and my mother spoilt them outrageously; there was enormous competition to sleep at Mrs St John's.

We spent the whole month with our parents and had a wonderful holiday, climbing the Snowdon range and exploring the beautiful Welsh countryside, but nothing transpired that suggested romance until exactly one week before we were due to return to North Africa. The Overseas Missionary Fellowship (then the China Inland Mission) was to hold its annual conference in the school and Farnham's old college friend, Leith Samuel, was expected. Hearing that he had just arrived, Farnham ran down to the front door to meet him.

Leith and his wife alighted and Farnham greeted them and then turned to be introduced to the girl who got out of the back of the car – a tall girl with a coronet of brown hair round her head and freckles on her nose. 'Let me introduce you to Janet Thompson, a medical student,' said Leith. They shook hands and Farnham knew at once. He came upstairs with a slightly bemused expression. Fortunately, I knew the girl slightly as I had been at school with her, but as she was five years younger than me, our paths had not crossed much.

Janet's parents, who had been missionaries in China, were also attending the conference which slightly complicated matters but, on the strength of our old acquaintance, we arranged a picnic breakfast on the beach and I invited her. We swam in a cold Welsh sea and fried eggs; they looked at each other through the smoke of a bonfire and she accepted a ride home on the pillion of his new motorcycle. After that things moved fast and they became engaged five days later on the heathery slopes of Mount Tryfan, just two days before we were due to leave. It proved to be one of those marriages made in Heaven; God's good and perfect gift to one who had been content to wait.

John's wedding took place on the Saturday at Clarendon. Janet attended, and it could almost have been a double celebration, but her parents, startled at the unseemly speed of the courtship, asked her not to make her engagement public until after her final exams, which would take place about three months later. So next morning, when Farnham and I set off to North Africa on the motorbike, they said goodbye behind some bushes at the bottom of the school drive. They had known each other for a week *and* they would not meet again for six months.

The journey to North Africa took us eight days, and it was one of the most glorious weeks I can ever remember.

The motorbike bounced along to the sound of our singing – sentimental love songs or happy hymns of praise, for Farnham had discovered very suddenly what it meant to be in love. He had been given his heart's desire, and I think I shared a little of his ecstasy, and it partly overcame the sorrow of parting from my parents. The joy of it is still wafted back to me by the breath of new-mown hay or the scent of a beanfield. I can no longer give a lucid account of that journey, but certain moments stand out, vivid and golden. I remember the very first morning after we left. We had intended to reach Dover the evening before and cross on the night ferry. But Farnham decided to stop off and visit a friend, Maurice Wood, to share his news, and of course we missed the boat. It didn't matter. In those days we could just as well cross in the morning, so we padlocked the bike by the side of the road and climbed the bank. We had a sleeping bag and a small cushion apiece, strapped to the panniers of the saddle, and we made ourselves comfortable and fell asleep.

I woke early in the morning to the sound of voices. It was only half light and I was alone. I peered over the top and saw my brother fast asleep at the bottom of the bank, his legs stretched out in front of him, while a couple of puzzled policeman surveyed him. 'Hello,' I said. 'Is anything wrong?' 'Nothing yet,' replied one of them solemnly, 'but if you don't wake your hubby and tell him to take his legs off the London to Dover Road, he'll get them cut off.'

Our luggage was minimal – a saucepan, a small frying pan, eating utensils and a water bottle, a change of clothing, a big bag of rice, and a Bible – nothing else as far as I remember. We bought bread and a large heavy sausage at Calais to slice in the rice, and although it smelt rather strange after a day or two, we persevered. I remember the long, straight French roads, lined with poplars, flanked by fields of sunflowers and patches of scarlet poppies, sometimes running beside great rivers where we stopped to swim. And then the unforgettable sleepy smell of pines as we drove through the forests of Les Landes.

I remember swaying giddily, only just winning the struggle to keep awake. There were no crash helmets then, and I knew that a fall would have meant almost certain death, but we were not afraid. We were far too joyfully alive to consider the possibility.

I remember the smell of paraffin and the satisfying bulk of rice and old sausage eaten at sunset, after which we would snuggle down in our sleeping bags behind some friendly hedge and sleep soundly. I remember crossing the border into Spain and zooming upwards round hairpin bends into the cool heights of the Pyrenees, and a little green valley by the side of the road with a mountain stream gurgling through the grass. Buttercups, forget-me-nots and grass of Parnassus grew beside the water, where we picnicked and washed and drank deeply and I seldom read the words, 'He makes me lie down in green pastures and leads me beside the still waters' without thinking of that place. There were rainstorms, too, in those high alps. One night we were drenched, sleeping out of doors was impossible, so we stayed in a wonderfully cheap village inn. I suppose I looked incredibly young and innocent, but the innkeeper's wife insisted on coming to my room and tucking me up, and kissing me goodnight with a string of Spanish endearments mostly ending in 'issima'.

From the cool heights of the Pyrenees we zigzagged down to the scorching plains north of Madrid to the strange red rocks and barren fields, where the crops had all been harvested. For the next three days we changed our habits. We rose about four in the morning in the great pre-dawn silence, lit our primus, gulped down scalding cups of tea and set off chewing our bread and sausage. Darkness paled to pearl grey, shot with fire in the east as the sun rose and the cocks crowed and the world woke.

By eleven o'clock we seemed to be riding through a curtain of fire. We would seek some shade in a eucalyptus grove or under an overhanging rock and stretch out to sleep, and once we shared the shelter of a stone wall with a family of Spanish gypsies.

I slept long and deeply, and woke to find them all grouped eagerly round Farnham; he was fluent in Spanish, and was reading them the story of the prodigal son. At four o'clock we would set out again on our southward journey, and the wall of fire gave way to the soft coolness of evening and the amazing pageant of sunset over the burnt, desolate landscape. Then on through the night beneath those fierce southern stars, singing to keep ourselves awake, till about eleven o'clock when we would snuggle down in some ditch and sleep again.

I remember the flat summit of the Sierra with its bracing mountain air, and the breathtaking moment when we looked down and saw the jewelled blue of the Mediterranean lying thousands of feet below, with Gibraltar crouching like a fierce old British lion to our left, while far away but very clear, lay the coast of North Africa. All that late afternoon I clung frantically to Farnham's back as he zoomed round those hairpin curves that led to the coast, but we slept luxuriously that night on the beach, after soaking off the dust and dirt and soreness of the journey in the warm sea. We camped near a fisherman's hut, and when we woke early in the morning a group of perfectly naked, smiling little children brought us a great platter of oranges and olives. Goodness and mercy had followed us and protected us all the way. As we crossed in the ferry to Tangier, the dolphins leapt and flashed in the sunlight. We were starting a new era.

A new nurse had come to the hospital and in the spring Farnham was going back to England to do further surgical training, work for his fellowship and marry Janet. The way seemed open for me to move up to the town in the mountains.

We went up together on the motorbike to spy out the land. The rains had fallen and we bumped up the steep road. It was hard to believe that we were within a few miles of the little town, for there was nothing to be seen but rocks and stones, covered with that thin veil of green that appears so swiftly when the first rains fall on the ground. But we drove to the crest of the hill and there just below us lay the town, sheltered between two arms of rock and set in emerald, for above the town towers a great cliff, and out of the cleft gushes a flood of clear, ice-cold water that never dries up, and the drought cannot touch it, for its source is hidden deep inside the mountain. Part of it tumbles away in a foaming stream and part of it is carried by pipes to the town, so that there were splashing fountains in nearly every street. But long before you see the houses you see the watered fields and the green, green gardens. Here in this sheltered valley the parched land has become a pool and the thirsty land streams of water.

Mohamed met us and took us to his home, where the family expressed their welcome by one stew after another – fish stew, mutton stew with vegetables, chicken stew with olives. When we were almost torpid, we set out on a house-hunting expedition, and one of them seemed suitable. It was small, but it had windows and a roof from which I could see the winding road that led eastward into higher mountains and the autumn gold in the valley below. It looked down into the village inn, where the town donkeys lodged, joined at night by the very poor and homeless, who could sleep on the straw for about three farthings. It is supposed to be like the place where Mary laid her baby, and that pleased me and compensated for the probability of there being a very strong smell of donkeys in the hot weather.

We arranged to take the house in three months' time and drove off early next morning. As we left, Mohamed, as a parting present, thrust three live hens into my arms, and their struggles and squawks added interest to our departure. It is not easy to carry three live hens on the pillion of a motorbike, but they settled down quite soon, and as I turned to look at the valley, beautiful with daybreak, the early morning shadows long on the hills, I knew for certain that I should come back. The lines had fallen unto me in a pleasant place. Yea, I had a goodly heritage.

The three months passed quickly. Christmas at the hospital was a happy time, and it seemed strange to think of leaving it all. Then on February 11th the telegram came late one night. My dear grandmother had died at her home in North Wales.

It was my first personal contact with death in the family, and I had often wondered what it felt like to know that someone who had always been there through life was there no longer. When work was over next day, I ran to the top of the cliffs overlooking the Straits of Gibraltar and tried to adjust to my loss. But no sense of loss came; only an amazing, glad sense of proximity and companionship. I felt almost as though I could stretch out my hand and touch her. Separation of distance and the veil of old age and a wandering mind were all done away with for ever. We had been close in spirit before, but now we were united. And I realized the meaning of those words, 'the whole family in heaven and on earth ... that neither life nor death can separate us from the love ...' She was in Heaven, a place to which I was allowed constant access. Never had there been less sense of loss, never more consciousness of a comforting human presence, strong and brave and bright as she had been before her mind clouded. Just as I was anticipating leaving all European companionship came that close sense of that dear presence. The comfort was greater than the sorrow.

8

up to the Mountains

In the end, when the time came for me to say goodbye to Farnham and take up residence in the mountain town, I did not go alone. Evelyn Pike, my former English teacher and life-long friend, travelled out and came with me. We arrived on a March evening and slept at the little Spanish hotel. My house above the inn had been taken by someone else, and we had to start our house-hunting all over again. It was rather a blow, but the words, 'God having provided some better thing', came to me clearly, and we spent the first day looking for it.

Mohamed was full of enthusiasm. I think that we saw some four or five houses in all. The first was depressing. It was down a sort of drain and had no windows whatever. The numerous Spanish population who lived on either side of the drain were loud in their welcome, but I thought not. We went to look at a second house, but the key had been lost, so we gazed through the keyhole into a black void. Mohamed thought we were being a little hard to please. He obviously considered my liking for windows unnatural. The third house was too tiny, the fourth too expensive. The fifth appeared to be the better thing that God had provided, and we found it in the evening.

We climbed a narrow staircase which led to two monastic little rooms with uneven, whitewashed walls and barred windows, but the stairway led to the roof. The moment I saw the view from the parapet, I decided to take the house. It overlooked the market place, and by the sunset light the sellers were packing up their stalls and loading their donkeys. Two storks sailed overhead, each alighting on one leg on the ivied ramparts of an old fort. Just beyond it the little houses rose up, one behind the other, tier upon tier of orange lichened roofs against the rock of the mountain. The colours in that last light were indescribable; vivid oranges, pinks, soft browns and greys, while here and there a gleaming white mosque towered up and cast its long shadow over the town.

Evelyn (who was staying for two or three weeks) and I collected some second-hand mattresses, a low round table and a cupboard, and settled in fairly comfortably. But we soon discovered that there were certain disadvantages. In heavy rain, the water poured down the roof stairs and twice coming in from visits in those first weeks in that wet March, I was met by my saucepan floating across the floor like a boat, and I spent hours up to my ankles coping with the floods. Cats tended to fall down the open area of the roof and die on my premises while I was away. Bugs pattered from the rafters of the attic, and I went to buy insect powder. There were several customers in the shop, and they were most sympathetic and eager to show me the whole collection. 'This is for the bugs on the roof,' they said, 'this for the bugs in your bed, and this for the ones on your body and clothes.' They seemed surprised that I failed to buy the lot, and I later discovered I should have done so.

But Evelyn had to leave, and the first night alone in that little whitewashed house was one I shall always remember. My door was strong and well bolted, but I dreaded being left to sleep alone in the middle of this Muslim city. I got ready for bed and opened *Daily Light*, and the words might have been written in gold: 'He that keepeth thee will not slumber. Lest any hurt it I will keep it night and day.' Suddenly there was no fear, nor was there ever any unfriendly disturbance by night. The promise held across the years.

The first two or three months were lonely. Farnham had gone to England and visitors were scarce. Apart from Mohamed's family and one other household, whose daughter had been in the hospital, the town was suspicious. Except for a few Spanish women married to Moroccans, no foreigner had ever before lived inside the city walls, although there was a flourishing Spanish colony outside. I studied Arabic hour after hour and tried to talk it to Mohamed's mother while she taught me to tease sheep's wool, or to Zohra while she got the distilled scent from roses and orange blossom. But I was not really unhappy. The mountains and valleys outside the town foamed with blossom and irises, poppies and marigolds. Mallow and crimson dwarf gladioli made bright carpets on the fields.

I started to re-read the old missionary biographies, among them Padgett Wilkes of Japan, and one sentence struck me very forcibly: 'Power is a dangerous weapon. Our God is a jealous God. He will not entrust it to anyone who is not wholly sanctified.'

It was a time of learning and growing and discovering what the simple presence of Jesus could mean when there was no other companionship and no one else who could talk English. Also somewhere during those months, the lost manuscript of *Treasures of the Snow* turned up. It had been found in a phone box and miraculously recognized and returned through several stages to my mother. I finished writing it, reliving in thought that idyllic year in Switzerland with all its happy memories. So on the whole the promise again held true: 'The solitary place shall be glad for them.'

Just outside the town lived Miss Vokes and Dyllis from the Emmanuel Mission. To them I sped joyfully on Sunday for our dinner of fried eggs and chips. We did not meet during the week at first, for we did not wish the town to think of us as in league, but that Sunday fellowship was some of the sweetest I had ever known. Miss Vokes was a choir leader and taught us cantatas and anthems, conducting the two of us in her living room as though we had been at least fifty strong in a music hall. I counted the days till Sunday.

Then in the evenings the little boys started coming. Many of them had been turned out of their homes because there was not enough food to feed the increasing family (by ten years old they were considered capable of scrounging for themselves). They roamed the town in bands, begging or stealing, and some went home at night, but some who came from villages slept on the steps of the mosque. One came to the door begging bread, and I gave him some. The word went round, and next night at dusk I had six or seven eager, bright-eyed little boys knocking on the door. They assured me they were all orphans, homeless and starving, and I let them in and gave them bread and treacle. Never having tasted treacle before, they were ecstatic. They crouched round the low table, licking all ten fingers, and gazed round the room in search of something to steal.

I told them the story of the Good Shepherd in faltering Arabic and showed them a picture. They laughed delightedly and when they left they blessed my ancestors and wished me peace. A spoon and a piece of soap had disappeared, but the boys were so shocked and offended when I mentioned this to them on the next evening that I finished up feeling almost ashamed of myself. Night after night they came, and I learned how to make bean mush and spiced lentils and to look after my property. As soon as they had finished eating and licked their fingers clean, they would look up with angelic countenances and ask for a story.

But the teachers in the mosque were getting suspicious. The boys were questioned and forbidden to come, and I wondered what had happened. They stayed away for three or four nights, but they missed their supper and decided to risk it. There was a sharp knock on the door one night, and

I opened to find an apparently empty street. Then I was nearly bowled over by a rush of flying little bodies hurling themselves from hidden doorways into my passage, and the door was bolted behind them. They grinned up at me and supped on bread and black olives, because I had not been expecting them, but they all seemed delighted to be back, and I, unaware of what had happened, was delighted to see them. It was quite dark when they left.

But as soon as they reached the street, pandemonium broke out. Men were lying in wait with great sticks, and the children who failed to dodge and escape were cruelly beaten. Return was impossible, so they decided to regain the favour of the other side by shouting names at me and throwing stones. A dead cat appeared on the doorstep and our happy evenings seemed all forgotten.

Except by one. It was nearly midnight a few nights later when I heard a knock on the door. I got up and looked out of the window and saw a small boy standing under the street lamp, beckoning urgently. I went down and opened. He pushed in past me and bolted the door behind me, and then he kissed my hand, bowed to the picture on the wall of Jesus blessing the children, led me upstairs and set us both down. His expression was joyful and triumphant. Tonight he was alone and he did not need to pretend to be a pitiful orphan or a ripe saint. He was just a happy little boy who had found a friend.

'The others won't come again,' he announced, 'but I will come every night. Now tell me a story and give me some bread.'

I tried to discourage him, but he was immune to discouragement. Night after night he turned up, usually waking me from sleep. Then one evening he arrived, obviously excited, and invited me to go with him next day and visit his mother.

'Your mother!' I exclaimed. 'I thought you were an orphan.'

He waved that remark aside as though unworthy of notice and promised to fetch me at two o'clock the next day.

He arrived on the dot and set off ahead of me. It would not do to be seen consorting publicly, so I followed fast up the narrow cobbled streets to the poorer part of the town. He stepped inside a door and I went in after him, just in time to see legs disappearing up a rickety ladder leading to a loft. Nimble as a squirrel, he ascended, and I started to climb clumsily and anxiously. I heard him announce, 'She's come.'

Gasps, giggles and general panic. I realized that none of them had believed him or expected for a moment that I would come. And as my strange pale face and blonde hair appeared at floor level, there was a second's stunned silence and then peals of laughter. I laughed too and climbed into the loft and sat down. There was nothing else to do.

Hamid was distinctly put out. This was not what he had planned. At ten years old he had a right to order his womenfolk about, and he commanded his mother to make tea. She hastened to obey him and blew up the charcoals, swallowing down her mirth. Then frantic searching, whispering and arguing as they realized that there was no sugar. However, it was clear from the oily substance in the clay bowl that they had been just about to have their dinner, so I suggested we ate together. They hesitated. Did Europeans eat bean mush? Hamid assured them that I did, and we gathered round with a piece of bread apiece and scooped from the central bowl. I was hungry and enjoyed it, for such is their skill with herbs and spices that even the food of the very poor tastes delicious. And soon their shyness melted and they plied me with questions. How often did I wash? How much rent did I pay? How old was I? Why was I not married? We were getting on quite well when Hamid intervened. 'Too much noise!' he said. 'Now she will tell you a story, the one about the lost sheep.'

Inquisitive neighbours were climbing the ladder, and the loft was beginning to fill up. I did my best, but women are not as sharp-witted as little boys, and they were quite unused to my accent. All I could see on their faces was open amusement or blank bewilderment. They simply did not know what I was talking about. I faltered miserably and Hamid came to the rescue at once. He rose to his full small height.

'See,' he said, 'I will tell you the story of the shepherd who had a hundred sheep and lost one.' (He stooped, absorbed in counting an imaginary flock.) 'So he took his lantern and went to the mountain and sought and sought.' (He was roaming the room, shading his eyes, lifting his imaginary lantern high in the air.) 'Listen, he hears it cry.' (He crouched in a corner, bleating pitifully.) 'The wolf is just about to eat it, but the shepherd is not afraid. He rescues it and lays it on his shoulders rejoicing.'

The little crowd watched fascinated and silent as Hamid toiled the length of the attic, his shoulders bowed beneath his burden, his hands raised to hold his sheep.

Near the doorway he paused, lifting his head, and began beckoning and calling, 'Come, my friends; come, my neighbours, I have found my lost sheep. Let us rejoice and have a great feast.' The audience were riveted. As he finished they laughed and applauded. But Hamid turned to me. 'Now tell them what it means,' he said.

I tried, falteringly enough, but their interest had waned with the end of the story. No one was listening unless it was Hamid's sister's little girl, Tamoo, who peeped out from behind her mother and smiled shyly. I smiled back, and had a strange feeling that here was some new beginning.

'Bring that little girl to me,' I said on impulse. 'I will teach her to read and knit.' I said goodbye and went cautiously out backwards. The ladder was really most perilous. But I walked home thinking long thoughts into the future. One day men, women and children would turn to Christ through the vivid, gifted drama and preaching of their own people. It was our job to find them and train them.

9

First Contacts

There was a great need for medical work in the little town. A Spanish doctor came up three times a week, but most of the men in those days would not allow their wives to unveil, let alone to undress in front of a foreign man, so there was virtually no treatment for women and children. I had hoped I could use my nursing knowledge to help them, but weeks went by and I was still looked on with hostility and suspicion by the town in general.

'My times are in thy hands' is one of my favourite verses. Looking back now, I can see that I needed those quiet months to study the language far more thoroughly before I started to make contacts with people. I had gone through the fat Arabic grammar and could at least make myself intelligible on simple subjects when at last the break came. The wife of a wealthy citizen had had her first baby boy and an enormous feast was planned for the seventh day. The sheep had been killed, the bread baked, but the baby sickened and refused to feed. The guests gathered quickly, for it was important to get the feasting over before the baby died, if it was going to do so, and they arrived in large numbers. But the young mother yearned for her son to live. She whispered to the servant girl, 'I've heard there is an English nurse in the town. Run and fetch her.'

I followed the girl to the large house. In that windowless room the air was thick and steaming with the fumes of food, and the baby was gasping for breath. I thought it had pneumonia, but being too weak and breathless to suck, its immediate problem was dehydration. I did what anyone with any comon sense would have done; boiled up a mug and spoon on the glowing charcoal and expressed the breast milk, feeding the child drop by drop with the spoon and adding tiny doses of sulphathiazol. And as I did so, I prayed.

There was dead silence in the room. The boiling of the utensils was to them almost a kind of witchcraft. 'Baz!' they exclaimed. 'She boiled the spoon!' They gathered round to watch, and God had mercy, for the baby thrived and patients began to come to my door until I could no longer cope with them. Many of them in any case needed a doctor. I started a dispensary three times a week and made up a few standard bottles of medicines and lotions from raw materials ordered from England, and procured by way of the hospital in Tangier a supply of tablets, worm powders etc. I also bought a few antibiotics, precious as gold because they were still so rare and expensive. I had a variety of patients; tough village men who wanted their teeth pulled (in a number of cases the tooth had been broken by the village barber and only the stump remained), desperately anaemic girls who had given birth at thirteen or fourteen, spotty undernourished babies, children with coughs and parasites, and head sores with the endemic head lice. Even mules were sometimes pushed through with horrible saddle sores, flattening the excited, laughing patients against the walls and causing chaos. It was one thing to get the beast in and another to put it into reverse and get it out. To turn it in such a small room was virtually impossible, and a flick of its tail would have cleared the table.

Often there was little I could do, but I was helped by the extreme sensitivity to drugs in those who had never had them. Their response to antibiotics was almost miraculous. Yet there were difficulties and mistakes, often due to our mutual lack of understanding. I remember being called to a two-year-old who as far as I could tell was desperately ill with pneumonia. I dissolved a sulphathiazol tablet and coaxed the child to drink it, advised as to his care and put two more tablets on the cupboard. 'One at twelve o'clock,' I repeated many times, 'and one at four o'clock. At eight o'clock I will come.'

I returned as promised. The child seemed cured and was bouncing up and down. The tablets reposed where I had left them. 'Why did you not give the tablets?' I asked. She gazed at me blankly. 'You said twelve o'clock and four o'clock, but we haven't got a clock,' she replied.

I remember being fetched by a man who lived in a village about eight miles away to visit a boy of fifteen who three days previously had fallen backwards into a cauldron of boiling water. The family was finding the smell unbearable and needed help. The father had brought a mule, but on those very rough mountain paths I usually preferred to walk. The village lay in a deep sloping valley between two arms of rock – little collections of thatched mud huts surrounded by green, green fields of Indian corn. In one of these lay the boy, groaning and burnt from his waist to his knees. The blisters had been plastered with a kind of black herbal paste and were obviously infected.

It took between one and two hours to clean him, although he was incredibly brave. As well as his dressings and the precious penicillin, I had brought a clean sheet for bandaging, and we tore it into strips. I returned two days later to repeat the dressings with another old sheet and he seemed much better, and the burns looked clean. I pointed to the dirty strips. 'You must wash them in the stream,' I said, 'and boil them for many minutes. Then you must hang then on the line to dry and I will roll them up.'

I returned after another two days and got a great welcome. When I asked for the bandages, I was greeted with roars of laughter. The conversation went as follows:

'Did you wash them?'

'Yes, yes, we washed them in the stream.'

'Did you boil them?'

'Yes, yes, we boiled them long on the charcoal.'

'Did you hang them up to dry?'

'Yes, yes, we hung them on the line …

Gales of mirth. ' … and a goat came and ate them up.'

But in spite of all, the boy recovered and the village began to recognize me. I arrived on one visit just as a bridal procession was winding down the opposite side of the valley, the bride heavily veiled and riding a mule, and all the men of the village accompanying her with flutes and drums. Suddenly the poor girl found herself abandoned. There was a wild rush across the valley and I was surrounded. 'Aspirinas!' they shouted, 'Aspiri-nas!' (aspirin being the only form of Western medicine that they knew).

There was a man of another village who needed fluid drawn off from his abdomen every three or four weeks. I would set out with the troca and cannula and needles well sterilized in a boiled aluminium jug covered by a boiled cloth. The procedure had to be done outside, as the hut was too dark, and the man would seat himself comfortably against a tree trunk. All was ready and I was washing my hands when the goats suddenly came home round a rock in a big rush. One old nanny put her back leg right into the sterile jug and it took a very long time to collect firewood, light it, and boil everything up again.

But in the autumn Farnham returned with his Janet. They came up for the first weekend of every month and saw a few cases, sometimes advising them to come to the hospital (for some this was an enormous adventure and expedition). This was a great relief, a lifting of the responsibility, but ultimately one knew that the healing was of God, and where my knowledge reached its limit, he so often took over. In the summer of the following year, Marguerite from Switzerland joined me for a time, and I learned what it meant to have someone quietly praying while I dealt with the sick or tried to preach the gospel. But I think I was still alone when a well-dressed man came to the door and said that his wife was possessed with a devil and he understood that the Jesus I prayed to could cast out devils. I had not met a challenge like this before, but I offered to go with him and see the woman. Sure enough, she was muttering, flinging herself wildly about, and in a society where there is no psychiatric treatment, this sort of thing is indeed a calamity. The only treatment is to tie the patient to a stake in the wall and to continue to live round her.

But as I watched her and heard of her symptoms, I felt no sense of evil. I thought she was having fits and I just felt deeply sorry for her. I remembered that the Lord had power over sickness as well as over evil spirits, and I asked to be allowed to go home for an hour and then return. The challenge of this power remained.

I started to pray, but there was no sense of peace or assurance or any breakthrough. I seemed to be praying to the ceiling, and the air was oppressive with a deep sense of failure. I found myself crying out, 'Lord, what is the matter? Why don't you speak to me?' and almost as though spoken, the answer came back. I was reminded vividly of a period in my life when I worked with a woman I just could not get on with. 'You didn't like her and she didn't like you,' that voice seemed to be saying, 'and you didn't care. You had other friends and you didn't try to put it right. Write and tell her you're sorry.'

It was the last thing I wanted to do, but too much depended on it. 'I'll write tonight,' I promised, and somehow the sense of God's presence was restored. I went back to the house and prayed in the name of Jesus, and the woman became quiet and recovered. The name of Jesus was vindicated, and they acknowledged his power, although as far as I know none of them ever came to trust him. But for me it was a step forward, a reiteration of the truths that God was trying to teach me. 'Power is a dangerous instrument, and our God is a jealous God. He will not entrust it to anyone who is not wholly sanctified.' And I have come to believe that 'wholly sanctified' means clean and obedient at that point where God has shined his light. We have a merciful God, and he does not shine his noonday sun in the morning. If he showed us once for all the unguessed depths of pride and selfishness in our natures, most of us would despair and give up. Little by little, life reveals, and the gentle challenge comes over and over again, 'Wilt thou be made clean?' and on each occasion that we answer, 'Yes, at any cost!', he accepts us and comes to sanctify us and works through us.

10

Fatima and her Friends

Little Tamoo did not forget my invitation. She arrived next day, scrubbed very clean, her hair strained back in two tight pigtails. Her face was brown and perfectly round, and her black eyes very bright. Marguerite and I called her the currant bun, and within a few days her friends started to come with her and we found we had a school on our hands.

But on that first morning just her mother Fatima came with her. And of Fatima and her mother Zohra I can write freely, because they are both safe in Heaven. Fatima announced that she had come to work for us and proceeded to tell me her life story. When she was about eleven years old, she was married by her parents' arrangement to a middle-aged man she had never met. Her little son was born when she was about thirteen, but she did not know she was pregnant until quite close to term. The baby died, but Tamoo was born two years later and grew to be the light of her eyes. But her husband was a disaster. He was a drug addict, and practically all the money he earned was spent on the weed. He would lie for hours puffing away, eyes half closed, while his wife and daughter dug for edible roots on the mountainside or simply went hungry.

They were hungry when they arrived. I needed help, for by this time parents and children were surging in, and although I could hardly pay her anything (our finances were stretched to the utmost limit), I suggested that they ate breakfast and lunch with us. I never regretted it. Fatima quickly became the cornerstone of the whole work. She chattered to us in Arabic and taught us the culture and the art of making a good meal out of practically nothing; and the children loved her and confided in her. Patients came to the house unafraid if she was there, while villagers opened to her homely, down-to-earth presence. We wondered how we had ever managed without her.

From her point of view, however, we had some strange habits. Every morning we read and prayed together, and at first this was incomprehensible to her. 'Can an old cat learn to dance?' was her attitude. But Tamoo loved the gospel stories, and gradually Fatima began to listen. That story about five thousand people being fed from five loaves and two fishes, for instance, that really made sense. She asked for that one over and over again, and began to realize that God sometimes answered prayer.

Then one morning she arrived sobbing bitterly and furiously angry. She had gone home the night before to find an empty house. Her husband had gone to another woman and taken everything they possessed – blankets, cooking pot, everything – and she had no appeal apart from bribes and influential friends, and of those she had none. She sat for a long time cursing him, calling him names, and weeping. She never wished to see him again, she sobbed.

'Then why are you so angry he's gone?' I asked.

'I'm not crying for my husband,' she replied angrily, 'I'm crying for my blankets.'

We shared what we could, and Marguerite stitched some curtains. The essentials of life were very cheap, and for a time she was, perhaps, happier without the man. But one day she arrived almost mad with grief, and this time there was no comforting her. Her husband had taken Tamoo as a little servant, as his new wife was pregnant, and once again there seemed to be no appeal. It was not etiquette to visit the house of your ex-husband, and the only time she ever saw the child was at the well. These were miserable meetings, for Tamoo looked thin and dirty, with sores on her head and arms. She cried to come home to her mother.

And then the possibility of prayer dawned on Fatima, and she suggested that we asked God to bring her daughter back. To my weak faith it seemed an unlikely event. The new baby was due, and little slaves of seven are extremely useful, but we started to pray daily. I cannot remember for how long we prayed, but it was mid-winter before the answer was given.

Winter in that little town was a dreary season. The snow lay thick on the mountains, and pools of black slush gathered in the cobbled street. The wind whistled between the houses, driving the sleet, and the little shacks on the outskirts leaked abominably. The children in their wet rags steamed and sniffed round the charcoal brazier, but they still had to go out and beg. On that cold night of wind and rain I was glad to get into bed and go to sleep.

But I was woken by a loud knocking and I ran to the window. A woman stood at the door, bowed with some heavy weight under her haik, and beckoning frantically. I went down and opened the door. Fatima almost fell through it. She flung off her haik, revealing Tamoo gasping and coughing on her back.

There was no doubt the child had pneumonia. So we propped her up with pillows and tucked her in bed. We gave her antibiotics and cough mixture and a hot drink, and she fell into a restless sleep. And then Fatima told her story. Neighbours had told her that her daughter was ill, and she was lying awake grieving for her with the rain dripping through the roof, when she said she was suddenly conscious of a presence in the room. She could not tell how, but somehow she knew it was Jesus, and he said to her, 'Go and fetch your daughter.' Fatima explained that this was impossible. It was raining hard, she could not go out alone in the dark – and it was against all convention to visit her ex-husband. But the presence and the voice persisted, 'Go and fetch your daughter.' So she got up and wrapped her haik round her and went out into the night.

Arrived at the door, she stood for a long time, listening. She could hear a child crying, but no one took any notice. In the end she tried the metal ring and to her amazement the door was unlocked, and she stole inside. It took another long time to persuade herself that the house was empty except for her crying child, but at last she dared approach the bed and lifted Tamoo on to her back. No one stopped her, for there was no one there. She hurried through the dark, silent streets to our house, like Peter freed from prison, wondering if it was all a dream.

Her father never asked for Tamoo again, and the incident was quite easily explained. He had gone away for a night on business and his wife, who was very young and foolish, saw that Tamoo was seriously ill. 'If I am here when she dies,' thought the poor creature, 'my husband will say that I am responsible. It would be better not to be here.' So she took her baby and herself off to her mother's house for the night. But what no one could explain was the presence of Jesus caring for that child and restoring her to her mother, and Fatima did not try to explain. She accepted what had happened in a matter-of-fact way, and it was probably at that point that she decided to become a Christian. After all, if he could feed five thousand with five loaves and two fishes, nothing could surprise her any more.

She grew fast. She had a real hunger to learn and to share what she knew, and at some point along the way we started the women's meetings on Wednesdays. At first just a handful came, haphazardly. I suggested two o'clock, but no one had a watch except me, and they turned up at any time up to seven o'clock. Fatima loved these sessions, but I found them discouraging. The women were far more interested in why I was unmarried and what I had in my chest of drawers than in the gospel I tried to preach, and there were times when I felt like giving up.

I remember talking to a friendly, smiling group and gradually becoming conscious of one woman only. She was a village woman and I had seen her before, but she gazed at me so intently, so drinking in all that I was telling her, I felt I was talking to her alone, pleading with her to understand and believe. I stopped and waited. Would she ask any question or show any sign of real understanding?

She got up and came towards me. She started pinching me gently and feeling me up and down. Then she turned to the other women. 'Too thin,' she announced confidentially, 'no flesh on her. She'll never get a husband.'

But there was one encouragement. Fatima's old mother, Zohra, was a water carrier. She carried heavy buckets of water from the river banks or from the fountains, and those who employed her paid her about twopence a load. It was hot, weary work. She was always the first to arrive on Wednesday afternoon, and the last to go. She would sit through session after session, wide awake and talkative when the tea was brought in, but when the reading started she would yawn loudly. 'Your words are so good they bring rest to my heart,' she would say as she stretched out on the mattress behind the other guests. She would fall fast asleep while I battled on in my faltering Arabic, competing with her snores. It was like having a noisy pig in the room, and it upset me quite a lot, and on several occasions I was on the point of asking her not to come.

But to my everlasting gratitude, the Lord restrained me and I never said those words. Perhaps I realized the tiredness and drudgery of her life and what it meant to sit and drink tea and rest for just one afternoon of the week in a house that was a little prettier than her own. The time came when Zohra stayed awake and listened. There was a new sort of brightness and energy about her and as she helped me wash up the tea glasses I commented on it.

'You understood something today, didn't you, Zohra?' I said.

'Of course, now I understand, since last week when you talked about me.'

'Talked about you?' I could not think what she meant.

But then I thought back and remembered that we had learnt the verse together in the literal, colloquial Arabic: 'Jesus said, "Come unto me all you who are tired and who carry heavy burdens, and I will give you rest."'

'That was me and my water buckets, wasn't it?' she questioned. 'I'm the only one who carries heavy burdens. And all this week, as I carried the water up and down from the river, I have said, "Jesus, Jesus" and the buckets haven't been nearly so heavy as they were before.'

I felt so thankful she had gone to sleep before I had had time to explain that verse. I would have told her that her sins were the heavy burden, and that would have spoiled it all. Jesus met her right at the point of her conscious need, her tired shoulders and her aching back, and he walked the rough paths with her and gave her relief. Later he would teach her of other burdens. She had started to learn ...

Then something happened that turned the little trickle of ladies into a positive flood till there were three, four, five roomfuls one after the other. Someone hearing that children came to the house sent us a parcel of toys – among them a clockwork mouse. It was a most attractive beast; you wound it up and it set off at great speed, turning at right angles, rushing round in circles. I thought it would be fun to let it off in school after the Bible lesson, just before the children went home. Had it been a bomb, it could not have first alarmed and then amused them more. At its first glorious entrance, making straight for their feet, and then darting away, they screamed in terror and leapt on the mattresses with their dirty feet on my *nice* covers. This mouse had obviously gone mad or was possessed with an evil spirit, and some were in tears. But when I tried to allay the panic by explaining that it was only a toy, they screamed the louder with excitement and joy. 'Again! Again' they shouted, rushing to meet the mouse, leaping out of the way and doubling up with laughter. I had the greatest difficulty in getting them to leave at all.

It was Wednesday and the little group of ladies would stray in sometime during the afternoon. We put a dozen cups on the tray, but by 2 pm it was obvious that things were not going according to plan. More and more ladies were arriving, most of whom I had never seen before. They greeted us smilingly, drank tea and listened patiently to the talk I gave. More women were arriving, and I told them to wait downstairs. I was confused. What was happening? Was a revival breaking out?

At the end of the first talk, I suggested to the first lot that they left to make room for the second. But they looked at me sweetly and patiently and said, 'We came to see the mouse.'

So the mouse performed again and yet again. He was almost as successful with the ladies as he had been with the children. They too screamed with alarm and laughter and jumped on the mattresses and would not go home. The ice was broken and they started to come regularly on Wednesday afternoons, sometimes as many as forty or fifty drifting at their leisure between lunchtime and sunset. It was a social occasion in their drab lives, and for most of them probably nothing more. But occasionally one would come back, wistful and questioning, drawn by her sense of need, so we started a little daily Bible study group at midday after the children had left. None of them could read, but Fatima was learning, and she shone at these gatherings. Her homely explanations were far more intelligible than mine, and she taught them to pray about everything. They prayed about the children and the goats, and the rent and the harvest, and they experienced wonderful answers. She longed for her neighbours to hear and understand, for she had the true heart of an evangelist.

The Lord's presence was very literal and real to her. When I first read her the story of the resurrection and told her that Jesus was alive now and with us, she was extremely startled and looked all round the room. In matters of truth and honesty I had to teach her, but when it came to faith, I was the learner. He was there unseen and could do whatever was necessary.

Then came the time when I had to go down to the town in the valley, so I told the group not to come at midday next day. Fatima looked at me in surprise. 'But we can come alone,' she said. 'But none of you can read the Bible,' I objected. 'It doesn't matter,' she replied. 'We know the hymns and we can pray, and we remember the stories.'

So I left her the key and they gathered. I asked her next day how they had got on. 'Oh, we had a wonderful time,' she said. They obviously had not missed me in the least. 'Tell me what you did,' I said. 'We prayed and we sang hymns and I told them a story.' ' How many of you were there?' She counted on her fingers. 'There were seven of us – I and my mother and my daughter, our neighbour and her two friends ... , and the Lord Jesus in the midst. Yes, there were seven of us.'

I remember catching flu and becoming really ill. Marguerite had had to leave because the government had refused to renew her visa, but Fatima and Zohra and friends nursed me with strange herbal remedies, oranges, spaghetti and small fried sardines. I had a very high temperature and no voice at all and on Monday I told Fatima to tell everyone that the house was closed for the week; that there would be no school, no ladies' meeting and no dispensary until further notice.

It was Tuesday afternoon that she sat down beside me and broke the news. 'Two ladies from a village came today,' she said, 'and asked when the ladies' meeting was. I told them to come tomorrow.'

'But, Fatima,' I croaked, 'I told you I wouldn't be up for several days. I couldn't possibly talk tomorrow.'

'Oh, but the Lord's going to heal you tomorrow, in time to take the meeting,' she said. 'I've asked him. Otherwise those women will go back to their village and they will never hear the gospel. I can help you, but I don't know enough yet to speak at the meeting. So tomorrow you'll be well.'

I felt desperate and worried feverishly all night. I did not wish to be healed. I felt very ill and I wanted to stay quietly in bed. My headache was worse in the morning and my voice a whisper. Surely Fatima would realize that she'd made a mistake. I lay very quiet and looked as sick as I could.

She was very quiet too, until about twelve thirty, when she arrived with some spaghetti. 'You must get up soon,' she said. 'The women will be arriving and I must arrange the room.'

'But, Fatima, I feel so ill and I can't talk.'

'The Lord is going to heal you. I told you.'

I was actually lying in the room where the meeting would be held, so I angrily rose. I hoped I would faint and that would teach her.

But I didn't. As I dressed, the fever seemed to ebb away. My head felt clear and light. When the women arrived my voice was strong and normal. We held three or four groups that day and there was no sense of strain or weariness. I was glad to go back to bed in the evening, but I had turned the corner. And I was amazed. Fatima was not.

'I told you,' she said.

II

The Children Come

When winter drew on, the children swarmed to the house. My new helper, Bente from Denmark, arrived to take Marguerite's place. She loved children and again lifted much of the load. I started to write *Star of Light*.

The plot of the book is fictitious but based on many true incidents; the old, childless wife in the village where I stayed, superseded by a new, attractive young mother; the beggar who hired the blind child to sit with him in the market; the babies repeatedly left on missionaries' doorsteps; and above all, Hamid. Hamid who was turned out of his home because food was scarce, who worked for the doughnut man and stole my eggs and my watch and anything else he could lay hands on. Who brought me a starving kitten as a Christmas present and who recognized that the way to Heaven was written in the Book, and that therefore he must learn to read. Hamid would arrive for his lessons in the middle of the night. He became a very large part of my life, and I still go back to see him every year. The little town, so impoverished and destitute under Spanish rule, has flourished under the Moroccan government and is now quite a prosperous tourist centre. Well-dressed, middle-aged gentlemen greet me enthusiastically and are grieved to discover that I cannot always remember which little, ragged, hungry, barefoot boy was which.

I think Mohamed first brought Hamid. He was a small, spotty-faced boy with a shaved head and an enormous ulcer on his shin. I gathered that he had been knocked about a good deal, for he would not let me come anywhere near him. I had to put the cotton wool, ointment, dressing and bandage in one corner of the room and stand in the far comer issuing directions. If I approached a step, he was out of the door like a startled rabbit.

But he allowed me to pray for healing from my corner, and gradually the ulcer dried up. Set free from pain, he became more friendly, and the day came when he turned on leaving and remarked earnestly, 'Your heart is good, your teaching is good, your food is good. May God have mercy on your ancestors.'

He started to gang up with the boys who came every night for their supper of bread and lentils or beans, rug-making and Bible story. They were on the whole a tough, gallant little crowd, fully engaged in begging, scrounging and stealing and well able to survive. The girls who came in the morning were much more pathetic. They were not homeless, but they were mostly very poor, and many were sent out early to beg, so they came to school when they could and left when they must. We gave them breakfast of bread and olives and coffee made from ground, burnt barley, goat's milk and sugar, and this was a great attraction and drew as many as we could squash in. Many of them were called Fatima and their surnames were vague and changeable, so the register went something like this: Fatima Spotty-head, Zohra and Tooma Goats, Fatima TB, Fatima Hunchback, Rahma Sores-on-arms, etc etc. Their heads crawled with lice and so did the hems of their garments. We sometimes had an afternoon when we tried to cope with the heads, which was a losing battle, but greatly enjoyed by all. Shrieks of laughter as the lice fell out into the basin!

When they first started to come, I was afraid. In cold weather they gathered in the room where I slept and I remember praying about it. 'Lord,' I said, 'I don't mind the body lice. I can deal with those. But I can't see the head lice. How can I cope?' But the Lord was very merciful. In the years I worked with those children, I often picked the lice off the hems of my clothes, but I never once, as far as I know, had one in my hair. The psalmist talks about God promising to be a shield to his head, and I experienced that in a very practical way.

Tooma was the littlest of our scholars. She had an older sister, Zohra, who brought a baby on her back called Fatima. They all slept with a small herd of goats, which their mother took up the mountain during the day, while Tooma begged in the fish market, and people threw her the odd sardine. She would arrive in school with the fish pinned to her filthy little dress, and she was not savoury. Being the youngest, she always made straight for my lap, and in spite of substantial pinafores, the mixed smells of stale fish, goat and unwashed child seemed to penetrate every part of me. One day I spoke to her sister about it. 'Zohra, could you wash Tooma's dress?'

She was rather offended. I seemed quite unreasonable to her.

'We haven't got any soap', she said.

'If I gave you some soap, could you wash it?'

The idea of soap was attractive, and the three went off together. It was a cold, rainy day, and in quite a short time they were all back, Tooma in a sopping dress that clung to her, but both she and the dress looked a different colour.

'But, Zohra', I said, 'why did you put this soaking dress back on her? She will be ill.'

It appeared that it had never come off her. There was no substitute, so Tooma and her dress had been put in the bucket all of a piece, to her great satisfaction. I removed the wet garment and dressed her in an old petticoat of mine and a warm pyjama coat of my brother's tied round the waist with a string, and she minced off down the road, no doubt imagining herself dressed in the latest European fashion. It was at this point, early in my stay, that I wrote to friends in England asking for old, warm, children's clothes, and they responded magnificently.

School consisted of an hour's knitting, breakfast, reading and Bible stories, and with Marguerite's and then Bente's help in the classroom, and with Fatima organizing the food, all went well. But wool was a problem. Friends in England and Switzerland sent us left-over balls of all colours, and the children joyfully knitted their own rainbow-striped pullovers, but the wool went very fast. We used raw sheep's wool, which we teasled and dried on the roof, for the boys' rugs, but we couldn't mix the two kinds, and to buy proper skeins of wool was financially impossible.

There came a Friday when I sadly told the children that they could come on Monday for reading and Bible stories but that there would be no more knitting for a time. The wool had given out and we must just wait for the next parcel.

Zohra was very angry. She was a thin, sharp-faced child with a most determined character. Her baby sister Fatima lived on her back, and if Zohra sat down, Fatima usually screamed. But Zohra intended to learn to read, and she intended to knit pullovers, first for both her little sisters and then for herself, so she walked tirelessly up and down in the passage, learning her letters and clicking away at her needles. Bente and I would work away at the knitting in our spare time, for such persistence deserved success, and now, today, just when Tooma's pullover was within a few days of being finished, there was no more wool. She scowled at us.

Suddenly her face brightened. 'You told us God answers prayer,' she said. 'Let's ask him to send us wool by Monday.' She placed the empty suitcase in the centre of the mat and the children with one accord gathered round it, lifting their hands palms upwards like the beggars in the market place, and Zohra prayed: 'Oh, Lord God, send us wool by Monday.' And I looked on with a sinking heart, for how could wool come by Monday? Parcels, if there were any, always went to Tangier, and my brother was not due for another week.

There was a sudden commotion at the front door; a banging of numerous noisy little boys, all shouting 'Te-le-phoon!' I left all and ran. The big house at the bottom of the street boasted a phone and would call me for urgent messages, and it was always an exciting occasion, with children rushing after me down the street, waiting outside to hear the news. As I went inside and picked up the receiver, the whole family gathered round, eager and expectant.

It was Farnham. 'There are visitors from England coming next week, so we're coming tomorrow instead,' he said. 'I've just been down to the customs and collected an enormous box of wool from Switzerland.'

Zohra was not surprised. 'I told you,' she said. 'And I shall need some red wool.' But the incident made an impression on her, she listened more carefully to the Bible stories. Then one day little Tooma arrived, breathless and exhausted, with Fatima bouncing on her back. Her mother was ill, and Zohra had had to take the goats on to the mountain.

Zohra returned within a week; but something had happened. She was quieter and less aggressive, and she looked happy. A day or two later she lingered behind. 'I want to tell you something,' she said. 'The first day I took the goats up the mountain, I was very frightened. I'd never been up the mountain alone before. But I remembered that Jesus said, "I am always with you." And I wasn't afraid any more.

'Then I was hungry and thirsty, and I had only a small piece of bread. But I remembered that Jesus said he was the bread of life, so I ate my bread and I wasn't hungry any more. And I went on a little and I found a stream bubbling up amongst the stones, and I drank, and I wasn't thirsty any more.

'Then a mist came down and I couldn't see the goats, and I feared to lose them. But I remembered that Jesus promised to answer prayer, so I prayed. The sun shone through the mist and the goats came back. So now I know.'

Such a simple little story, but then she was a simple child. She learned to read quickly and soon mastered the little reading primer we had made, which a kind friend who was a printer photocopied for us. It consisted of nine pages, a few sentences on each, and some simple black and white illustrations. It spoke of the purity and beauty of Heaven, the barrier of sin, the birth of Jesus, the story and meaning of his death. It told of his resurrection and ascension and finished up with three little prayers – a prayer for forgiveness, a prayer for the Holy Spirit of love, and a prayer to the Good Shepherd for protection and guidance from earth to heaven.

Mufaddla, who came to school each morning from an outlying farm, loved her little book. She could soon read it fluently, and one day she begged me to let her take it home. Being still inexperienced, I let her do so. But the next day she did not come back, and later I found the book torn up on the doorstep. Bente and I felt very sad, for she had been such a bright, intelligent child, who had seemed to understand so much and to respond so quickly. Now she was just another snatched back.

I saw nothing of her for months. Then one day her father came to the door, all smiles. The brother was ill out at the farm, and would I please come along and see him?

I left Bente to cope with the house and went on my own. Down through the cobbled streets and out on to the main road that wound upwards and eastwards into the mountains, with its wide views across the valley and more mountains beyond. The farm stood off the road, screened by fig trees; a low thatched hut with the family living one end and the livestock the other. It was rather dark inside, but I could see Mufaddla squatting among the goats. But I turned my attention to the boy on the bed. He was coughing and feverish, and they agreed to come for medicine. I made the usual polite remarks and left.

I had not gone far before there was a rush of feet and a small hand was thrust into mine. Mufaddla, bright-eyed and tousled and distinctly goaty, was smiling up at me. 'Come to the top of that little hill,' she said. We climbed together and stood looking down at the roofs of the hamlet, the olive groves and fig trees, the deep green of the patches of Indian corn.

'That's my brother's farm,' said Mufaddla, pointing to a long, low hut. 'And that's my grandfather's house. But you can't see my home.'

'I can,' I said, standing on tiptoe. 'It's down there behind the fig tree.'

'I don't mean that one,' she said rather impatiently, 'I mean my real home, up there with God.'

'Yes, I know, Mufaddla, but who is going to lead you there?'

'Jesus, my Saviour,' she whispered.

Then she was gone, flying down the hillside, out of sight among the greenery. But she had told me all she wanted me to know, and I went home comforted. Jesus said, 'This is life eternal, that they might know me.'

But perhaps the child who gave the most joy was Alia, the slave girl in the mayor's house. Her mother, a widow far from home in a distant village and starving, had brought her little two-year-old daughter to a distant relative of her dead husband in the town and sold her. The child had grown up as a little slave. She was not cruelly treated, but she was desperately overworked in the large house. She must have been about fourteen years old when she appeared at the door, a towel over her head. I could not see her face. A mumbled, 'My mistress says come.'

I followed her and found the mayor's wife sitting in a beautiful curtained room, with her precious first son on her lap (there had been three daughters). The baby had whooping cough and was vomiting every feed. He was desperately thin and dehydrated and exhausted with coughing.

The house was near, and I went three or four times a day, to feed the baby and administer the medicine, and to feed him again if he wanted. And very gradually he grew better. Sometimes in the evening the mother would want me to stay and chat. I tried to tell her about Jesus, who had power to heal. But she turned away nervously and changed the subject. I left her rather sadly at the end of the fortnight. The baby was feeding well and gaining weight and there was no reason to keep on visiting. There were so many others.

It must have been three weeks later when I was startled by a violent hammering on the door. Thinking there had been an accident, I ran to open, only to find a breathless girl on the doorstep carrying a large basket of vegetables. She pushed past me without invitation and stood in the passageway looking up at me. 'Do you remember me?' she asked. I had to admit I didn't. 'I was the servant in the mayor's house. I used to listen behind the curtain when you talked to my mistress. You talked about Heaven. She sent me to the market, but I ran all the way and now I can stay for five minutes. Can you tell me the way to Heaven in five minutes?'

I fetched the little Wordless Book of the illiterate and we went over it. The brightness of heaven, the darkness of sin, the atoning blood of Jesus, shed on the cross for sinners, the white purity of sin forgiven. (The third page means nothing to them the first time, but I have had women say, 'Tell me again the name of that man who died for me.')

She understood enough to lift her hands palms upwards like the beggars in the street and say, 'O God, give me a clean heart.' Then she bolted. And it was some time before I saw her again.

But her mistress noticed the difference in her. The old sullen, defiant look had gone, and there seemed to be some secret content. One day she questioned her. I do not know what was said or how the child explained, but Alia was suddenly allowed to come and learn. She would turn up on a Sunday at a highly unorthodox time at the morning service. I asked her one day to tell us what difference it had made to her knowing Jesus. She considered. 'I suppose I am no longer afraid,' she replied.

About two years later, her master planned to marry her to a countryman who would have taken her far away from us. But she was quietly confident that this would not happen until she had learned to read. 'I know I shall have to go in the end,' she said, 'but not until I can read the Word of God.' The day came when the man was coming to legalize the engagement. She sent us a message. 'Pray for me,' she said. And the tiny group of Christians gathered in my house and prayed for her deliverance. We sang the Arabic translation of an English hymn which Fatima loved – 'The soul that on Jesus hath leaned for repose, I will not, I will not desert to its foes. That soul, though all hell should endeavour to shake, I will never, no never, no never forsake.' Later on in the day she sent a message that all was well.

I asked her what had happened. She had been asked the customary traditional question, 'Will you marry this man?' And to everyone's amazement and indignation, she replied that she would rather not. Her rejection would have been speedily brushed aside had it not been for the man himself, who lost his temper and shouted that if she did not want him, there were plenty of girls who did, and that he would not take her at any price. Her master, who would have received the bride price, was not pleased. That did not worry Alia unduly. God had heard her prayer and for a time at least she was safe. When she finally left to go, she could read her New Testament haltingly.

Most of these girls were married by their parents' arrangement at the age of about fifteen and shut in. It was difficult to keep in touch, as the in-laws were not always welcoming. Many of the young husbands migrated to the big cities and settled there. Sometimes even now, when I return for a few weeks each year to Morocco, I find one of them again. They nearly always remember just one thing from those old days – the little hymn that we sang almost daily in Arabic:

There is a beautiful country.
The gates are closed.
No sin can go in.
O Lord my God, give me a clean heart.
Take away my sin in the blood of my Saviour.
Lead me on the road to your house, O God.
Then receive me with joy.

They repeat the words with laughter and enjoyment, for those old days were happy ones. How much they understand I do not know. But I remember that the thief on the cross knew much less theology than what is contained in that little hymn. Yet he was welcomed in.

Many years later I went to an Arab Christian conference in France, where a number of women told how they had become Christians. Most of them had attended missionary sewing or knitting classes when they were children, and heard the Bible stories, but none of them had really dared to accept or even believe at the time. But years later, when they heard the same message on the radio or through another Christian, it all came back to them – the warm room, the kindness, the tea and biscuits, the bright colours of the wool – and somehow they wanted to prolong the memory and they listened. And suddenly it all made sense.

It helps us to believe what is sometimes hard when working with Muslim children – that our labour is not always in vain in the Lord.

12

Out to the Villages

It was not long before we began to get invitations to visit the sick in the villages. We put aside a day in the week for this. We loved these days. Both Marguerite and Bente were great walkers, and if Fatima was with us we were doubly welcome. First we would set out if possible in the cool of the dawn, before the sun had risen above the towering rocky crests behind us, when the valleys were swathed in mist and the rest of the world still asleep. We found that with a supply of malt and iron tonics for the anaemic young mothers, a bottle of gentian violet for sores, some eye ointment and worm medicines and sulphur tablets for babies with diarrhoea and vomiting, one could partly revitalize a village.

And gradually we made friends and were often invited to spend the night. The kindness and hospitality of these villagers knew no bounds. In the quiet of the evening, when they had finished their work in the fields, they would crowd in, bringing their sick, and later as they lingered we would talk to them. The word hurry was unknown to them. 'Come on, come on,' they would say, 'the night is yet young.' And they would laugh delightedly over the lost sheep and the prodigal son, and clap their hands. And just occasionally, very occasionally, a more wistful look would steal over somebody's face. They had glimpsed something of the meaning behind the story. Sometimes they would steal back later and ask questions.

But it was very different when Fatima talked to them. There was one woman who lived in a distant village, and she and her son often dropped in on us when they came to market. They were eager to hear more of the Bible teaching, and they begged Fatima and me (I was alone that autumn) to visit them once a week. 'I will gather the whole village,' she would say, 'in the evening we will all come.' So Fatima and I and little Tamoo would set out on a Monday afternoon, returning in time for Tuesday school in the morning.

I shall never forget those long walks over the barren hillsides, the scent of camphor heavy on the air, the brown and golds of the landscape so clear against an eggshell blue sky ... dense blackness of autumn poplars in the last rays, the incredible colours of sunset behind us, and the warm smell of dying bracken.

Before we reached the village, we had to cross a river, with marshy ground on each side. Although it was not deep, it was a formidable barrier for Fatima and Tamoo, who were not used to wading; and besides, it was usually getting dark. Fatima would plough on, moaning and chuntering under her breath, and I would catch the gist of it. 'Oh, what darkness! Never mind, the whole world is lost in the darkness of sin, and the light of the world is Jesus. I don't know how we shall get down this bank. I hold on to you and you hold on to my daughter, and may the good Lord hold on to all of us.' (Bump ... bump ...) 'Though it's a long way over these ditches, but for the sake of the Lord Jesus I would go further than England.' (Slosh, as she stepped into a bog.) 'I'm in the mud. All we like sheep have gone astray. Look, here's a man ...' (Collision with a man, who asks for medicine for sores.) 'Yes, come along to the neighbour's house tonight, young man, and you will hear about the Lord Jesus, who will cure you of your sores and cure you of your sins.'

When we actually reached the river, I took Tamoo on my back and we all waded forward together, and the chuntering got more agitated. 'O Lord, hold on to me, hold my hand, and hold tight, my daughter, and don't fall in, for it's a deep, dark river, like the pit of sin from which the Lord Jesus rescued us.' But we always got over safely, and then things would warm up. The old diary describes a typical visit to that village.

'Arrived at 8.30 pm after a three hours' walk and sat gratefully on a mat in Yamana's yard. The world was like a beautiful picture framed in the mud doorway. A twisted old walnut tree, emerald fields of Indian corn, the turquoise strip of river in the valley. Soft, dark outlines of mountains against the apricot sky.

9 pm   Flatpan bread and eggs, after which we set out with lanterns to the teacher's house,

heavily armed with sticks against fierce dogs. Over several ditches, and we arrived to a great welcome from the teacher, to whom we had given a gospel in the spring.

10 pm   Mint tea

10.30 pm   Talked to a full house

11 pm   Eggs and tomatoes

11.45 pm   More talking ('the night is yet young')

12.30 am   Tea

1 am   Hymns with the violin

1.30 am   Huge potato and partridge stew

2 am   Felt ill, persuaded them to pull a mat near the door and fell asleep.

3 am   Big yellow dog rushed in. Huge excitement. The household was still laughing when I woke at 7 o'clock.

7.30 am   Tea

8 am   Read 1 John with Fatima.

9 am   Tomato and eggs

9.30 am   Talked to the women. More talk to the men.

The teacher seemed in earnest ('If he really paid my debt, then I must believe in him. No one else paid for me.')

11 am   Huge bowl of macaroni, and we all ate from a wooden spoon which we passed from one to the other.

11.30 am   Read them the prodigal son, and Fatima spoke to a group of women. ('We have come to tell you how to be Christians, so you can come to Heaven with us.')

Back to Yamana's house. Very hot, and washed in a bucket in the cow house. Very dark, with five cows. Dressed in imminent danger. Discovered all the kids peeping through a crack in the wall.

Another houseful. More talk. Fried fish. More tea.

Duly arrived in another village. The heat was too much, and I made my own sleeping arangements. Talked and visited till midnight. Lay down on the floor with the family, three cats and 50,000 fleas, and they locked the door. We were hermetically sealed; cats fighting, purring, yowling most of the night. Leeks and garlic hung just above me. Buttermilk ripening at my elbow. Could not sleep till 4 am for lack of air, and woke suffocating at 5.15. Everyone snoring, so crept outside into the cold, fresh dawn. The sky was bright with stars, but there was a pink glow in the east and trailing mist. It was still dark, so I bathed at the source of the stream and then lay down again on the threshing floor and watched the sun rise. Then I slept on the clean husks until breakfast time, when I reappeared, to the relief of the family.'

After breakfast the group of villagers gathered again, eager to listen. 'I'm going home with my heart wide open,' said a man. 'When you come again, stay five days and I can learn it all.'

I sat on the verandah in the sun, combing my hair. My hostess came up and stroked it admiringly. 'Nothing,' she murmured, 'not a single louse.'

Fatima, as time went on, became fearless on these occasions and would always take her turn. When Bente or I spoke, they listened with an air of friendly enjoyment, sometimes drifting into seriousness. When Fatima spoke, the silence was tense and shrewd. They watched her unblinkingly. But she had a gift for story telling and would weave a wealth of local detail into the parables which often made them laugh in spite of themselves. Her favourite story was the lost sheep. 'Tell me this,' she would say, as the story drew to a close. 'Why did the shepherd go out all night to look for that sheep? He was a rich man. What made him go?'

There was a buzz of speculation. Truly it seemed strange. In their minds the owner of a hundred sheep was akin to a millionaire. Rich men do not go out into the mountains to seek for a single lamb.

'Then I will tell you,' she would say. 'He went to look for that sheep because he could not rest until his flock was complete. All his heart was with that missing lamb. And that is why we have come tonight. There are many Christians in other countries, and indeed in this land. But the Lord is not satisfied. He wants you here in Beni Isi and

Amis ...' Here I stepped across the open doorway, where across the valley the lights of other villages twinkled in the hollows of the black mountains. She had never been to Bible college, but in a land where man of necessity holds life so cheap she had learned to know the heart of the Father, which can never rest till his family is complete, to whom every individual is infinitely precious.

There were occasional drawbacks. I was once sleeping soundly in a village in the fasting month of Ramadan, when the family eats by night. About 2 am I was woken to find a table set by my bedside and the family sitting expectantly round a large plate of savoury stew. In front of me as the guest of honour lay the supreme delicacy – a little dish of goat's eyes staring at me balefully in the dim light! But on the whole visits to the village were pure joy, and it was a sacrifice for the one of us who had to stay behind to keep the routine going. Of all the species of human nature, the Moroccan peasant with his earthy sense of humour and simple kindness and sense of hospitality is one of those whose company I most enjoy.

We never went uninvited. As hosts they were unsurpassed, but to strangers they could be hard and suspicious, and the dogs who guarded the entrances through the prickly pear hedges were large and fierce and had probably not had rabies injections. We prayed for the scattered hamlets and waited until God opened the door. And he often did just that in a wonderful way.

There was a village across the valley where we longed to go. From my house we could see it perched on the hill above the main road. But no one had visited it, and we had no contact. Then one early morning after a night at Yamana's, we walked down the road and to our joy a bus was coming our way. We climbed aboard, confident of reaching home in good time for school.

When we reached the turning that led off to our little town, we asked the driver to stop. He was a surly Spaniard and refused to do so. 'This isn't a bus stop,' he said. 'You must wait until I stop five or six miles further on. Then you can walk up to the town from the other side.' This would mean an extra four or five miles climb up a very steep, shadeless hill, and the day was getting hotter and hotter.

I was very annoyed, and showed it, saying what I thought of the driver, muttering futilely that I intended to report him. Fatima was puzzled by my behaviour. 'Did we not pray this morning that the Lord would guide us?' she asked gently. 'Why are you so upset?' Frankly I was shamed into silence. God's voice seemed to speak very clearly, 'What I do thou knowest not now, but thou shalt know hereafter.'

The bus stopped far down the valley and we stood gloomily contemplating the steep turning that led back to the town, wondering if one of those rare buses might come along. We had forgotten that we were standing at the bottom of the hill that led up to that unvisited, prayed-for village, when a woman's voice behind us recalled us and we turned round.

It was not a market day. She had come down the hill alone, and this was unusual. Where would a woman go except to market? And then they always travelled in groups or families. She carried a bundle in her arms and came towards Fatima purposefully. 'Is that the English nurse?' she asked, jerking her thumb in my direction. On learning that it was, she said, 'Then introduce me.'

Fatima did so. The woman drew the cloth from the bundle and showed me a baby with about the worst infected eyes I had ever seen. They were tight shut, the lids swollen up like blue grapes, pus pouring from below the matted lashes.

'How long has she been like this?' I asked. 'Three days.' 'Why did you not bring her earlier?'

And then the story came tumbling out. 'I didn't know. I had never heard. But last night as I slept, I dreamed a dream. Someone came dressed in white and said, "Take your child to the English nurse." I said, "I don't know her, nor where she lives." But the voice said, "Go down to the main road at sunrise and you will find her there." So I came and here you are.'

There we were indeed. The hill seemed less steep and high than we had expected as we climbed it together. With treatment and three-hourly shots of penicillin, the child's eyes seemed much improved by the early evening, when she left us with medicine to take home. Best of all was a loving, eager invitation to visit her village on Saturday and to bring the Book.

Bente, Fatima and I set off at midday on Saturday. It was the first of several visits. It was a large, scattered village, and we prayed that we might find the house quickly. We need not have worried. The news had spread, and the first woman we met took us straight to our friend's house. And to our joy the baby's eyes seemed quite healed. Quite a crowd collected on the grass outside the hut. There was much laughter as we gave out simple medicines. Then our friend said, 'Have you brought the way to Heaven?'

They listened open-mouthed as we explained the Wordless Book. One seemed to listen with her heart as well. She walked with us for part of the way when we left, holding my hand. And she said, 'Give me a book like that and then I could look at it every hour and learn the way to Heaven.' We gave it her. We did not realize that our days were numbered.

13

Endings and Beginnings

We should have realized that the opposition must soon start. I had been in the town nearly five years and things appeared to be going well. Perhaps we had forgotten to be cautious enough. Numbers were increasing rapidly, the dispensary was crammed three times a week, fifty to sixty women were coming to the women's meetings on Wednesdays in shifts of about ten at a time, and the children's work was going on happily, and on Fridays we did our visits to villages. It seemed like a season of calm weather, and then the storm broke.

It started with a summons to Bente, my much-loved fellow worker, to go down to the Danish Embassy in the coastal town. She was told that there were complaints about our activities, and her visa for living in the district was cancelled. She returned broken-hearted but was comforted by Psalm 37. On her last day we went out to a village and came home to find the house spring-cleaned and spotless with Fatima and all the children installed ready for a party and farewell service. Bente left next day to start working in the hospital at Tangier and I walked home with a strange sense of foreboding.

I was summoned next. Being British I needed no visa, but complaints had been received about our visits to the village across the valley and I was not to go there again. I thought sadly of those dear women, and especially of the one who had said wistfully, 'Is there anyone who can stop me from losing my temper and telling lies?' Would anyone ever tell her again?

Zohra the water carrier arrived a day or two later, frightened and very excited. She had been taken to the police station, questioned, threatened and released. As I went through the market I saw a soldier seize hold of one of the school children, but I went to her rescue and he let her go. Then Fatima arrived to tell me of a dream she had had. She had been walking beside a stream when suddenly the water had come flooding over the banks in a dark rush. She had been carried away down the valley and had felt herself drowning, when someone in a white robe had come to the edge of the flood and had stretched out his hand and pulled her ashore. 'Something is going to happen,' she said quietly, 'but Jesus will bring us through.'

Children were questioned in the market and there was an ominous sense of impending disaster. Then one day Fatima did not arrive. I set out to look for her and met the family being escorted by police to the local Court House.

We took no notice of each other, but as I passed Fatima smiled and pointed upwards.

They were there all day and by evening I felt I should go down and see what was happening. They were sitting together looking fairly cheerful and I was taken in to the Basha, the city governor. He was courteous, but firm. They appreciated the medical and the welfare work but all Christian teaching must stop at once, and the group in the Court House were never to visit me again. A guard would be put at the bottom of the street, and if any disobeyed they would be beaten and imprisoned.

The guard at the end of my street suddenly fell down dead three days later. He was rather a nice man, and I felt dreadful about it, but the incident made quite an impression and no one wanted to take his place. The group kept arriving one at a time very late at night or in the small hours of the morning, some of them almost seeming to enjoy the adventure. But I knew we could not go on like that. Outside the town the two ladies from the Emmanuel Mission had rented a house and were making friends with the people round them. Our lot, in time, could quietly transfer to them.

The waiting days seemed long and depressing. The school was closed, the dispensary empty. I went out on the autumn hillsides and talked to the villagers going to and fro to market, often treating the deep, painful cracks on their leathery feet. One day about 2.30 pm I was approached by a group of five – two men, two women and a donkey – and I was asked if I would go with them to see a sick man in their home village.

I was suspicious. 'Where is this village?' I asked. 'Near, very near,' they replied. 'Just on the other side of the mountain.'

The mountain itself looked a formidable barrier, with its upper slopes of deep pine forest, but I thought we would probably cross over before sunset, and I agreed to go. I had never been to the far side of this particular mountain. We set off pleasantly enough and climbed for two or three hours. The shadows were lengthening when we plunged into the forest, and the stony track grew narrower. The sunset light blazed through the dark foliage and we were still climbing. Once or twice I asked if we were getting near to our destination. 'Near, oh very near,' they replied.

Darkness fell and one of the men lit a lantern and we stumbled along in silence, the fir boughs brushing our faces. Then to our right there was a gleam of light in a clearing, a collection of small mud huts lighted by candles and charcoal fires, a woodcutters' colony.

'Is this the village?' I asked, much relieved.

'No, no,' replied the men, 'ours is over the other side of the mountain, but it is near, very near.'

We stumbled off into the inky blackness ahead. The lantern showed one step at a time and we had gone some way before I began to realize that something was wrong. The women had stayed behind at the woodcutters' camp, and I was alone on this wild, dark mountain with two unknown Muslim men, going I knew not where.

I was really frightened. Retreat was impossible through those black, rocky woods. There was nothing to be done but to go on, and to cry out for God's protection.

I cannot explain what happened next. It is something I have experienced only three times in my life in moments of physical danger and fear. I can only say that suddenly I knew I was perfectly safe. I could almost feel the everlasting arms around me, almost sense the warmth of the shadow of his wings. We came out of the forest and the night wind was clean and cold on our faces, and the sky above us a blaze of stars. We crossed the crest and began to travel steeply downhill, slithering on the loose rock. We came to a great boulder, and as if it knew what was expected of it, the mule lay down and the men started unpacking the saddle bags. They handed me a piece of bread and a blanket, and told me to sleep against the mule's belly, where his legs would keep the draught off me, while they would snuggle up against his spine. They sounded as though they were showing me into their best bedroom and I realized that there had been nothing to fear. They were kind men, and they assured me again that the village was near, very near. In the morning we would soon arrive.

The blanket smelt of horse and garlic but it was warm and I slept soundly, only waking at sunrise to the amazing panaroma of crests aglow with light and glimpses of the silver sea where the heights level down to the Mediterranean coast.

The men smiled at me and asked me how I had slept (how could I ever have suspected them of treachery?) and they assured me that breakfast was in sight. We jogged on downhill for about two hours, travelled through a long defile and there at the end was the usual prickly pear hedge enclosing a group of thatched mud huts. We had arrived.

I was welcomed with the usual charming hospitality and fed with pancake bread, fried eggs and mint tea. The man I had come to see seemed to have a bladder infection and they arranged to come the next day and collect suitable medicine for him and for a few other sick folk I was able to see.

Afterwards I tried to talk to them about the Good News of Jesus and they listened politely. But it was no good leaving my little store of Gospels with them for they assured me that not a single person in the village could read. They begged me to stay and travel with them, but I needed to get back home. I set out alone, got lost in the forest and arrived back at midnight, weary but very happy.

I can't remember much about the weeks that followed, although I know they were sad weeks. Farnham was urging me to come down to the hospital and start a home and nurses' training school for Moroccan girls who were interested in Christianity. It was a hard decision, but one small incident seemed to act as a pointer.

A homeless boy called Absalom who worked with a weaver and slept under the loom turned up one day with a terrible ulcer extending almost from his knee to his ankle. I knew he needed bed rest and hospital treatment but he refused to leave his job, fearing to lose it. All I could do was dress the huge sore, cover it and pray over it. To my amazement it started to heal.

He came every day and seemed to have great faith in our prayers together. I started to read the gospel to him and he listened without comment. But one day he arrived very early in the morning, obviously frightened and disturbed. 'I have had a dream,' he said, 'You must tell me the meaning of my dream.

'I stood at the beginning of a dark road and at the end of the road there was the cross where Jesus died. I wanted to go to it, but there were enemies hiding along the way, ready to spring out on me and hurt me. But beyond the cross, on the other side, there was a place of safety. Tell me, what does it mean?'

Did God mean us to lead these ignorant, frightened people to the cross, the world's greatest battlefield, and leave them there unprotected? 'Behind the cross was a place of safety.' Had the time come to gather some of them into a shelter where they could learn and grow for a season, without fear and distraction? The idea of a nursing school might well be 'a place of safety' for some of these young, lonely believers.

I went home to England for Christmas and stayed for a short time to think things over. Home was wonderful, but the wealth and materialism of the West seemed a strange contrast to the poverty and hunger of those I had left. Was the spoilt child with his heap of presents really any happier than Hamid when an orange or a biscuit came his way? – and where was true happiness to be found – in what we have or in what we are? The verse, 'In thy presence is fulness of joy' became very precious to me, and I started to write *Rainbow Garden,* where Elaine finds the secret of true happiness.

I spent two memorable months at the Shebeen Mission Hospital in Egypt, watching how they trained girls of minimal education, and received much helpful advice. Then, having finally decided to move down to the hospital at Tangier, I went back to the mountains to collect my belongings, only to find that Fatima had continued to gather the poorest children and was feeding them and teaching them in her own house. It was a sad parting. I left on a cold, rainy day and passed little Zohra crouched sobbing in the market place. But the whole small group found a spiritual home with the Emmanuel Mission outside the town and that witness continued for some years. My dear, ragged little boys were re-gathered and loved through their early teen years by a converted Teddy Boy and his wife, Albert and Margaret Thomas. In the end, all Christian workers were forced to leave the area, but middle-aged men still enquire eagerly for Mee-stah Too-muss on my visits back, and there are a number of Gospels hidden away under looms or in the dark recesses of little shops. Sometimes, too, a prosperous, middle-aged shopkeeper will be slightly indignant when I cannot at once remember which ragged little boy he used to be.

How do we, who work among Muslims, measure the achievement of those years? A few bodies healed, for a few desolate children the memory that someone cared, and a few, so very few, who came to a living faith in Christ with all that means of suffering and family division. Only four remained openly avowed Christians in the years to come and no church formed. I believe there are some *secret* believers, but they are *known* only to God.

When I was home on furlough, I got talking to a lady in the train. She asked me about my work and I told her I was a missionary nurse. Her comment was as follows: 'I think you missionaries do a great deal of harm. These people have their own religion, and by trying to impose your views upon them, you're forcing them into a different culture, dividing them, and introducing unnecessary problems. Why can't you leave them alone?'

It would be so easy to agree apart from two basic beliefs not shared by that lady, nor by the TV reporters who have been known to say the same thing – basic beliefs that transform the issue. Firstly, do we really believe that Christ is so eternally precious that he is worth infinitely more to them than all that they may lose, even life itself – whom to know is life eternal? And secondly do we believe in the priceless, measureless, eternal value of one redeemed soul to God? If we do, let us press on; if not, by all means, let us leave them alone.

Looking back on these first years in Morocco, I wrote *Three Go Searching, The Fourth Candle* and *Star of Light,* and then the biography of Hudson Pope, the well-known Scripture Union evangelist among children. During this time, too, my aunt Miss Swain arranged to have a book of my verses published.

14

The Hospital at Tangier

The Tulloch Memorial Hospital stood on the edge of a cliff looking out over the Straits of Gibraltar. On a clear day you could look across to the Rock crouching in the sea, like some grand old lion, and behind it, the coast of Spain. To the west the Straits broaden out into the Atlantic and by the light of those wild sunsets, the great historic sites were almost visible – Cape St Vincent, Cadiz, Trafalgar. To the east, one turns to the beautiful curve of Tangier Bay, nowadays an extended city of highrise hotels and flats and tarmac roads; but when I first went out, the empty golden beaches rose into rolling hills, reached by rutted tracks, so dead and brown in summer, so emerald and flowered when the rains fell.

The hospital had been started in 1889 by Dr Churcher in an improvised Moorish stable, and named after young Edwina Tulloch who had died of typhoid fever, in her first year of missionary service. Others had followed, and a building had been erected to house twenty in-patients, an operating theatre and an Outpatient clinic. In 1938 a large new wing was added for Outpatients, radiology and dispensary. A ward for TB patients was built on top of this, and towards the middle of the century it had become a small, modern, well-equipped hospital, the only Mission Hospital in the whole of North Africa's Islamic belt, as far as Egypt.

It had a heroic history. Doctors and nurses had laboured and died, while some had hung on single-handed. In 1906 during a typhus epidemic, not only was the hospital crammed with patients but the sick had erected tents in the streets around so as to be within reach of their only source of help and comfort. Dr Roberts and Nurse Ida Smith, weakened by overwork and lack of sleep, both succumbed to the disease and died within a week. Then with no medical staff left it seemed as if the light must go out, but it never quite did. By the end of the week, Ida's sister Georgina (also a nurse) had arrived to do what she could until further help was sent. She too died within a few years, probably also of typhus, but the little hospital remained open. In those days, and for a long time afterwards, it was the only place for hundreds of miles round where the very poor could be treated free, and they came by their thousands, sometimes from distances of a hundred miles or so, trudging down mountainous tracks from distant villages, bumping along rutted roads on donkey back or in rattling buses, they came and came and came ...

In the busy Out patient department, an effort was made to keep the numbers of morning patients down to a hundred and twenty and to see them in order of arrival (some for the doctor, some for the nurses, and some for X-ray). It was extremely difficult to do this satisfactorily as the sick started to arrive at 4 am. They were given boards with numbers, but many could not read those numbers, and names were little better as identification because about half the people who came were called Fatima or Mohammed. Surnames and addresses were vague. Their tricks for jumping the queue were endless! Some would bribe the early comers to change boards, some would try to erase the 0 from the 100. Sometimes a solitary innocent-looking woman would suddenly lift her haik and out from its folds would emerge a cluster of children, like chickens from under their mother's wings. Each needed to see the doctor, she would assure us, but she didn't want to bother anyone by getting more than one board! When the doors were shut the more determined would sneak round the garden and hide behind the bushes at the nurses' entrance, hoping to creep in under cover of one of them going in to work. If caught they would consider it extremely funny and expect all to take the same view, not always shared by somewhat weary and exasperated staff. When the waiting room was full, a short gospel message was given by one of the workers, usually under very difficult circumstances. The speaker must have felt very often that it was an impossible task to gain attention from any of the hundred and twenty or so parked along the waiting room benches, pushing in at the door, squatting on the floor etc. However, over the years we heard of some who heard and listened and came again just for the message – several times repeated every morning – and began to think seriously about the Lord Jesus from that simple introduction.

My brother Farnham joined the hospital staff in 1945 and assisted Dr Anderson until 1948, when he himself became medical superintendent until 1975, the year in which the Moroccan government took over the hospital, putting in their own staff. Farnham was, I think, in some ways the most Christ-like man I have ever known. He had certain advantages. His wife Janet was a skilled GP and acted as anaesthetist, making a perfect complement to himself in every way. He had a great gift for understanding, picking up and using languages, and as he quickly acquired a very good grasp of Arabic and as he had already studied French and Spanish, he was well equipped to cope with the multi-cultural environment of Tangier. Then there was the staff; two doctors later joined him – Julian Carlisle from Harrow, UK, and William (Bill) Campbell from the States, both with special skills and both more involved in the medical rather than the surgical side of the work, which was Farnham's prerogative. Both were true brothers in the life and work of the hospital. The nurses, too, were a loyal and dedicated team. Not that they always approved of Farnham; his amazing capacity for work could leave frailer souls in despair, and the saints can sometimes seem exasperating to the less saintly. But they were loyal to his principles, and on the whole they loved him and recognized him for what he was – a man of God.

Through the long, grinding and often disappointing years he never lost that God-given characteristic of seeing the individual as special and unique, that will leave the ninety and nine and go after the one. In that hot, thronged, clamouring Outpatients, with its milling crowds including the rude, the impatient and the totally unconventional, he looked with unhurried compassion and understanding on each, and his patients knew it and almost worshipped him. He could not bear to send anyone away unhelped or abandoned. He would go up to the wards with some travel-stained old man from the mountains who needed an eye operation and a bed for the night, and having been finally vanquished by the nurses ('No, repeat No, there is absolutely no hope of a bed, it is quite impossible to admit anyone else'), he would look thoughtful. There was probably a corner down at the house – Janet would rig up something. There was in fact a tiny guest room, which Janet kept immaculate, as guests of all nationalities had a way of arriving at all hours, often quite unexpectedly. One such visitor arrived from England, and Janet led her confidently to the little room where the bed had been made up with clean sheets. It was a shock to the lady to find a grizzled head on the pillow, its eye covered with a blood-stained bandage. Farnham never could resist the sight of an empty bed!

He was an accomplished surgeon, and as later government hospitals and private clinics opened in the town he specialized more and more in eye surgery. In 1963 he went back to England to take his Diploma of

Opthalinology to be better equipped to set up a specialized eye department in the hospital. Before that the hospital had to cope with anything and everything surgical and medical. Here he often experienced God's enabling in a wonderful way. He told of a morning when, as he was crossing from his home to the operating theatre, he was stopped by a tourist. The man explained that he was a surgeon on holiday, and having heard about the hospital, he wondered if he might watch a few operations.

It was an unusual request, but Farnham agreed gladly and invited him to assist. All went well, until a patient was brought in with what had seemed like a perforated gastric ulcer – a common and relatively simple surgical emergency. However, when the abdomen was opened, there turned out to be not this, but a rare condition requiring an operation Farnham had never done before. Farnham decided he would have to work from the surgical manual. It was then that the visiting surgeon (or was he an angel in disguise?) made his quiet offer: 'Would you like me to take over? It just happens that I have specialised in this condition.' Swiftly and with expertise the operation was performed while Farnham watched and learned and thanked God.

Farnham's early letters back to his parents show with what high hopes he went out to Tangier, how intense his interest was in his patients, what joy he felt over his surgical triumphs, and what spiritual longing he had for those around him. The realization of the crushing strength of Islam dawned on him quite quickly, as extracts from his letters show:

*'The men are very difficult; I can well understand why
so many men missionaries from this country have gone
home in despair. They seem so unresponsive and there are
complications wherever you turn. Every avenue through
which you might approach them seems blocked ... They
read and pray so easily, but not one is out and out for the
Lord, and it seems to mean nothing to them. The Church
here at present is very small and very dead, but it is simple
and run on New Testament lines. It could be wonderful if
the Spirit of God breathed on it ... '*

More and more he was coming to depend on the power
of prayer, his own prayers and the prayers of others. He
wrote: 'Unless I am careful about the planning of each day,
things pile up and I go to bed late and have no inclination
to get up in the morning; the old, old story!

'Through reading *Behind the Ranges* (the life of J.O.
Fraser of Lisuland) I have been shown afresh the value
of systematic prayer from those who are one with us
in the work. My heart is so crushed by the news we
have just received, that our only baptised unmarried
girl on the compound has become secretly engaged
to a Muslim. You can well imagine, when there are so
few, how precious each one is, and what a bitter blow
an event like this is to the little church. It would have
been prevented, I feel, if someone had been praying for
her regularly. I would like to ask half a dozen or so of
you friends at home to attach yourselves each to one
of these Moorish converts out here. If each was hedged

about with prayer, it might prevent the devil making off with the next one. One never knows when he is planning to strike next. Would you undertake to pray for this one, really faithfully every day?'

And again:

'The forces against us are so strong that unless we are prepared to put everything into the fight, we shall get nowhere. At present we are suffering defeat after defeat in this battlefield, and your letter has come to me as a warning. I realise that the situation will continue to deteriorate unless a counter-attack of the most costly nature is made. God's message to me yesterday was from Hebrews XII: "Ye have not yet resisted unto blood striving against sin." I was given the same words on my birthday in the words of Ramon Lull who wrote 600 years ago: "It seems to me that the Holy Land cannot be won in any other way than that whereby Thou, O Lord Jesus and Thine Apostles won it, by faith and prayer and the shedding of blood and tears."'

But it wasn't all sadness; there were flashes of joy over reports of other work, or some gleam of light from the Bible. He wrote:

'I loved hearing about F. (a worker in Southern Morocco) and the five years with no results, followed by blessing, and now there are 30 meeting together to worship. It made me scream with joy! Perhaps one day I can go down and visit there.

'I have just read Revelation in Arabic, and parts of it made me cry, because it is so wonderful to know that one day poor Hamid and Fatima will walk in white raiment and have all their tears wiped away. If only more of these people in Morocco could hear the Gospel.'

He saw clues and pointers to blessing in the lives of some older missionaries:

'Miss Glen [in whose house he chose to live when he first arrived in Tangier] has worked here for 35 years and shows no sign of weakening. She has survived typhoid and cancer and has seen results because she has given her whole life to the people, i.e. she has always had them living with her. This of course calls for the sacrifice of all privacy, but it wins their lives. Perhaps it is not possible for married people to live like that and illustrates what St Paul writes, "The unmarried man cares for the things of the Lord" (I Cor. VII:32) . Miss Glen and Mr Elson [who ran a school for orphaned boys] will have a great welcome from all their girls and boys in Heaven.'

Yet as the years went by, there was a quiet work of grace going on in a few hearts, but not until 1955 was he allowed to see an open, obvious move of the Spirit. It was in that year that Farnham wrote an account of a Sunday afternoon service in Tangier. It was during the annual Moroccan Christian Conference and five had been baptized.

'Mr Acton spoke well on the first chapters of Acts, and many were helped, especially the girls. The men always seem slower, but A. from Tetuan and the two Xauen boys gave good testimonies. A. from the TB ward has been hotly attacked this week. There are some fanatical Muslims up there who seem determined to get rid of him or his faith ...

'Sunday night: Thank you ever so much for praying for us; we've had a wonderful day! Heaven on earth! God has really spoken to people and we have seen hard, matter-of-fact Muslims converted and deeply convicted of sin; and I am deeply convicted for my lack of faith. Mr Bocking took the afternoon meeting and put up a blackboard with a simple picture of the way of life and the way of death. Then he drew a book underneath and asked any who wanted to become Christians to come up and sign their names in the book of Life. There were some very mocking men present and I did not expect anyone to come forward, but ten girls went up to the front. Among them were T. with her plaster leg and Z. on her crutches, F. who has always been so proud, but still no men. After the meeting L. came to me and said, "Go up to my brother's room, he needs you." A. her brother has always been very nice and sensible, but has never given any indication of interest in Christianity. He works as an orderly in the men's ward and is in fact a well taught Koranic student. I went to his room and found him crying, and he said he must accept Christ and give his testimony in the church that night. He was very upset about his former immoral life, but now knows that Christ has forgiven him. So we had a beautiful last meeting when A. spoke on "Grace and truth came by Jesus

Christ", a verse that seems to fascinate him. After that Mr Acton spoke on prayer in the church and we had a prayer meeting. Rejoice with us! We have seen today that God can save anyone and I'm sure it is only a beginning. Pray much for the men in the TB ward. They have heard all about it and are furious. But God is greater and if they kill us at least we can say, "Lord, now lettest Thou Thy servant depart in peace, for mine eyes have seen Thy salvation."'

There were many ups and downs, and discouragements often came in clusters to knock out the faithful, often weary workers. Of the small group of Christians in Tangier, several, and it seemed to us always the most gifted and the most needed, died young, and of those we can speak freely. H., converted in Mr Elson's school as a lad, survived two years of cruel imprisonment for his faith.

On his release he bore faithful, open witness as a church leader, until he died of cancer in his forties. He was a gifted preacher and Bible teacher, and much respected by his fellow workers. Although these men reviled him as a Christian, when someone was needed to look after the union money, H. was the only one they would trust and so he became union treasurer.

A. who had the gift of writing beautiful Arabic hymns (very different from the rather doggerel missionary translations) died as a young man of leukaemia.

M. was converted on the TB ward; he came from the far Rif mountains, a pious Muslim who told us later that when the doctor came to read to them the words of Jesus at night, he longed for a gun to shoot him. But he came to love the doctor dearly and wondered at the kindness and care bestowed on him. Mrs Kent, the hospital matron, who was becoming increasingly crippled with arthritis in the later years of her missionary life, would climb the steep stairs up to the TB ward every night to read John's Gospel with him, and his heart was won. He became a ward orderly when his TB was healed, and married a Christian student nurse. For some years he worked in the men's ward, a gentle Christ-like figure, but died of heart failure in his thirties. On the night of his death, he sent for the doctor and asked him to read the opening verses of John 14. 'I go to prepare a place for you' were his last breathless words, spoken with great joy. Z., also converted in the hospital and trained as a student nurse, was the brightest of our girls and showed every sign of becoming a strong leader amongst the women. She died suddenly under anaesthetic during a tonsillectomy in her twenties.

Why? O why should they be taken from us when we needed them so badly? Has the Enemy more power to hurt in his own territory? Did their Lord know that the way ahead was just too hard and transplant them to perfect them in a fairer climate? We shall never know, but we did know the devastation these bereavements caused, blow upon blow it seemed to the little struggling church. But the work had to go on, and we prayed that although we were knocked down we should not be knocked out or accept the depression and despair which at times seemed the only ways of reacting to such devastating discouragements.

Farnham did not see church and hospital as separate work. Many of the converts became hospital workers and several of the leading Christians were employed in some way by the hospital – so it was inexorably one work and everyone knew that. The local paper made an attack on the hospital at one time and said, 'If you go to the English Hospital [as it was often called although staff were of many different nationalities – English, American, Danish, Swiss, Swedish – but we all spoke English], then your body will be healed, but your mind poisoned by the teaching you will receive.' We took this to be a backhanded compliment. It certainly did not stop anyone, as far as we know, from coming to the hospital and still they continued to come.

Some travelled very long distances and arrived like weary pilgrims at the end of a journey, and to such the doors were always open. One of the most touching cases I can remember was that of an old man who came from the far Rif mountains. Outpatients was just finishing when we heard the tap of a stick in the stone passage and a fine-looking old tribesman with a beard like a goat was led in by the Outpatient orderly. He was blind with double cataracts and had travelled over one hundred miles, partly on foot. Could we make him see?

Farnham examined him and thought that he could; he asked who had guided him.

His granddaughter had guided him, he replied, and she was going to stay with him and look after him. He would not need any other nurse; in fact he implied that he would get on better without them.

Farnham explained that apart from the nurses in training, we could not have a young woman loose in the men's ward at all hours. She would have to find lodgings and wait for him. He said that she was not exactly a young woman and they could not possibly be separated. I went to investigate.

The passageway where they had waited was almost empty, but curled up under a bench lay a tiny child of about five years old, her cheek pillowed on her arm. It was the guide and nurse, worn out by the long journey, taking her rest where she could find it.

So we admitted them both into the men's ward and the nurse snuggled up against him and slept and slept. Sometimes she woke and we would see two dark, bright eyes peeping over the quilt. It was highly irregular to admit relatives into beds, but at first they seemed hardly human; he more like some noble old animal with its young, and she in all habits, domestic and social, was entirely kitten-like. All she wanted was some warm spot close to the one she loved where she could curl up and go to sleep.

But on the day of his operation they had to be parted. She was taken to the women's ward where she continued to behave like a kitten, but now a stray mewing kitten. But the ward helper took her home for the night and she was comforted. Next morning we dressed her up as a nurse and tied a doll on her back in Moroccan fashion, and she was yet more comforted.

A day or two later she was taken back to her grandfather and lifted on to his bed. His eyes were bandaged, but he held out his hand and she kissed it. Then she fished down the neck of her dress and drew out seven stale crusts and arranged them on the sheet, guiding his gnarled old hands towards them. At every meal since they had been parted she had saved her bread for him.

Then one day, hand in hand, they went back to the Rif mountains. The operation had been successful and he could see. We have never heard of them again. Like most of those patients who live at a distance, they came into our lives for a few days and then disappeared, usually healed and happy. But now and again links were formed which have lasted until now.

A., a well educated boy, arrived from the neighbouring town with a long-standing eye complaint. He had heard the gospel on the radio, but we did not know this at the time. He had recognized it as the truth and wanted desperately to know more and see if it really 'worked'. But he had a problem; he was a devout Muslim and believed Islam to be true too, so he decided to play safe and follow both ways for the time being. He continued going to the mosque, reading his Bible and the Koran, praying in the name of Mohammed and of Christ, but he found no peace of heart. Hearing that there was a hospital run by Christians away to the West and making his eye the excuse – although he had no expectations of help in that area – he decided to go and investigate.

He arrived in the middle of a busy Outpatient day and he had to wait a long time before he hinted very shyly that he had come for some eye ointment. Farnham was used to such hints and offered to put him up for the night as he lived far away, sensing that the lad was searching for more than eye ointment. That evening they read the Bible together, the first of many sessions, as A. came regularly at weekends when he was free to learn more. That first evening Farnham was led to Matthew 6 and the verse 'No man can serve two masters', and this came like the voice of God to A. He knew that he would have to decide and he knew on which side lay truth and light. He took his stand for Christ, and in the years that followed faced the usual conflict and persecution. He became a hospital orderly and later trained in a Bible School, and has now become a full-time worker for God among Moroccans in Europe.

Visiting sick people in villages was a work shared by the evangelist, doctors, nurses and Moroccan helpers. Usually on Saturdays a group laden with medicines, dressings and simple Arabic tracts would set off in the old hospital van, with a representative of the patient who had probably walked miles to be our guide. I will tell of one such visit in Farnham's words – '"There's only one more river to cross," said our guide as we climbed out of the car and started to push it out of the mud, where its back wheels were firmly stuck. Only one more river bed, but about five miles of waste, undulating land. There was no road, but our guide, a black-bearded country man in a loose brown and black striped jellaba, kept pointing eagerly ahead; for somewhere among those low hills there nestled a village, and in the village was a hut, where a woman lay on the floor desperately ill.

'With a final tremendous bump we topped the last rise and the village lay in the hollow below us, shimmering in the heat – a collection of thatched bamboo huts surrounded by a hedge of prickly pear cactus. Every child and every dog in the settlement had come out to meet us; but at the sight of a motor car the younger children gathered up their long skirts and scuttled in all directions with shrieks of terror and delight.

'"My wife is here," said our guide, and we stooped down and followed him through the low entrance to where in the semi-darkness a youngish woman lay on a rush mat. Her six children hung around the door – beautiful, shy, dark-eyed children, smiling into the doctor's face.

'The woman had nephritis. The husband would come back with us in the car, fetch the medicine, and walk the twelve miles back, as he had walked the twelve miles to fetch us.

'Out in the sunshine we came, to find the whole village had collected to meet us. A crowd of men, smiling and friendly, squatted in the shade of the thatch. The women stood at a little distance, staring, and the children caught hold of our hands and pressed around us. For half an hour we had a little village clinic, treating sores and headaches, giving out worm medicine and eye ointment, advising on the feeding of babies, etc.

'These people were shepherds and tillers of the soil, and we read them the story of the lost sheep. When the sheep was found, they threw back their heads and laughed. "Can you read?" said the doctor when he had explained the story. They laughed at the very idea. "There is a boy who can read but he is at the mosque in the next village today. He will read to us – leave us a book. The rest of us are like beasts. Come again and tell us another story from your book."

"'Yes – come again, come again," cried the children clustering around the motor, and rushing squealing up the hill as the engine started.

'But we have never been again. There are so many little villages nestling among the hills, so many sick in the big slums of the city, so many thronging the doors of the little hospital – and so few to go to them.'

So the work of the hospital carried on year after year. There was faithful sowing and little reaping, and the fruit was indeed hand-picked. Through the witness of the medical work and the daily preaching of God's Word in Outpatients and the wards, Christianity is respected in Tangier today, although the hospital as we knew it was shut nearly twenty years ago.

People stop one in the street and lament the closing of the hospital and weep for the doctor they loved. 'He was not a Muslim,' one said, 'but he will be in Heaven. His heart was clean.' People knew what we stood for even if they rejected our message. 'She worked at the English Hospital,' I heard a taxi man say – looking at me. 'There they treated us all as equals – they never took bribes. The doctor was the kindest person I ever met.'

I often thought that these lines written by Matthew Arnold of his father could have been said of Farnham:

If, in the paths of the world,
Stones might have wounded thy feet,
Toil or dejection have tried
Thy spirit, of that we saw
Nothing! To us thou wast still
Cheerful, and helpful, and firm.
Therefore to thee it was given
Many to save with thyself;
And, at the end of the day,
Oh, faithful shepherd! to come
Bringing thy sheep in thy hand.
FATIMA
'He shall gather the lambs in His arms.'

Written on the death of a Moorish child who had been brought into hospital incurably ill from a distant tribal village. She only longed for her father who had returned home and whom it was impossible to trace. On the night of her death he unaccountably arrived and carried her off to die in the Fundak – the roofless lodging place of the beasts of burden and of the very poor.

'I will die in my father's arms,' she said. 'Amid scenes and faces I know,

Where donkeys stamp in the Fundak yard
Where straw is scanty and cobbles are hard,

And the vermined squatters cook on the shard,

'Tis there that I long to go.

Not among faces foreign and kind

Would I plunge to the straits of death,

But under heavens starry and free

In the well-known haunts of poverty,

Held to the heart that yearns for me

Would I yield up my rattling breath.'

And through broken speech shall the Questing Love

Surge to her last alarms,

That scorns no channel to heal and bless,

Unperceived, through man's gentleness;

She shall rest in her final helplessness

In the Everlasting Arms.

Loving, unloved; seeking, unsought;

Knowing, the while unknown; Denied all access,

pursuing His quest, The tide steals in on her long unrest:

Through the peace of a father's ragged breast

He shall gather and bear His own.

15

My Life at the Hospital

I started my new life in Tangier with seven teenagers. We lived to begin with in a basement, but later moved upstairs as numbers increased, to the beautiful villa which had been the doctor's house until Farnham built his own bungalow in 1956. This was the Student Nurses' Home, called Dar Scott, i.e. the House of Scott, named after Lady Scott, the kind local patroness who gave substantially to the setting up of this first school of nursing for Moroccan girls. The girls were mostly sent to us by missionaries from all over the country and from Algeria, and were those who had become interested in Christianity, if not already committed Christians, and wanted to learn more. So we taught them anatomy, physiology, basic nursing skills and the Bible. This training was something of an innovation in Morocco, as nearly all the nursing in the government hospitals was done by men. For a girl it meant appearing unveiled in front of men in the men's ward, and a European sister had to be present all the time in those early days, or the girls' parents would never have allowed their daughters such laxity of conduct. The girls soon proved their worth.

In spite of their very limited education and the early age at which they came to us (fifteen to sixteen), they all turned out to be innately clean, quick to learn, kind and professional in their behaviour. As far as their nursing was concerned, it was in almost all cases a success. A few went on to England or Switzerland to gain certificates, and some obtained responsible posts in Moroccan hospitals. The majority left after two or three years to marry, and no doubt their training helped them in the care and bringing up of their children.

Spiritually, the picture was not so bright. While they were with us they seemed to respond to the Christian teaching, but I was still only beginning to discover the stranglehold of Islam and the spiritual warfare involved in the release of its followers. Of those who have stood firm and become recognized as active disciples of Jesus I cannot write, as they are alive and vulnerable. But there are those few from among the student nurses and those who worked for us in the hospital who remained true, and for them we thank God. Of these some have left the country and can live openly as Christians, and others serve in the quiet, limited way which is at present all that is possible to a Christian woman living in a 100% Muslim country. Only a very few have let their light shine more clearly and have suffered. One saw Jesus. 'It was worth it all for those few seconds,' she said afterwards. 'He was there beside me. He was so beautiful. He didn't stay, but I knew he would come back.'

Not all by any means continued as Christians, but a few did, and those who stayed in Tangier joined the little

Arab Church which continued to meet there for many years. Fatima and her family, who followed me from the mountains after a time, became part of this group, but she was a country woman through and through and never quite adapted to town life.

My life at this time was made up of varied activities. Much of it as far as I was concerned was routine, living with the girls, teaching them and overseeing their leisure hours. Farnham and Janet's six children also played a big part in my life, as it often fell to me to look after them if there was an emergency operation or Janet needed a well-earned afternoon off. The dear Grannies (my mother and Janet's), who both came to live with us, also needed care and attention. Janet and I shared this between us with the very loving, capable help of several faithful Moroccan ladies.

The milk clinic for mothers and babies was close to my heart. It was for undernourished and starving babies. They were weighed weekly and given milk powder (provided by a USA relief programme) and vitamins by the hospital. It was naturally very popular, as if breast milk failed, other milk was far too expensive to consider for the type of women who came to the hospital and babies were expected to survive on bread and mint tea, with disastrous results. It was satisfying work. The babies would arrive with huge heads, sunken eyes, bloated stomachs, and stick-like arms and legs, lying inert and whimpering in their mothers' arms. The transformation was rapid once the feeding started and over a few weeks or months their eyes grew bright, their little heads lifted and they began to sit up. The sad monkey-like faces grew child-like and chubby and their weight steadily increased. By the end of a year when they started to cut their teeth, we would try to say goodbye to them. We would explain to them that now they could join the family round the beanpot and leave room for another baby at the clinic. But it was the hardest thing in the world to get rid of them. There were endless reasons to bring them back, endless tricks to prolong the connection, and in many cases we never really did get rid of them. Within two or three years they would come trotting back to Sunday School. Auntie Edith, an older Danish missionary, started a school for them, as many families could not spare their girls to go to school or pay for the shoes and books required for attendance at grammar schools. In the summer holidays we organized day-camps, teaching them from the Bible before taking them for picnics and games on the beach. Many of them became very really 'our children' and grew up to join the student nurses in some instances.

One day an illiterate woman from a distant village arrived with a very sick baby in her arms. She was urged to leave the baby in the ward but felt unable to stay. There were other little children at home and goats to be cared for, and the terrible fear of her baby dying without her was strong. She took the medicine and turned to go. But it was very hot and the way was long. Janet suggested that she and the baby should spend the day together in her home. She would give the child three-hourly penicillin injections and feed it with a pipette, and when the heat cooled off a little they could start back to the village.

S. agreed and sat quietly in the little living room where a cool breeze swept in from the sea. Between treatments, Janet showed her the Wordless Book, with its black, white, red and gold pages. We have showed it to hundreds of illiterate women and they have smiled and nodded and forgotten. Just occasionally one knows it to be true and such a one was S. Her baby's condition improved during the day, and she went home knowing that something life-changing had happened.

She kept coming back to hear more at possible and impossible hours, hungry for any crumb of teaching anyone could give her. One Sunday morning she happened to arrive at the time of the little Arabic Communion Service, and sitting there with that small timid group something happened again. 'I have understood,' she said afterwards. 'Jesus said, Come to me. Jesus said, Follow me. Jesus said, Take up your cross, and that is what I am going to do.'

Her next baby was almost due, and we did not see her for some time. Several weeks later, when I was sitting writing at a table, she suddenly stormed into the room, apparently very angry. She carried the ex-baby on her back and the new baby in her arms, and she brought her fist down on the table with a crash.

'You never told me,' she exclaimed, and burst into tears.

I got her to sit down. 'What did we *never* tell you?' I asked. Then it all came pouring out; she had gone back to her village and witnessed joyfully to her new-found faith

('I thought they would all want to know,' she said.) But the neighbours were suspicious and hostile, and when her baby was born no one, not even her own mother, would help her. It was a long and difficult labour and only her seven-year-old daughter stood by her, and only four or five of her neighbours came to the seventh-day feast, so beloved of all village ladies. She had not known it would be like that, and she hated the lot of them.

I asked her if she felt she had made a mistake. Was the way too hard? Did she want to turn back? She gazed at me in astonishment and once again the fist came down on the table: 'Never, never, never,' she cried.

It was true, we had never really told her. Time had been so limited and we at the hospital had been so busy. So we went through the Gospels picking out the passages where Jesus warns his disciples that they will have to suffer. She seemed to calm down so we started again, tracing through the Lord's teaching on forgiveness and she listened quietly, until we came to that supreme, shining example of forgiveness – the words of Jesus on the cross, 'Father, forgive them, they know not what they do.'

Down came the fist on the table again. 'I don't believe it,' she said.

I asked her why not, and she replied that it was impossible. No human being could ask forgiveness for those who were hammering nails into his hands, and I suddenly realized what I had not formulated before – that she was right; no human love could respond like that, but this was not human love; this was the love of God ... the very love that he offered to share with us; the love of God shed abroad in our hearts by the Holy Spirit.

I was talking beyond my experience, but she seemed to understand at once. This was the answer to her need. 'You mean,' she questioned, 'I've got to go home ... and the first woman who has a baby ... I've got to be the first to go and help her?' She looked at me wonderingly.

'Of course, I was never going to speak to them again ... but then you see, you never told me.'

I cannot write freely for her family's sake; I can only say that S. went home to love as Jesus loved and to overcome evil with good. In an amazing way she has proved that it works, and the love of Christ indwelling and reaching out through a simple human life will draw people to himself. There are some today who would say, albeit secretly, that through a glimpse of that gentle compassion shown to them in the life of a simple village woman, they have come to believe.

Another woman came from a distant village and was admitted to hospital for minor surgery. She stayed only a few days, but again was shown the Wordless Book and asked to take one home. She was very shy and rather inarticulate, and we did not know how much she had understood, nor did we especially remember her. There were so many.

It was probably about two years later that she suddenly appeared with five or six ragged, bright-eyed, excited little village children attached. She strode in waving her Wordless Book. 'Don't you know me?' she cried, seeing our surprised faces. 'I'm your sister in Christ. My sins are forgiven. Now I have brought my children. There is no school in our village and I want one of them to learn to read to me from your Book. You can have which one you like – this one – or this one – or this one. Keep him and send him to school until he can come home and read the Bible to me.'

It seemed a reasonable request, and I chose a nine-year-old who was thrilled to stay. He fitted in well and enjoyed the local school. But he had never slept in a bed before and seemed a little bit cold and lonely. After two weeks I took him back to his village for the weekend. No hero returning from space could have had a more excited and enthusiastic welcome, and I promised to return on Sunday afternoon to take him back. When I arrived there was a feast prepared and we ate bread and read together and he was ready to come.

The car stood just outside and I had not locked the door. When I opened it I found that Muhammed, aged seven had got there first. He had entwined himself inextricably with the brakes and could not be pulled out, and from somewhere between the front seats a voice said, 'I'm coming too.' It seemed the perfect solution. Two in a bed would be warm and cosy, and two going to school would be companionable. They stayed with us for two years until a school started in the next village and they were able to continue their education from home. I can only say that their reading achieved its object.

16

Nephews and Nieces

Farnham and Janet's six children were a continual source of occupation and pleasure. Soon after he married, Farnham decided to build his own house, with much local help. It was a stone's throw from the Nurses' Home and at the bottom of the hospital compound, a small house on the cliff top with large windows looking directly across the Straits of Gibraltar. At first it boasted one large bedroom and a tiny one with bunk beds for Paul and Oliver. Over the years these two children were followed by four more – Clare, Danny, Martyn and David. Later the two dear Grannies joined the family. At each addition the house grew a little larger as other rooms of various shapes and sizes were added to it.

This house became a centre for Moroccan Christians, medical students, visitors of many nationalities, hippies in distress, the sick and needy of every description. In the middle of all this the children grew up (also with a good deal of local help). They have turned out loving and caring people and look back to that crowded little house with nostalgic pleasure.

One of the English nurses (Gwen Theakston) working at the hospital during this time, wrote the following limerick which illustrates the house's varied use. It was to celebrate Farnham's completion of a sofa/settee to use in the sitting room. Farnham also had a reputation for driving the old hospital van and his ramshackle motorbike far too fast!

There was a young doctor called Sinjun
Who said, It's my honest opinyun –
That given the floos (money) and plenty of juice (petrol)
I could make my bike go like the wind – un.
It's my intention to make with a sort of invention –
A settee that expands to meet the demands
Of the house by the sea at a quarter to three
When folk come to tea,
There'll be room – don't you see?
There'll be bishes (bishops) and mishes (missionaries)
And other strange fishes,
A jubbly* or two and a hippy with flu,
A baby with measles, another with sneezles,
For they all come to tea at a quarter to three
(Do come and join us then!)

* jubbly = country man from the mountain villages.

Children attract children, and the place swarmed with them – the smartly dressed offspring of American missionaries, business people and diplomats; the scruffy older brothers and sisters of the milk clinic babies. They were welcomed indiscriminately and played endless noisy games on the old tennis court at the bottom of the garden.

Certain incidents with the children stand out in my memory.

We had the use of a battered old van and later a car, and I remember a Saturday afternoon in the spring, going as we often did into the country for a picnic. From January till April the hills behind Tangier are glorious with wild flowers – first heavily-scented narcissi, then blue irises, hyacinths, mallow, small crimson gladioli, marigolds, buttercups and multi-coloured vetches. Farnham's children loved to join the girls and me on these flower-gathering expeditions. Paul had an endearing lisp and I can see him aged about three squatting on a patch of emerald green grass, munching a handful of it. 'Pauli eat grath,' he was mumbling to himself, 'Pauli die, Pauli eat more grath, Pauli die more.' Providentially Paul did not die but lived to go back to Morocco, after his medical training in the UK, as a surgeon in a government hospital.

I remember David at six years old apparently possessed of a devil, suddenly rushing from his flower-picking to the van, jumping in, taking off the brakes. The van, parked on a hill, took off pretty smartly. I was some way away and there was nothing I could do about it but stand and pray – but possibly the worst moment of my life passed in amazed wonder as I watched the van turn gracefully and come to rest in a ditch on the other side of the road – and it wasn't David steering either!

Oliver was the perfectionist and poet. At Christmas time he had to have his own tiny tree as well as the big family one. He would spend hours decorating it and gazing at it, lighting the candles in the dark and seeing who knows what worlds of beauty and joy. But he also liked to live by rule and he hated to be one moment late for school. He would ask me the time every few minutes. Once when I was working I failed to look up, merely saying it was still quite early. There was a grieved silence and then he remarked, 'Auntie, I do *wish* you would take life more seriously!'

Clare, the only girl of the six and thus specially precious, had the distinction of being the only one forgotten and left behind on a seaside picnic several miles from home when she was three years old. When Janet arrived back at the house and counted the children as they jumped out of the van (her own and others), Clare was missing. Very agitated, she went back to the beach where half an hour before they had packed up the picnic, to find a contented Clare sitting on the old road sweeper's lap, sucking a boiled sweet. She was not the least worried, for were not all Moroccans Daddy's friends, and would not Mummy for sure come back to fetch her?

Danny had a vivid imagination, and it was hard to tell whether the amazing adventures that he related so charmingly had really happened or not. But he had a wonderful knack of saying the right thing and cheering everyone up. I once travelled to England with him and we were staying a night with friends in Madrid. It was blazing hot and the plane had had to make an emergency landing in Seville, so it was midnight before we finally reached Madrid airport. I carried a sleeping Danny to our host's car, almost too tired to speak. The kind host, who had been waiting for five hours, seemed in a similar condition. When we finally reached the car and staggered into it, it would not start. We had to leave it and continue the journey in a taxi through the dead suburbs of Madrid, passing through dark grey street after dark grey street in the early hours when even Spaniards were asleep. Danny suddenly woke up.

'Where are we?' he asked.

'In Madrid,' I replied drearily.

He peered out of the window. 'Then I do think Madrid is the interestingest place I have ever been to,' he exclaimed enthusiastically, and somehow the fog lifted!

Martyn and David, the two youngest, were inseparable. David was the leader of a gang of little Moroccans. There was one rather disreputable family of six small children who were flooded out of their house near the beach and took refuge in our basement. They all seemed more or less the same size, pasty-faced and underfed, but Martyn and David loved to spend the evening drinking mint tea with them. During the day they would pour into the garden below the doctor's house and roll down the grass slope with shrieks of laughter, repeating the performance again and again. David never seemed tired of rolling with them. Martyn would join in for a time, but enough was enough, and I remember him marching into the house, flushed and with grass in his hair, and remarking with great vehemence, 'It's not that I don't like David, because I *do* but I do *wish* there was just *one* person out there who had some *BRAINS.*'

I started a Sunday evening group known as Young People's Fellowship for English-speaking children, and we always started off with biscuits and Coca-Cola (a rare treat in those days). David, aged about five, was allowed to join us for the refreshments and singing and was an enthusiastic member of the group. One day he came up to me looking thoughtful. 'Auntie,' he asked, 'could we have some fellowship, just you and me alone?' I was delighted. He was such a merry little clown – perhaps something more serious had penetrated. I asked him when the fellowship should take place. 'Tonight,' he said, 'when I am in bed in my pyjamas – just me and you.' I arrived in his room with a children's Bible under my arm. He was sitting up in bed waiting for me. He gazed at me suspiciously.

'Where is the fellowship?' he asked.

It took me a moment or two to realize my mistake. I fled, and parking the Bible, ran to the corner shop for a bottle of Coke. We spent a happy but secular half hour. Fellowship was Coke – neither more nor less.

I remember journeys with some of the children – there always seemed to be a good many of them. The journeys were taken on the whole light-heartedly, and on one occasion travelling across Europe we stopped late at night in Spain. We laid the sleeping children in their sleeping bags in a row on a moonlit field, and we adults stretched out beside them. We did not realize that because of the heat Spaniards dig their beetroots by moonlight. We woke to find ourselves surrounded by a startled, noisy group of Spanish labourers with hoes wanting an explanation. But when they saw the sleeping children, they were all kindness and courtesy. *'De nada – de nada,'* (it is nothing) they cried, waving their hands, and they dug their beetroots weaving around us till sunrise.

The family was fortunate. The children grew up in that happy era when the government paid boarding school fees for the children of British couples working abroad with a salary under the minimal limit. One by one, aged nine, they left for school in the UK. The most exciting days of the year were when the family and any of my girls off duty would go to the airport to meet the plane bringing the 'big children' home for the holidays. The girls were considered part of the family, and we would travel in convoy to the airport. I remember the little flying figures rushing across the tarmac clutching collapsing parcels, especially at Christmas time. I remember the embarrassing noise of the reunions, only no one was embarrassed; David triumphant at getting his hand-made wooden bookends safely through the customs. 'I packed them right at the bottom of my suitcase, the customs man never even saw them,' he exulted gleefully, as though he had successfully transported a bomb! Every small accomplishment was aired and appreciated and new experiences shared. A special family concert was given for Paul who had been learning the piano for one term. 'Paul will now play a piece,' said the announcer solemnly.

'Paul will play theveral pietheth,' was the spirited reply, and he proceeded to do so.

Farnham and Janet excelled at picnics and took the children camping during the holidays. Anyone who liked could join in the fun as they pleased. I doubt if there are any more beautiful beaches in the world than those either side of Tangier, and I could never decide which I liked best; the Atlantic side with endless golden sands stretching all the way to Rabat, huge breakers, and rocky cliffs, or the soft Mediterranean coast, with little inlets, calm blue sea and clear, transparent water.

There were lonely roads to the districts far off the beaten track where even a twelve-year-old could learn to drive the car in safety on sick visits to villages with Daddy. Sometimes there was a feast to partake of on arrival of roast sheep or fowl, freshly slaughtered for the occasion. Weddings and feasts such as that celebrating a baby's birth added colour and gaiety to life.

I remember an occasion when the hospital staff were invited by a grateful patient to spend a night in his village and to be present at the final marriage celebration of one of his relatives. We were to witness the departure of the bride at midnight to go to her husband's house. The older nurses found plenty of reasons to refuse the invitation (it was blazing summer weather and a long journey), but Farnham and I thought we would take the girls who were eager to accept, and we set off one afternoon with our guide, Paul and Oliver tagging along too. We drove in the old hospital van until the path petered out and then we left the van with a guardian and set out on foot. It was one of those villages which was 'near, so near, just over the next hill', but the next hill recurred six or seven times – the old familiar story. It was nearly sunset when we arrived, sweating and exhausted, but the feast revived us. The bride went off around midnight to a deafening burst of lutes and tambourines, and we lay down where we could and slept soundly.

We had intended to leave at dawn and reach the van before the sun really gathered strength, but it was not to be. The sick of the village had already gathered, and Farnham had to conduct quite a long Outpatients before they served us with a ceremonial breakfast. It was blazing hot before we were allowed to leave, and we walked slowly while the sun rose higher and higher.

We had trudged some miles when Paul suddenly collapsed. We were not far from a tiny village. We laid him down and covered his head, but there was no shade and our water supply was nearly finished. A river bed lay ahead of us, but the river had dried up. To our left was a collection of mud huts, hardly a village. Someone hurried there to ask for the loan of a donkey and if possible, a mattress.

They were kind and concerned, but they could not help. Every donkey had gone to market early that morning, and there was not a beast left in the place. There was nothing for it but to try and carry Paul (a sturdy nine-year-old) between us and stagger on.

It was then at the time of real danger and need that we learned afresh, as we have done over and over again, the truth of God's promises. Just as we prepared to move on, we heard the sound of little hooves, and a small donkey driven by an old man rose up out of the river bed, a little further on. The man had been gathering rushes and had tied them in two neat bundles on either side of the animal's flanks, forming a perfect mattress for a child to lie on. He was only too happy to earn some extra money and laid his great straw hat over Paul's head and shoulders and set off merrily. Before long we came to a river bed that had not dried up and Paul was laid in a pool and revived, after which we all splashed in the water too. It was rather warm and muddy, but we were not fussy and we travelled on homewards praising God for his provision. The old man was happy too, rewarded beyond his expectations for we were very, very grateful.

17

Questions People Ask

The question of the child looms large in missionary circles today, and so it should. Do children suffer from a life less materially comfortable and with fewer 'things' than they would have in their own countries? Are they adversely affected by the busy lives their parents often lead, a house open to visitors of every kind, and later the inevitable separation that school and college bring? Are parents justified in subjecting their children to such a life?

From my own observation I would say that on the whole these children do not suffer, provided that special times of privacy with their parents are strictly kept. Having less in the material realm is probably a good thing; little treats and gifts are the more precious. The children are forced to use their own initiative and imagination and to provide their own entertainment. The home-made plays, concerts, drama performed by kids dressed up in tablecloths and their parents' clothes, can be far more exciting than an hour spent in front of a video.

There is also the education of mixing with other cultures and nationalities; life abroad is often colourful, unconventional and seldom boring. These children grow up as part of a worldwide brotherhood, at home with all types of people. They experience, too, that early sense of family unity, as they see their parents' interests largely narrowed down to the purpose for which they came to the land of their calling, i.e. to preach the gospel, often linked with relief of suffering or providing educational facilities which would otherwise not be available to the local people. All this without the bewildering outside conflict of entertainments, extracurricular programmes etc, and the strain of keeping up with the Joneses. Such children come at a young age to share the interests of their parents. The coming of a soul to Jesus is rejoiced over together; the plight of another less fortunate child is a shared subject of prayer and caring.

Of course there are casualties – some rebel in their early teenage years and will try out a different lifestyle, seeking their own philosophy of life. But, as the years pass, life without Christ can be a soul-hungry, disappointing affair, and they will never quite forget that 'in my Father's house there was bread enough to spare'. Also, as with all Christian parents, there are those strong, invisible cords of love and prayer drawing them back to their true resting place. 'It is not his will that one of these little ones should perish.' 'This is the will of God, even your sanctification.' 'If we ask anything according to his will, he heareth us.' Let us then rest on this promise and take heart.

Most of our young people look back to their childhood years abroad with happy nostalgia, and we have been greatly encouraged by the number of missionary sons and daughters who have grown up to train and return to the country of their childhood or engage in full-time Christian work elsewhere.

I have often been asked whether God's work is best undertaken by the married or the unmarried. There seems to me to be place for both, although there are obviously some jobs which the unmarried can more easily undertake. I believe that a simple Christian home, uncluttered by foreign gadgets, where husband and wife love and honour each other and where happy children are brought up in the nurture and fear of the Lord and where the doors are ever open to welcome all who come, whatever their race, class or creed, is a very real lighthouse in a dark land. Perhaps there is no greater witness to Christian unity than a truly Christian home. One example of this especially comes to mind.

In the '60s our homes were beset with hippies! Morocco, where up in the Rif mountains marijuana can be picked in handfuls, was the largest centre for the hippy migration, next to Katmandu. They came by their hundreds – many of them beautiful young men and women in flowing robes and long hair, sickened by the materialism and false values of their own societies in America, the UK and many European countries. They came to seek an alternative lifestyle. Sadly, the only alternative many of them found was drugs and all their attendant evils. Many were mercilessly robbed, cheated and sometimes beaten up. The cheap hotels and dirty basements where they squatted bred frequent diseases, and the girls often became pregnant. Some went out of their minds through LSD. In their distress they turned to the hospital by their dozens. Later, in answer to many prayers, a YWAM team came to live on the hospital compound and opened a hostel for them, where many found an alternative lifestyle in Christ.

But there was still no hostel when Peter suddenly arrived in my brother's living room during a family meal, clad in only a scanty pair of bathing trunks. He was over six foot tall, and his whole body, face and limbs were blistered with sunburn, and his eyes were bright with fever. He had been swimming on the beach and lay down afterwards in the midday sun and slept for several hours. On waking he found that all his possessions – wallet, passport, money, tickets – had been stolen and he was suffering from sunstroke. He tried to reach his lodging in his trunks, but he was conspicuous, to say the least of it, and the police arrested him for immodest behaviour. At the police station he was made to stand next day for many hours against a wall in the blazing August sun. When he was on the point of collapse, they pushed him out on to the road.

Where was he to go? With a mocking crowd of screaming children behind him, he somehow managed to reach the hospital, but the hospital was closed for spring cleaning. However, the cleaners assured him that down at the bottom of the garden he would at least find a doctor. So he arrived in the middle of lunch and staggered in through the open door.

The little house was full to overflowing, but Janet put him in David's bed, while David obligingly slept on a mattress on the floor. (David and Martyn were quite used to this sort of thing – 'We don't mind people in our bedroom at all, Mummy,' they once remarked. 'But must we have old women?')

The burns, though not deep, proved to be fairly extensive and became infected, smelling horribly in the heat. Peter was a quiet boy, disillusioned with the hippy life and rather noncommittal. A Christian medical student spent a long time talking to him, and we all tried to cheer him up. But when he left us to return to England with a new passport and money borrowed from the Embassy, no one felt they had got to know him very well.

Then the letter came. It was a restrained letter of thanks and only the last paragraph betrayed his real thoughts. 'I have found a church and have started to attend regularly, and I think now that I am a Christian. I stayed in your house for nearly three weeks, and I have never been in a house where so many people of so many types and nationalities came in and out. Yet all the time I was there I never heard an irritable or impatient word. If that is Christianity, then I want it.'

Is not that the heart and crux of all our work – all Christian witness worldwide – so to live day by day that those who watch us will say, 'If that is Christianity, I want it'?

Not all contacts were so rewarding, and there were many discouragements and apparent failures. There were dark patches, struggles, times of bitterness and near despair; also apparently unreasonable physical attacks, which for me took the form of frequent migraine headaches. One of our number committed suicide. There was strong temptation to yield to discouragement and disappointment with our seemingly fruitless labour, to envy those in other parts of the world where churches were being formed and souls won for Christ. Were we wasting our lives? Had we mistaken our call? There were those apparently strong missionaries who returned home after a few years, exhausted by physical and emotional breakdown or simply through sheer discouragement.

I remember the unnatural attacks that seemed to fall on one small American mission whose activities counted for God and who dreamed of a radio programme. A young mother and her baby died in childbirth; a fine new young worker contracted polio and was permanently invalided home. A young son died, a baby died, another was born with brain damage, and a mother was so damaged by giving birth that she could never have another child. A husband was shot by thieves and suffered grave internal injuries, and later an only son of twenty who went back to the States to enter university was shot for his wallet containing a few dollars. In the end, as a mission they were all turned out of the country and again we asked, Why? Why? Only after many years did the reason for these fierce attacks become clear, for it was through their efforts and vision that Monte Carlo Radio, the transmitting station set up by Hitler to announce his victory over Europe, now beams the gospel nightly into all the North African coastal countries.

To those of us struggling on against what seemed to us hopeless odds, the sense of failure could be crippling and the temptation to give up very strong. Also in a small, very hard-working community, in a very hot country, with the frustration of a difficult foreign language and little outlet beyond the confines of one's job, the attacks on relationships could be deadly – and this in spite of the normal deep ties of fellowship.

But help was given. I remember the visit of a Swiss pastor, who spent his life going from mission station to mission station with a very simple message. No Christian can be possessed of an evil spirit (the Holy Spirit will never share his residence with a messenger of Satan), but in a Christless country where Christians have dared to launch an attack on enemy territory, the counter-attack will be strong and definite and the oppression of evil spirits should be quickly recognized. He urged us to give them their rightful names (pride, jealousy, resentment, discouragement, depression) and to seek out a group of trusted friends and ask their help in binding and rebuking that spirit or spirits by name and claiming the victory. Where we obeyed, situations were healed and relationships were restored.

So some of us learned the vital, soul-saving lesson of forgiveness ... *Firstly* to others. So often the supposed slight can be ridiculously small – a look or partially heard remark, a criticism repeated third hand, at the end of a long, exhausting day. Thus a nagging secret resentment is born and the enemy keeps it alive and blown up out of all proportion, to the detriment of health, happiness and effective service. We so often suffer because we cannot forgive or we cannot accept forgiveness, or sometimes a mixture of both. *Secondly*, we have to learn to forgive *ourselves*. The sense of failure, the deep discouragement, the feeling of guilt is very great. We tell ourselves missionaries should not fail or be discouraged.

We can forgive only by looking at the nature of God's forgiveness.

He delights to forgive *(Mi. 7:18)*. *We cherish our grudges and find it hard to be reconciled. It wounds our pride to take the first step, but the Father on the housetop could not stop himself – he ran to pour forgiveness on the prodigal.*

His forgiveness always takes the initiative *and our very repentance is the result of his seeking. He never says, 'He was in the wrong; he should come to me.' Rather the Shepherd took every step of the long road to forgiveness himself, and the sheep never took one to meet him. In fact he never took a step at all. The sheep was carried back on the tide of the Lord's forgiveness.*

His forgiveness actively destroys the evil it forgives. *It is so strong, so loving, so purifying that it actually cleanses the heart in which it operates, as light scatters darkness. His forgiveness forgets. When God pardons a sinner, he instantly sets him in unclouded, unbroken communion with himself.*

His forgiveness sees us through *the natural result of our failure. 'I am with thee,' said God to Jacob – 'I will bring thee again' (Gen. 28:15). We might say, 'After all, he brought it on himself; he deserves all he gets.' Divine forgiveness saw him right through.*

Lastly, his forgiveness expresses itself. *Many times doubt and a sense of strain drag on between two people who both long to be right with each other, because through shyness, fear or reserve neither can pluck up courage to discuss the matter. God on the other hand proclaims his forgiveness (Ex. 34:5-7).*

(From *A Missionary Muses on the Creed*, pages 31-33)

So we learned to live as a loving, forgiving community of people of very varying ages, from very different backgrounds, but one family in our Lord Jesus, holding on to one another in love with the assurance that our labour was not in vain in the Lord.

18

A Tribute to my Father

One night in September 1956 I had a very vivid dream. I saw my father lying on the ground reaching out to me across a barrier that I could not climb. Next day the telegram came. He had had a severe heart attack and the condition of his heart was such that he was not likely to live long. A missionary came from another station to look after the girls and I flew home, my first trip in a plane.

While the rather anxious hours passed I seemed to see him moving through the years as in a film. He was home seldom enough between meetings, visits and speaking tours in North and South America, Australia, New Zealand, North and South Africa, Palestine and all over the British Isles, to see his children through rose-coloured spectacles. No one could say that we were always easy to manage, but our father never realized it. He left the heavier side of our upbringing and all our serious training to our mother, never doubting that she was far more competent than himself in such matters. And on his short visits the usual rules and regulations went west. They were riotous occasions of merriment with games of bears under the nursery table, charades, camp fires, picnics, midnight feasts and long, long tramps over the hills or to Upton-on-Severn. Yet this abandonment caused none of the usual disillusionment or unruliness that so often follows treats and irregularities; for he obviously considered us good children, and as many others will too, we temporarily became what he considered us to be. Besides he was so infectiously happy that no one wanted to spoil it by being contrary or unruly. Without a word on the subject he would leave us with the abiding impression that goodness was desirable and utterly joyful, the only real fun in the world.

His influence over us must have been largely unconscious for he very seldom actually taught us anything at that age. Although he could speak delightfully to Sunday Schools on occasion, he did not consider himself gifted with children, and he left all the simplification of spiritual matters to his wife, of whose patient, thorough Bible teaching much could be written. She could come down to the level of the smallest, but he would retain his own level, only sometimes opening a door and allowing a little child to catch a glimpse of mystical glory far beyond it, and yet the more beautiful for being only vaguely understood. I remember how he lifted me, as a seven-year-old, on to his knee and almost shyly, in a voice that sometimes trembled with emotion, read aloud all nineteen verses of Mrs Cousins' hymn based on Samuel Rutherford's last sayings, 'The sands of time are sinking, the dawn of Heaven breaks.'

And the result? I was thrilled and transfixed. There was the feeling that Daddy had trusted me to share something that mattered to him, and there was a whole new world of bright imagery to explore and revel in, and eventually, after many years, to understand. In a surprisingly short time I had learned all nineteen verses off by heart, and the old Scottish divine would have smiled had he watched the little brown tomboy in the red bathing dress climbing a perilously steep waterfall in a stream bed and murmuring to herself:

Deep waters cross my pathway,
The hedge of thorns was sharp.
Now all these lie behind me,
Oh, for a well-tuned harp.

Another memory is of him arriving home a day earlier than expected, after a long absence abroad, and walking up alone from the station and meeting John in a pram, wheeled by a local girl who was helping temporarily. The round St John face and something about the pram struck him as familiar. He stopped and gazed.

'Excuse me,' he asked with his customary politeness, 'but could you tell me ... is this by any chance my baby?'

'I'm sure I couldn't possibly say, sir,' replied the girl haughtily, and made off in a hurry.

He was gloriously hospitable. 'Do drop in to tea,' he would urge strange families at the Sunday morning service. Sometimes, however, he would fail to mention it at home and an enthusiastic group would arrive at the front door just as we were finishing tea. ('I'm afraid you were expecting six, but we're only four!') My mother was a genius at carrying off these situations but we children rather spoiled her efforts by relapsing into helpless giggles. The family learned to be ready for anything and Sunday tea became a standing joke.

Yet apart from slight lapses of memory he was the soul of courtesy and always treated his wife and daughters like queens. He loved to help in the house, but apart from looking after babies, at which he excelled, his efforts were not always successful. Some rather elegant ladies were once expected to tea and my mother, who was not very well, went off to rest after dinner, making my father promise to wake her in time to prepare. She was only woken at the last minute by her beaming husband. 'Nothing to worry about, darling,' he proclaimed triumphantly. 'All is ready,' and he ushered her excitedly into the sitting room to a table laden with piles and piles of thick, sparsely buttered doorsteps. The ladies were actually arriving. There was apologetic whispering and laughter in the passage, but our guests were sports; they munched gallantly away and the party was a great success.

In the combination of our mother's simple, straightforward teaching and the sense of our father's mysticism that was beyond us, there was a strength and safeguard against the modern tendency, resulting perhaps from oversimplification of divine truth, to consider religion the property of the flannelgraph and the Primary Sunday School, and to abandon it in adolescence. We might wriggle and yawn and feel bored in the Sunday services, but none of us looking at that shining, lifted face, or listening to that voice that trembled with adoring love could maintain for a moment that the Breaking of Bread was really boring, and it left us with a feeling of mingled sadness and expectation; sadness because we were small and wicked and incorrigibly merry and so could see nothing, and expectation because we might one day grow up and understand and see what Daddy saw. And perhaps that was why so much of our play centred round the story of King Arthur and his Knights and the Holy Grail, and the character that I invariably impersonated on my lonely rambles was Sir Galahad. What the Holy Grail was, none of us knew, but one must be very pure in heart, like Daddy, to see it.

So while our mother mourned the passing of the years and the tumbling babies that seemed to turn into tough little boys and girls overnight, he exulted in each stage of our growth and bent his scholarly mind to each new achievement. He delighted in the exceedingly amateur family orchestra and would become absorbed in a game of chess with a very small son. He would give the same concentrated consideration to the mis-spelt literary efforts of a little daughter as he would to his Greek commentary; in fact he was the only person to whom I was not ashamed to show them.

With that sanity which so characterized him, he recognized himself as a man set apart, and of such certain standards are required. He recognized us as ordinary, healthy children, and of such certain other standards are required; and he never confused the species. Provided we were not malicious, he did not quell us when we mercilessly mimicked our elders and betters (and some of us were truly gifted in that direction) but he never spoke one discourteous word about anybody and we never heard an impatient or unloving word between him and our mother. He encouraged us to enjoy ourselves and he loved to give us treats; but we knew he denied himself and kept under his body; and this positive, radiant holiness that went on its own way, seldom criticizing or scolding, was extraordinarily constructive and controlling.

So we grew up and he watched and waited, never trying to force upon us the spiritual riches he had stored up for us until we were ready. But during our teenage years he began to introduce us to his own methods of Bible study and each of us could testify that he opened up the Book to us as no one else had ever done.

As a teenager and later, I loved to go with him to summer conferences for young people when he was in England, and see the very evident appreciation of his listeners and how often he was the centre of a group of eager young men and women or engaged in private session with one or another. It may have been the absoluteness of his standards or the superhuman demands he made on them; it may have been the tender humour and understanding with which he mingled those demands, or it may have been his own humility. At all events many hundreds of people wrote after his death from all parts of the world and all spheres of life to pay tribute to the profound influence he had had on them in their early years, and some of these are men and women who have become mighty leaders for God. 'He did more to make Christ real to me than anyone else', wrote a missionary wife in Zimbabwe. He appealed equally to the simplest person and to the most intellectual.

I remember a talk he gave once on Luke 4, where Jesus, as his custom was, went to the synagogue on the Sabbath day. He emphasized the importance of example, quoting John Bunyan's words, 'I was very careful to give my children no occasion to blame, lest they should not be willing to go on pilgrimage.' Not an easy thing to say, with a lynx-eyed son or daughter sitting in the audience weighing up every word; but in the matter of practising what he preached he passed the test every time.

We wanted to share him with our friends, and as we approached or reached university studies we had for some years in the Easter holidays what we called 'The Applegarth Conference' (Applegarth being our second home in Malvern). To this lively group of young people he and my mother gave of their very best. Morning and evening sessions were given over to serious study and discussion, and the afternoons to wonderful picnics and rambles and high teas organized by our mother, who took the whole crowd of hungry, noisy creatures straight to her heart. They discussed their problems with my father with unusual freedom because he was never shocked or surprised, and his humour, sympathy and broad understanding must have led many a rebellious, puzzled young Christian into right decisions and paths of peace.

Something he said to us and which I wrote down went as follows (the arrangement of the lines is mine):

You can have this world's peace

And enjoy it

Provided you shut your eyes to the future

And shut the gates of the soul to yesterday.

The peace that Jesus gives

Is precisely the opposite.

It throws back the gates of yesterday,

Showing sins forgiven.

And as for tomorrow

It opens its gates and shows the future

Radiant with promised grace

And with the sure hope

Of seeing His face.

He was equally in demand at large Bible study conferences in different parts of the world with his amazing knowledge of the Bible, the result of countless hours of patient study, self-tuition in Hebrew and Greek and notes that filled thousands of loose-leaved sheets. There was a legend, probably not far from the truth, that he could give the reference for every verse in the Bible, and the children he knew best when he lived at Clarendon School in later years used to love to shoot unexpected texts at him. But they seldom, if ever, succeeded in catching him out, not even the small, golden-haired girl who fixed him with a diminutive forefinger and stated solemnly, 'Thy wife shall be a harlot in the city', and my father replied with equal solemnity, 'Amos 7:17'. after which they both relapsed into a state of mutual admiration and glee.

'Mr St John, I'd give the world to know the Bible as you do,' said a lady to him at the close of a meeting. 'Madam,' he replied, 'that's just what it costs.'

But he always stressed that the Bible is never an end in itself. It is the path by which you reach Christ, and he never considered any study really worthwhile unless it affected one's daily conduct in a practical way.

For many years he travelled extensively, and for years in the 1920s and '30s used to visit the States each summer. He was offered the headship of a well-known Bible college there; and though the prospect greatly attracted him, he felt it was not to be.

His was an ever apparent joy, rising from depths of praise that spilled over in sparkling enjoyment of life's pleasures. Often during the war he would come and take me out from hospital and, not really at home in any red tape atmosphere and probably dreaming of his next sermon, he once unconsciously settled on a seat in Outpatients forbidden by large notices to the public. Sister hurried up, all starch and indignation, but his beaming innocence disarmed even that lady and she retired smiling. He was so certain she had come to welcome him to her domain, so cordially delighted to be there. Then he and

I would sally forth to Kew Gardens or for a trip up the Thames, and his radiant pleasure in the expedition would banish for a few hours all the horror and strain of war and the wounded and the raided nights, and I would go back feeling strangely refreshed and balanced.

And how much his letters meant, specially to his children, as they followed us to Lebanon, to Morocco, to Australia where John was in the Navy. His letters were never long, but strong and pertinent to the needs of the moment. When I was grieving because my activities had been checked by government regulations he wrote, 'If we look at the Government action we may become bitter. But if we only look at the movement of the hands of God, our hearts become soft and tender, and we remember that if an under-shepherd is transferred to another piece of work in the factory of the Father, the Chief Shepherd can well care for the little flock.' Or to one who was facing a decision, 'I am heavily and happily burdened for you. The branching road of your immediate future stretches ahead of you and you will soon have to make a decision. Till that hour keep an open mind, hospitable to the truth as it comes to you, an open heart ready to entertain the demands of love, and an open hand ready to give and to serve.'

In 1952 he came and visited me in the mountain town in cold winter weather and bought me a new oil stove, with the inscription stuck on the top, 'She spreadeth out her hands to the poor; yea, she reacheth out her hands to the needy. With her new stove she is not afraid of the snow' (Prov. 31:20-21).

And now the plane was landing and I arrived home to find my father over the worst, but apart from a few expeditions in a wheelchair he was mostly in bed for the last eight months of his life. My parents' home at that time was a flat in Clarendon School in North Wales (now Kinmel Hall). They had come to live there when the school moved from Malvern through the kindness of Miss Swain, his sister-in-law, the headmistress of Clarendon whose love had followed him and the family all down the years and with whom he had the closest possible friendship. For the past three or four years when he had not been strong enough to travel, he had been school chaplain and had shared the senior Scripture teaching with Miss Swain, and many are the letters from parents and girls that testify to the life-long formative value of those sane, deep expositions of the Bible. 'Perhaps we shall never fully know all that his spiritual influence and teaching has meant to the young people,' wrote one parent, 'but we do know that he has done much to build up their faith and strengthen them in their following of the Lord.'

Even the younger children found him extraordinarily approachable. They would sometimes come to him with their small troubles, more often with hot, faded bunches of flowers and little home-made gifts. For his last Christmas they made him a tiny Christmas tree with presents on it, and he sat proudly in the shade of it for weeks.

For a while after I arrived he rallied and had time to enjoy to the full life's last gifts; his peaceful home, the increasing realization of the love of his friends worldwide, the gradual dawning consciousness that he would soon see the Lord. These were some of the ingredients of his deep tranquil content. In the last few years he had dedicated five of his eight eldest grandchildren, and the last public service he performed was the dedication of Evelyn, aged three weeks, brought by her parents from Coventry for the occasion. The service took place in the sitting room of our home with a few near friends invited. Michael, aged four, often came up with John, his father, at weekends. Jampa' was Michael's ideal. He was a gentle little boy and when my father became really ill Michael would lean his head on his grandfather's pillow and sit quiet as a mouse, keeping silent vigil. In the morning his first anxious question on awaking would be, 'Do you think Jampa has had a good night?'

The last months were weary ones. He had frequent heart attacks and could often draw breath only with oxygen. But he never once complained or lost his sense of humour and was always thinking out little ways of sparing my mother and myself as we nursed him. In spite of breathlessness he insisted on praying aloud in loving detail for absent members of the family. He was rejoicing in the hope of seeing his two eldest from abroad in July, but when he realized he would probably not be there then, he accepted that too. 'I've held them in my heart for forty years; they may be at the other end of the world but they are here all the time.'

There were times when the physical struggle swamped all else, but even then his heart was anchored. 'I feel like a little tug in a great storm,' he gasped. 'But I'm fastened to a great ship on ahead. It's going into port and can't lose its way.

'When I go in to see the King it will be bright, very bright – I'm the happiest man alive.'

His sons Oliver and John, who had arrived the previous evening, were both by his bedside with my mother and me when at 2 am he woke, fully alert and mentally clear. He was able to enjoy them both for about five minutes and then relapsed into semiconsciousness. The next day, Saturday May 11th, 1957, at 2 pm he looked up very steadfastly and stopped breathing.

The funeral service took place in the little country chapel of Bodoryn, amid the buttercup fields. The few beautiful wreaths and the hundreds of bunches of wild flowers picked by the children who loved him both spoke of resurrection. A great crowd gathered round the grave to sing 'How good is the God we adore'. When the guests finally separated, there was a wide, bright rainbow spanning the sea.

'I've never been to such a funeral,' remarked an old man from the village. 'It was kind of joyful-like all the time.'

Hundreds and hundreds of letters poured in from all over the world from high and low, old and young. Practically all spoke of the deep, strong goodness that had so attracted them. Many wrote with a sense of real personal grief. 'For us the light has gone out and the world is a poorer place', wrote the secretary of the North Africa Mission who loved him like a father. Yet thank God the Light still shines and the way is open to all who will follow.

19

Rwanda

After my father's death I returned for a short while to Morocco and then came back to England to be with my mother, who had to have eye surgery, and during that time I worked as a school matron at Clarendon, where we lived. It was then, in response to many, many requests, that I wrote an account of my father's life. My mother was supposed to help me and of course all her early memories were invaluable – but in some ways she posed a problem. She was so modest and self-effacing that, had she had her way, she would never have been mentioned at all, and, as I kept reminding her, where on earth would those five children have come from?

Towards the end of those two years, when my father's biography was already published, I received a letter from the Rwanda Mission asking me if I would write the history of the Revival, a movement that had started back in the '30s, spreading like wildfire through all the East African countries, and whose influence was felt in places all over the world. To me, accustomed to the Moroccan Christians in their ones and twos, the idea of hundreds turning to

Christ in repentance, born again and powerful radiant witnesses, was like cold water to a thirsty soul, and I agreed to take on the task.

I went back to Morocco early in 1965 and my mother soon followed and remained there till her death in 1976. She started by living with us in the girls' training home, but later we moved together to a small flat nearby. I spent that first year back in Morocco mostly reading and appraising the enormous pile of letters and magazines and reports from Rwanda submitted since 1921 when two young doctors, Leonard Sharp and Algernon Stanley Smith, pioneered a Mission Hospital. But the crux of the whole story is probably expressed in the summing up of Festo Kivengere, a man who came to Christ during those early years and became an outstanding evangelist in the '60s and '70s. He wrote, 'The aim of the first representatives of the Rwanda Mission who came to our country was to tell us about God and His plan of salvation; but because of the strange colour of their skin, their strange language and culture and their human weaknesses, the task of communication would have been impossible through human techniques alone. It needed the Spirit of God, the Spirit of might and order, the mighty wind which swept over the chaotic surface of the dark water before creation, to breathe over their efforts.

'In one sense those early missionaries were highly successful. Churches, schools and hospitals sprang up, and thousands flocked to them. Yet something was missing . . . so often there was a general assent to the new teaching but little real change in people's lives ... Then 20 years after the founding of the Mission that same Spirit came in new power. The Spirit which had created that longing in many hearts swept through the land, congregations and missionaries alike were caught up in another Pentecost. Silence gave way to praise, barriers were broken down in the presence of the Risen Christ. Men and women entered into the liberating power of Christ's Cross.'

I left Morocco early in 1966 and travelled via Brussels and Rome to Entebbe Airport. The first thing I noticed was the clean, washed air, the smell of rain and the luxuriance of the greenery. I was met and taken to the Church's house in Kampala, where I spent three or four days talking almost non-stop to Dr Joe Church and his wife Decie, a couple whom God had greatly used in helping pray in that mighty wind that had blown throughout the land. Although one no longer felt that roaring gale, one could see the results everywhere – for wind cleanses and energizes, sweeps away what is dead and withered and sets free what is new and alive. I listened fascinated to the memories of an old man who had seen the early beginnings of that mighty work of God.

Joe, who joined the team in 1927, spoke much of those early years of struggle and famine, of wounding from wild animals, of sickness and the deaths of fellow workers and little children; he spoke, too, of crowded churches and apparently enormous spiritual results. Everyone wanted to wear clothes and sing hymns and have medicine and learn to read their catechism and become a teacher. He spoke of the joy in numbers and statistics, and then of the gradual chilling realization of the shallowness of the work – just the outward form of Christianity with no real change of heart; the right words and actions masking the totally unregenerate life. He spoke of his own deep depression, the consequent wrong relationships with missionaries and nationals, and of the sickness and despair that nearly caused him to return to England. And then he told of a time when he had travelled up to Kampala from his hospital in Gahini with one strong resolution in his heart – to find the real secret of victory over sin.

As he was climbing Namirembe hill, a young African named Simeoni Nsibainbi stopped him and said shyly, 'You once spoke to me about surrendering all to Jesus. I have done that and have found great joy, but there is still something missing in me and in the Ugandan Church. Can you tell me what it is?'

The two men went home together and pored over their Bibles for hours on end, tracing the teaching of the Holy Spirit and the victorious life. Suddenly the answers Joe had known so long blazed into reality for both of them. 'God met with us', he wrote. 'He gave us no special gifts, just a transforming vision of the risen Christ.' I travelled south to Gahini, where the movement seemed to have started. The red earth roads were damp and bumpy, winding on through the green countryside sprinkled thickly with small fenced huts and patches of cultivation, with little children guarding herds of enormous long-haired cattle. Then the mountains appeared and we crossed over into the highlands of Rwanda with their breathtaking views of hills and valleys that always seemed partially veiled in a kind of blue mist.

I was surprised at the primitive conditions still prevailing in the hospital at Gahini – water having to be carried up from a crocodile-infested river far below, no sheets, and crowds of relatives round, under and if possible in the bed with the patient. But there was love and happiness and healing. I wandered round the grounds, beautiful with flame trees and jacarandas, and remembered those early beginnings.

There was the tiny prayer room where young Blasio, recognizing the spiritual dryness and strain in relationships, had retired for a week of prayer and fasting. It was here that Joe and Matron, strongly opposed to each other's methods, had publicly asked forgiveness of each other and of their African workers, to the amazement of the latter. 'Never before have we heard a white man own he was wrong,' they said wonderingly. And it was here that the spirit of prayer came upon them in revival power.

The Spirit of God was amongst them. For two and a half hours men rose, sometimes several at a time, overcome by conviction of sin. There was uncontrolled weeping and crying out, followed by overwhelming joy and burning love. One after another offered to carry the news of the Saviour's redemption to the farthest parts of the land. It had suddenly become so glorious, so sweet, that they simply could not keep silent. One by one they set out, to the extreme disruption of school and hospital routine and the intense annoyance of some of the more orderly minded. Truly they 'went out with joy and were led forth in peace', while to their newly opened eyes the mountains of Rwanda seemed to break into singing before them, and the trees in the valleys clapped their hands.

I visited Kabale, where in 1935 a young hospital dresser from Gahini, aflame with the joy of forgiveness and the love of Christ, had begged for a week's holiday to go and testify to his friends in Kabale. Lawrence Barham and the Rev Ezelcieri Balaba had been praying for years for God's breath of life on the dead, formal church at Kabale, and in this young dresser they saw that spirit of praise and testimony so lacking at their own centre. As a result they asked for a team of Christians from Gahini to visit them and to hold a ten days' convention for the three hundred teachers and evangelists.

And during these meetings men were convicted of sin and trusted 'Christian' leaders confessed that they had never been born again at all. Sums of money, stolen years before, were returned and a great longing was born in those who loved the Lord to go out all over the district and tell others about him.

It was a heart-searching yet joyful time, but it was not till those same teachers and evangelists had gone home to their scattered congregations amongst the banana patches that the real results of the convention began to be seen, and strange reports began to come in from the little country churches of Kigezi. Through these teachers, now born again, cleansed from sin and consecrated to God,

Christ himself reached out to the people. Men, women and children flocked to the churches, many brought there by dreams. Whole congregations would cry out and tremble before God and pray all night. Many would fall to the ground in paroxysms of grief and remorse as they saw their sins, and numerous stories are told of that time. Great was the joy of the little church when a man of evil repute stood up and recounted how he had been told in a dream to look up the number of a certain hymn and sing it. He woke and got up at once and found that the hymn was:

I lay my sins on Jesus,

The spotless Lamb of God;

And as he sang, he turned to the Saviour. Back at Gahini the outward manifestations of revival became progressively more violent, and in the summer of 1936 many missionaries felt there was cause for concern. But as the fierce, almost hysterical emotion passed, there arose something from the dust and ashes that no missionary could gainsay: a love and zeal that glowed and burned and must testify. More and more bands went out to preach in the villages, and wherever they went they carried the Saviour with them and crowds flocked to hear his voice, weeping through the darkness to seek God.

On an unforgettable day I sailed across Lake Bunyoni with Pat Gilmer to visit the Bwana leper colony. The canoe was dug out of a tree trunk and looked precarious, but the water was as smooth as glass. Exotic birds skimmed past us and the island seemed enfolded in the peace of the hills surrounding the lake. The bays and inlets were strewn with mauve and pink water lilies, and the soft colours of the reflections were beautiful beyond description.

The island, originally the lair of a wicked and much feared witch doctor, was bought by Dr Sharp in 1930, after the old man was arrested. It was then a deserted spot, haunted by fears and memories of evil, shunned by everybody, easily and cheaply leased to anyone who dared to take it. It is no longer, as at first, a receiving centre for lepers, for the new practice is to treat them in local clinics and Pat used to go round in her well-equipped van, giving regular treatment. But elderly patients, too maimed or too old to start life afresh, still lived there, lovingly cared for by two English nursing sisters and a team of African Christians, and a centre for training the disabled had also been started up. It was a happy place. We climbed to the crest of the island by firm paths between rows of huts, where men and women, some dreadfully disfigured, pursued their crafts and daily work, greeting us with smiles as we went by. On the highest point stood that triumph of architecture, the church, cruciform in shape, designed by Dr Sharp, with its seventy-foot tower and spire, a landmark for the whole lake.

And it was in this church that the spirit of revival began to move among the lepers. In 1936 a team from Gahini visited Bwama Island and a patient from Kigeme called Simeoni was deeply moved. He had worked as a nurse in the hospital and was a prey to terrible fears; fear of death because he was not saved, fear of life because of the progress of his disease. But to tell the story in his own words: 'That day I was pierced in my heart and more afraid than ever. A Voice said, "Repent", but Satan also spoke, "Repent, but don't give up sinning. Put those stolen medicines down the drain, but don't confess."

'But I found no peace, and then one day I could bear it no longer and I brought my sin out into the light and confessed. There was no other way. Friends said, "He is mad", but I have found peace.'

Shortly after this two more were converted and they became a team to pray for the others. The others resented it and persecuted and falsely accused them. Life was hard and bleak and one evening just before sunset, when the lake to each side lies level and golden, two of them entered the cool, dim church and began to sing. Perhaps they were weary of their diseased, ostracized life; perhaps Simeoni was thinking of his four little daughters buried by the shores of Bunyoni; in any case they sang over and over again the hymn with the refrain:

In the sweet by and by
We shall meet on that beautiful shore.

And as they sang, one patient after another crept into the darkening church to sing with them – the lame, the blind, the disfigured, rejoicing at the prospect of meeting one another on another shore. Soon the building was full and they sang and prayed until morning, on and on, while the sun travelled up the sky. Hospital work was apparently forgotten (one can understand why harassed, overworked sisters were not always completely in favour of the Revival). Dr Symons came over from Kabale to do the ward round and wondered where his staff were, but he, too, joined the great congregation and they sang on until they had no voices.

'I ached from being hugged,' went on Simeoni, telling the story some thirty years later. 'On the third day many, many people repented and were saved. My wife was saved too. I stopped worrying about my illness.' (Here his delight overcame him and he jigged gently up and down in his chair.) 'Slowly I got better and I prayed for a hospital for leprosy in my own country.'

God heard his prayer and later he went to the first leprosarium in Burundi, where for twelve years he worked as a male nurse and led many to Christ. In 1961 he was discharged and came to be the trusted senior worker at Kigeme Hospital. His face lights up as he tells the story. 'Because I was ill, I found Christ. I was in despair like Jonah in the belly of the whale. He brought me up, he lifted me out.'

Evelyn Longley wrote of many at that time bringing back clothes and blankets and all sorts of stolen goods; but perhaps the chief sign of revival was the new radiance and courage that shone out on ravaged faces, the new sense of the presence of Jesus in their pain and weakness.

And when a Christian patient does die, the burial of the old, diseased body becomes a time of great rejoicing as his friends talk together of his new body. 'It does not yet appear what we shall be, but we shall be like him.' Can there be any more joyful prospect?

Miss Longley and Miss Horton were the first of a succession of heroic lady missionaries who gave years of their lives to those suffering from that most feared disease. In these times when it is not uncommon for missionaries to return home with breakdowns due to culture shock, absence of social life, loneliness and overwork, it is good to remember Evelyn Longley, Grace Marsh, Janet Metcalf and Marguerite Bailey. They remained for years in that isolated place and, apart from the Sharps who came to live on the next island, the ladies had no European companionship except each other. They carried enormous medical, spiritual and administrative responsibilities, they dealt with the stench and horror of leprosy and bore the burden of the constant sorrow of hopeless, incurable pain and approaching death. Yet all made their home on the island and retained over the years good physical health, soundness of mind, a lighthearted sense of humour and a holy life of fellowship with God.

But in the mission as a whole there were very mixed feelings about the Revival. It was a time of joy and a time of sorrow, a time of conflict and of reconciliation, of wounding and of healing; and no hearts were more torn and perplexed than those of the missionaries themselves. They were often divided from the Africans and even more often deeply divided among themselves; and it is well to look back over this stormy passage of rough water and try to understand what caused such divisions and even in some cases such bitterness and estrangement.

First one must consider the background of these missionaries. For all their faith, courage and deep devotion to Christ, they were products of their age, and their age was that of post-war colonialism. And because the rural African loves a quiet life, he usually conformed exactly to the colonial conception in public. Very few whites knew anything about the real person behind the obedient, servile facade, and most of the missionaries were no exception, loving, devoted, but disliking any outward show of emotion; unconsciously patronizing, seeing themselves, because as yet no other vision had been given, as white beneficent chiefs among simple Africans who humbly accepted all they had to give, including the gospel.

But God had a different vision. He wanted to show the world a new concept of fellowship that would override caste, code, background, race, colour and prejudice. It was the only real answer in the world to war, hatred, racial superiority and apartheid.

The first hurdle to be crossed was Joe Church's insistence on an equal brotherhood of black and white – the only possible basis upon which a self-governed, self-supporting indigenous church could grow. But the germ idea caused consternation. Some missionaries prophesied no good at all from Mrs Guillebaud's habit of allowing the Africans to crowd into her house for Sunday hymn singing, or Joe Church's custom of letting them sit in his room as equals and share news from his letters.

It was Bishop Stuart at Kampala who first invited a whole team of African evangelists to stay in his home for a quiet weekend before the Mokone convention and showed publicly to the Christian community in Uganda that brotherhood on equal terms was both safe and desirable.

Then there was the question of excessive emotion; the shouting, the dancing and hysterical manifestations, so utterly repugnant to the English gentleman and soldier, so completely suitable for those just emerging from paganism who knew no other way of expressing overwhelming grief or extreme joy. It is easy to see after the lapse of years how much it was a matter of temperament; how foolish it was of the Africans to insist there could be no real work of the Spirit apart from crying and trembling; how unwise of the missionaries to try so hard to check what resulted in such joy and praise. But it is not easy to check true values in the very heat of battle.

There was no doubt that the African Christians who had passed through the emotional stage came out with a radiance and strength that left the tired, perplexed missionaries right in the shade. Some too were deeply humiliated by disclosures and confessions made by their trusted workers about whom they had written home so glowingly. What had all their years of work and prayer amounted to? Apparently nothing.

And then in 1938, when the difficulties and divisions were at their height, the harassed missionaries met for a conference on Lake Kivu in north-west Rwanda. 'God showed us something of what full surrender means,' wrote Dr Symonds, 'and we learnt that it was not an easy thing to be broken, and He requires this of us every day. We realised too more than ever, the possibilities of a life of real fellowship with each other and with the Africans. There is no doubt that many of them are farther along the line than we are. In their sight we are no longer "the Great White Man", but they long to walk with us and to grow. with us.'

There was a breaking and rejoicing such as had never been known before, and many are the happy testimonies from men and women who found a peace they had never known before in dropping all strivings and pretences, accepting criticism and facing reality; beginning at last to know because they were willing to be known.

God's timing is perfect. By 1939, when the mission had to enter the dark, difficult years of the war, the birth pangs of the Revival were mostly over and the Church had emerged purified and tried and ready to meet the increased demands and added responsibilities about to be asked of it.

It seemed at first as if all supplies from England would be cut off, and plans were made for living off the land. All pay and grants were reduced by 20% for Africans and Europeans alike. Nothing so forcibly proved the reality of what they had gone through as the way the Africans reacted. Almost without exception they accepted the cuts in their meagre pay without a murmur. 'Satan thinks he can make us poor,' said one young hospital dresser eagerly, 'but he can't. We have Christ now, and so we are rich.'

There is only one class at the cross, humble, forgiven sinners, rejoicing because God has forgiven them; and this forms a bond between them that cannot be broken. 'If we walk in the light, as He is in the light, we have fellowship one with another, and the blood of Jesus Christ His Son cleanses us from all sin.'

This special insight was given at a time when it was most needed. It was the only solution to the age-old social barrier between black and white, missionary and convert. It flared to its logical conclusion during the Second World War, the only answer to racial hatred and prejudice. All over the world men who were sick and scarred by fighting and bombing and killing recognized it; they saw that it worked and longed to understand the secret. So it came about that in the fifties calls came from far countries and teams of African and English brethren went together to share what God had taught them.

In the decade following the end of the war, teams travelled from East Africa to many parts of the world – to India and Pakistan, North America, Brazil, Australia, New Guinea and to various countries in Europe and Africa. It is probably true to say that wherever the teams travelled the message got across, because they went in simple dependence on the Holy Spirit, without trappings or attractions, simply to share what God had taught them. Because they longed for reality and were drawn by sincerity, whatever the colour of man's skin, pride, prejudice, complacency and pretence were broken down, sin was confessed, cold hearts caught fire, estranged parties were reconciled and love and fellowship were restored.

I travelled home with very much to think about and spent the next year in Morocco, living with my mother and the girls, but writing *Breath of Life,* from which much of this chapter has been taken. It was a strange story to write in a Muslim land, with the precious ones and twos struggling on, and a couple of faithful, prayerful missionaries retiring from a mission station in the south where they had worked for many years and seen no known convert.

'Oh Lord, how long?' one cried, and the answer seemed clear as I sifted through all that I had seen and heard. 'Oh Lord,' they had prayed, 'send revival ... and let it start in me.'

20

In the Steps of St Paul

When I was about thirteen years old, my imagination had been captured by the story of Onesimus, the runaway slave whose small history appears in the book of Philemon. I told my father that I wished to write a novel based on the incident, and without the flicker of a smile he accompanied me to the public library.

'My daughter wishes to write a novel set in Bible times,' he announced to the astonished librarian. 'Could you please show her the ancient history section where she can do some research on the period.'

I failed to see the wink that must have passed between them and felt very solemn and adult. I obediently researched and found out quite a lot about ancient Colossae and the Roman world. I wrote my story laboriously, mostly in pencil in a multitude of lined penny notebooks. The family applauded, but it never went further. Some years later the manuscript, almost forgotten, was lost in a move. But the idea never quite left me. And one day, when my sister Hazel was over from Beirut, spending a holiday with us in Tangier, I mentioned this old dream.

'Why don't you write it?' she asked.

'Because I can't write about places I've never seen,' I replied, 'and when could I ever go to Turkey and Greece and Rome?'

'Next year,' she replied promptly. 'Come to Beirut in the summer holiday and we'll drive back to North Africa together in my Volkswagen, and camp. We'll visit every place St Paul ever set foot in.' (Except the islands of the sea.)

So in 1966 I left, with some trepidation, for Beirut. It was not my first visit. I had been there once before when I was still working in the mountains. After about a fortnight of enjoying the life of Hazel's school and meeting some of her numerous Lebanese friends, we set off on the first stage of our journey. The little Volkswagen was well packed with the tent, sleeping bags, primus, provisions, water container and personal luggage. Crowds of excited friends came to the gate to see us off. It was quite emotional, but at last the gates closed behind us and we were out through the traffic, chugging east towards Damascus, with the great Lebanese range to cross. Up we climbed over the mountains with their stupendous views across the Bekaa plain, where to the south the snows of Hermon shimmered against the blue. Then down from that bright air to Damascus and on along the eastern plains of Jordan, arriving in Amman that evening, where we were welcomed and entertained by Christian friends.

Hazel knew everybody, and it was pleasant to tag along behind and be welcomed and entertained wherever we went. It happened again next evening after a thrilling day. I was seeing for the first time that place in the Jordan River where 'there was much water' (had Jesus really stepped down into that pool?) and dusty little Bethany. We got out and stood on the crest of the Mount of Olives, and looked down on the whole great panorama of modern Jerusalem, and then Hazel explained quite calmly that we were to stay with the keeper of the Garden of the Resurrection (the Garden Tomb) for three nights, and we would sleep in a little summer house a hundred yards or so from the grave.

The country was dry and barren in August, but the garden was lovingly watered all the year round. It was a mass of flowers. The Mottars had a delicious meal waiting for us and we sat for a long time talking and breathing in the sweet scents of the garden at dusk. Through the open window, half veiled by trees, was the tomb where Jesus may have lain. A few hundred yards away rose a little hill, seamed on one side with rocks which in certain lights bear a strange resemblance to a skull. Gordon's Calvary they call it. And the General insisted that if it was the hill of the Mount of the Crucifixion, then there must be a single tomb very close at hand, for 'in the place where He was crucified there was a garden, and in the garden a new tomb'. Seven years after the General's death, the garden tomb was excavated, solitary and empty, with the stone rolled back from the entrance.

The Mottars held us spellbound with the story of their recent lives. They were Palestinian Arabs who had come to Jerusalem on holiday with their nine children. While there, the war broke out between the Jews and Arabs and it became impossible to get back to their home. Their money was dwindling and the banks were unable to transfer. They and many like them were faced with the problem of real hunger.

Mr Mottar visited the bank daily, but nothing was coming through from his own account. A day came when they finished the last of their food for breakfast. So Mr Mottar gathered his nine children round him and read to them God's promises of provision in the Bible.

'We are going to see if the Bible is true,' he told his anxious family. 'I will go out with a basket and I will tell no one of our need, only the Lord. If I come back with an empty basket, then it seems the promises are not true. If I come back with a good dinner, then you can know that the Bible is a book to be trusted.'

He went first to the bank and stood in the long queue. Like most others, he was turned away empty-handed. As he went out, he met a local acquaintance coming in. The man stopped and spoke to him.

'How are you managing with all those kids, Mottar?' he asked.

It was a temptation to tell and ask for help. But Mr Mottar remembered his promise. 'We're all right,' he said quietly, and went on his way. 'That's true,' he thought to himself. 'With all those promises we must be all right.'

Not knowing where to go next, he sat down on a seat by the roadside, his empty basket beneath his feet. 'O Lord,' he prayed. 'All those little children!' There was much more than their dinner at stake. It was their faith in God.

He looked up for someone was speaking to him. His friend stood in front of him. 'I don't care what you say, Mottar,' he said, 'you can't be all right with all that crowd to feed.' He dropped a packet into the empty basket and walked away. It contained enough money to feed them for many days. The money came through, and later he was offered the job of caring for the Garden of the Resurrection, with a house on the edge of the garden. He did his work beautifully, for the place is a mass of flowers and shady trees.

Next morning at sunrise I ran out and sat beside the opening to the tomb and pretended I was Mary Magdalene on that first amazing morning when Jesus called her by her name.

We had just three days in Jerusalem; we drove south to Bethlehem, north to the Vale of Sychar, and back to Bethany and saw those old, old cave-like graves at the back of the village. Out of one of these Lazarus had come forth. We followed the road to Emmaus in the evening and crossed the Brook Kidron and climbed the hill to the Garden of Gethsemane where the twisted olive trees are said to be round about two thousand years old. It was hard to say goodbye to the dear Mottars and that quiet little flower-scented tomb. We shall never see Mr Mottar again for during the Six Day War soldiers broke into the garden and shot him at close range. Perhaps he who had loved the spot so much would have been glad to die in the very place where death was conquered.

So on the third morning we drove again to the crest of the Mount of Olives and looked back on the holy city and started north for our first night's stop in Damascus. The hospitality of Syria and Turkey is something I shall not forget in a hurry.

The landscape as one nears the Turkish border is incredibly lovely – hills and pine forests and far views. We stayed the night in Latakia with loving friends of Hazel's and drove over into Turkey the next day. Our aim was to reach Antioch. We did not hurry. The roads were rough and the Volkswagen dusty. It was incredibly hot, and we bathed in a river. We were to stay the night with a well-to-do Turkish family whose daughters were boarders at Hazel's school in Beirut. We decided to stop near the town and change and tidy up and rub over the Volkswagen.

We were just a little way from Antioch, looking for a suitable place to stop, when we saw the procession coming; two enormous cars hooting loudly. 'I think the President is coming,' I said to Hazel. 'We'd better get into the ditch.' We squeezed to the side of the road, but the cars drew up alongside of us and the family poured out, laughing and shouting. It was the welcome committee come out to meet their headmistress. We followed them back in our disreputable little vehicle, feeling extremely scruffy, and they led us to the most expensive hotel in Antioch.

That evening we feasted in their home and in the morning they took us to see the sights of Antioch. It lies among hills – a small town; but in the days of St Paul it was the third largest city in the world. Here we saw what is probably the oldest known Christian church. It is cut in a cave, and from its mouth one can turn and look out over the little city and the green, well-watered plain of the Orontes River. Inside, when our eyes grew accustomed to the gloom, we could discern the worn mosaic floor, the spring of water in the corner, the rough carving of a cross on the rock. From the back of the cave a secret passage leads to steps near the city wall, for the disciples were first called Christians in Antioch, and to worship was probably a risky business.

The rest of our progress through Turkey was a dream of sunshine, sunflowers, rough roads and sleepy little towns, and kindly peasants in bright, artistic costumes, harvesting their crops along the way, and eager to have their photos taken. Sometimes they tossed us bunches of grapes and once they presented us with a melon. We visited Tarsus, once a great centre of learning, now a small, rather bedraggled little place, crowded with mule carts. Beyond, to the west, rose the Taurus Mountains.

One night we slept in a small hotel where all the residents, including ourselves, lit their primuses in the long stone corridor and for the most part cooked macaroni. On another night we set up our tent in a camp site where whole families were employed picking melons. The tents were enormous and elaborate, housing grannies, babies, relatives, and we felt a little ashamed of our simple contraption (it was too small, and in any case our legs stuck out of the doorway), but we were loudly welcomed at the crowded coffee shop that night, and invited to dance and requested to speak English.

I especially remember a blue misty morning when we turned a corner and saw Lake Egridir just ahead of us. Turkey's weak point is its washing accommodation. We plunged in gratefully and picnicked on the little beach. I believe we found another camping site that night, for we were getting very close to one of the places I specially wanted to see – Homaz, the old Colossae and the site of my proposed book. Colossae, set on a high mountain above the gorges, the city where the slave Onesimus ran away from the service of Philemon and returned bearing one of the world's most gracious and immortal letters – the Letter to the Colossians.

Turkey makes nothing of the old Bible sites. It has changed the names of many of the old cities. Only because Hazel had done this trip before was she able to locate the place. We wound up a stony track, high above the road, and somewhat nervously entered the little market place.

It was a riot!! Tourists were almost unknown in Colossae, and an excited crowd collected. They obviously thought us very funny, and we spent a little time simply laughing at each other. But it was kind, hospitable laughter, and they insisted on serving us with free coffee at a little wooden table in the local inn. Then someone remembered; there was one scholar in Colossae who spoke English, and a deputation set off to fetch him and returned triumphant.

He also made welcoming gestures, but his English was limited to one sentence: 'See you fellows in de mornin'.'

We left amid affectionate, amused goodbyes and drove a little way down the mountain. It was late afternoon, and across the valley rose the strange white limestone crags of Pamukkale. We stopped for a picnic supper, and it was just here that our butane gas container suddenly caught fire and blew up in a small way. It was really rather a tragedy, but we laughed and laughed until we were quite speechless.

We drove up the opposite hillside and spent the night in a little hotel at Pamukkale, and bathed in the hot and cold springs. It was late evening, and the sun was setting down in the valley in a glory of green and gold. A hundred miles to the west, at the end of the Lycus Valley, lay Ephesus, and somewhere just below us, the ruins of Laodicea.

No one in Pamukkale could tell us exactly how to reach them, but when we gained the highway we stopped for petrol. The garage man knew no English and we knew no Turkish, but we threw out the word Laodicea and he nodded and pointed to a rough little track on the opposite side of the road. We bumped along it for a few hundred yards, then it petered out into a narrow path. We pressed on on foot and suddenly we found ourselves at the edge of a field where lay the ruins of the old, old city.

There was no mistaking it. 'I would that thou wert hot or cold.' Up above to our right lay the limestone crags, with heat emanating from the cataract of hot springs – a wonderful spot in winter. Over to the left, the ice-cold water from the cold springs cascaded down the mountain – a perfect retreat in the blazing summer weather. Kept apart, each stream proved a blessing. Mixed and lukewarm, they would have been useless.

There were clear signs too in the stones of rebuilding and new beginnings, for Laodicea was twice destroyed by earthquakes. After one of these the Roman emperor offered financial help, but the proud little city refused. 'We are rich, and increased in goods, and have need of nothing', was the message they sent back. For me it was one of the most moving experiences of the journey, as though that sad, poignant letter leapt to life again in the pages of the Bible and that final offer of hope rang out across the centuries, 'Behold, I stand at the door and knock.'

A long drive down the Lycus Valley brought us to Ephesus in the late afternoon. We explored for an hour in that special illuminating light of early evening, tinging the old stones with gold. We stood in the theatre where they shouted, 'Great is Diana of the Ephesian!' and followed the dusty little track up to the great temple of Diana, formerly one of the seven wonders of the world, now a few mildewed stones, in a swamp where frogs sit and croak.

After two nights in Smyrna we crossed the Bosphorus. What a thrill to be in Greece! I remember the first view of ruined Philippi and the river nearby where Lydia's heart was opened. At Thessalonica, we stayed at a children's Bible camp by the sea and spent a never to be forgotten evening with the children, sharing and singing and applauding their little dramas.

We crept out early for a swim and on reaching the apparently empty beach we removed our dresses and made for the sea. It was embarrassing to round the little sand dune and find ourselves suddenly in the midst of a crowd of modestly clad Thessalonians having a prayer meeting. However, it did not seem to worry them, and again we left this little Heaven on earth with real regret and almost a sense of tearing apart.

We reached Athens early in the evening, when the westering sun illuminated the Acropolis, set high and beautiful above the city. We were to stay with another friend of Hazel's who had visited her in Beirut and kept a home for elderly widows. But we had not mentioned supper and thought we would eat before arriving. We were discussing the price of a hamburger when a charming young man came up to us and said in good English, 'Can I help you?' He negotiated the right change and we thanked him and sat down on a seat outside to eat. A few minutes later our friend returned. 'Do you read the Bible?' he asked. We told him we did, and he said, 'I knew it.'

Then over our supper we really settled down to get to know each other. He had studied at Capernwray Bible College in the north of England. He ran a Christian bookshop in the town, where he sold books by Patricia St John translated into Greek. He was actually in process of translating one of them himself, and he found it hard to believe that the authentic article was actually sitting opposite him, dusty, sunburnt and devouring a hamburger.

I think there is nothing like the fellowship of Christians who simply recognize Christ in each other and reach out to him in joy. We found out that he was going to preach in Corinth on the following day. He had no car, so we offered to take him. His name was Angelikos, and he translated for us as we had no common language with anyone else, but the welcome of these people and their hospitality went right to our hearts.

The epistle seemed to come alive as they took us round the ruins of the old city, and we imagined other little churches surrounded by sin and temptation, yet battling through to victory. Once again we parted, probably never again to meet on this earth, but with the strong sense of permanency of the whole family in Heaven and on earth. What interested us most was the cripple boy we met there, who had been alone in his room for some years, unable to get out. But people visited him and one by one he talked to them of the Lord, and the result of those times was the forming of this little church, which was growing well.

We crossed by ship a day or two later to Italy and watched Greece receding against the soft sky that reflected the sunset ahead of us. We landed at Brindisi late at night. Next day we drove through the beautiful Italian countryside with its vineyards and grape-pickers and fascinating little white towns on the tops of the hills, and reached the suburbs of Rome in the late afternoon.

There seemed to be no camping site or friendly cottages that let rooms, and I wondered what to do. We knew no Italian. I had a little Spanish and I found it rather a help.

I marched into a shop and asked where we could find an inexpensive lodging. The effect was remarkable. The shopkeeper went straight to the phone and as far as I could make out, started talking about some Spanish Catholic Signoras. She returned smiling and nodding and told us to wait, which we did, totally mystified. An enormous car suddenly appeared and we were told with some ceremony to follow. We protested, but we were helpless against the waving of hands and the nodding of heads, and a chorus of '*Si, si, si*'. We protested even more when the car stopped in front of an enormous, palatial building and the driver told us to get out.

'It must be the biggest and most expensive hotel in Rome,' we whispered, preparing to flee, but there seemed to be no escape. He waved away every objection as irrelevant and we were led up the steps and greeted at the door by a sweet-faced Mother Superior, who had come to welcome her Catholic guests from Spain. We had been brought to the local convent.

We felt dreadful frauds. We produced our British passports and tried to explain that it was a mistake. We were only Protestants. She seemed a little surprised and disappointed, but remained welcoming and hospitable. We slept for two nights in a beautiful guest room under an enormous picture of the Pope and talked with the nuns, to whom our coming seemed a sort of exciting novelty.

I can't think how we packed so much into two days in Rome, but Hazel as usual knew her way round. I remember most vividly the roof of the Sistine Chapel, the carvings and inscriptions in the Coliseum and the catacombs, especially that little picture of the Good Shepherd scratched on the rock. How those early Christians must have felt their need of that shepherd care!

As we left Rome and set off north, I felt a sense of liberation. As far as Rome I had taken notes copiously of every place that concerned St Paul. Now I could stop studying and merely enjoy myself. Florence, Spoleto (where we stayed with friends) and then a hot, enchanting morning in Assisi.

That evening, as we travelled on through the high hills above Assisi, we had our first taste of really bad weather. The rain poured down, the road was twisting and treacherous. We had no plans for the night. Somewhere in the district lived a kind, welcoming friend who had taught at Clarendon, but we had lost the address and could only remember the name of the road. The town might have been anywhere. We had no hope of finding her. We cruised along in the dark, feeling lost and rather frightened, when Hazel suddenly gave a yell of triumph. She had seen the name of the road. Of course it might be in a different town, but it wasn't. We did not even need to ask more than once. Everyone knew the Roncos, and within a very short time we were safe, warm and dry, camping in the sitting room, again enjoying wonderful hospitality.

At Monte Carlo we stayed with more friends who worked with Radio Monte Carlo, that vast broadcasting station built by Hitler to announce his victory over Europe to the world, but now beaming gospel programmes all over Europe and to North Africa, Russia and beyond.

Now we were heading for home along the south coast of France and into Spain. Camping sites were plentiful and luxurious, the weather was perfect. We reckoned we had two more nights to go before crossing on the ferry to Tangier, when apparent disaster struck us.

We were waiting stationary at a busy crossroads a few miles north of Tarragona when there was a tremendous crash at the back of the car, jolting us forward and hurling us against the windscreen (it was before the days of seat belts). An enormous truck, whose owner had apparently fallen asleep, had rammed into the back of the car and cracked the Volkswagen engine in two. At first we were so thankful to discover that neither of us was hurt (although my arms and hands remained numb for several days) that we scarcely realized the predicament we were in.

The excitement and noise was indescribable. We were some way out of town, but crowds seemed to spring up from nowhere, quarrelling and arguing with Spanish heat. The police were screaming at the traffic jam, and the lorry driver seemed to be trying to turn our wheels. We discovered later that he wanted to prove that we were turning left and had not indicated. After a lot of wrangling and shouting, in the end a pick-up truck appeared and hoisted our car on top and took it to a garage in Tarragona, the nearest town.

We were taken in the truck and dumped on the pavement. It was quite dark now and starting to rain, and after ten o'clock at night. As we were nearing the end of our journey, we had very little money, and the camp site was far outside the town. Nor could we have carried our gear. We enquired about hotels, but were assured that every hotel was full, as it was a fiesta (a remarkably common occurrence in Spain). No one seemed to care, and we stood in the little street with our hand luggage and prayed. Just then a boy came up to us and said, 'I think I know a house where you could sleep.'

He seemed like a small, bright-eyed angel, but as we followed the streets became narrower and we began to wonder. We had obviously reached the poorer part of the town. He stopped at a tall house and beckoned us inside. He led us up a very dimly lighted stone staircase. By now we were definitely feeling scared. But he kept turning round and making encouraging noises. At last he knocked on a door.

An elderly woman opened it and after a few words of explanation she admitted us a little doubtfully into a small living room. We looked round. There were Spanish texts on the walls. We showed her our Bibles and within a couple of minutes we were all in each other's arms. The bond of the love of Christ is seldom felt more strongly than when Christians meet in a strange land with little common language; it overrides all barriers. That night in that humble little home we instantly knew ourselves to be one in Christ Jesus.

In a city of over 60,000, there were just sixty Protestant Evangelical Christians, and she and her family were among them. They were kindness itself and though she could keep us for only one night, as her families were arriving next day, she took us to the church and we met with a little group. They escorted us and our belongings to a small chapel by the beach, not yet registered for use but containing a tiny kitchen and toilet and ample space to camp. It was quite luxurious, and we were detained for four days while the garage searched in vain for a Volkswagen engine, much hindered by two fiestas.

Then we gave up in despair and decided to travel on by train and leave the car to be picked up later when it had been mended.

Why? we wondered. Everything had gone so well. God's guiding hand had been in evidence. Why should this delay have been allowed? We were almost at the end of our money. We had to go on the first morning to visit the British Consul, who could not speak one word of English. We needed funds sent out urgently from England. We needed to give a true account of the accident for insurance purposes.

It was here in that dingy office with a bored-looking Spanish official that I was given the gift of tongues. I knew very little Spanish, but I suddenly found that I could ask for what we wanted and give a lucid account of all that had happened. In spite of the lies told by the lorry driver, we were awarded full insurance costs six months later. Then as we left the office, somewhat dazed by the whole experience, we met the reason for our being in Tarragona.

An English lady stood on the pavement crying bitterly. When we spoke to her in English, she seized hold of us and sobbed out her story. She had never been abroad before and knew not a word of Spanish, but her elder sister, a school teacher, had persuaded her to fly out for a week's holiday. She had not enjoyed it much – the crowds and the cheerful jostling in the streets at night scared her. But her sister was there to look after her. Then on the fifth day of her holiday her sister had a severe stroke and was taken to hospital, paralyzed and speechless. Marjorie hovered helplessly at her bedside. The nurses told her to go and buy suitable food, but she dared not enter a shop. She wanted to arrange to take her sister home, but the air company was miles away in Barcelona and there was no one to help. She was in utter, hopeless despair. God heard the cry of the desolate. When we should have been back in Tangier, God guided us to her.

We went to the hospital and visited the sister and took Marjorie shopping. We were able via the Consul to get in touch with the air company and arrange for her sister to be taken by ambulance to the plane and flown home within five days, when another ambulance would convey her to hospital. She was well insured, so there was no problem. We kept Marjorie company and stocked her up with what she needed, and we left her confident that all had been arranged. A later letter from England confirmed that the plans had gone straight ahead.

So often we simply have to believe that all things work together for good, without seeing the guiding hand that traces the pattern. Like the workers in the weaving shed who see only the reverse side of the roll of carpet, the disastrous situation appears a tangled muddle, but you have to wait for the whole beautiful design to be unrolled up there with him. Just sometimes, to confirm our faith, he answers our questions now and shows us the reason why.

We travelled back to Tangier in the slow, hot Spanish train, with hearts full of praise, and in the months to come, with those sundrenched, carefree memories of our journey clear in my mind, I settled down to write *Twice Freed* – the story of Onesimus.

21

The Grannies

Janet's father died soon after mine, and we both fetched our mothers to live with us. For some years they proved invaluable as pram pushers, baby sitters, language teachers and general odd-jobbers.

They made themselves available to other families as well as ours, and when Mrs Radcliffe was taken seriously ill, six-year-old Will tried to comfort her by saying, 'It will be all right if you go to Heaven, Mummy, because Granny St John will look after me.'

But the years took their toll, and Granny Thompson gradually became crippled with arthritis. Then Granny St John fell on the stairs and broke her ribs and never really recovered her strength or her memory. By the early '70s they were both permanently bedridden and beginning to lose their memories. Yet for about six years the bedroom they shared became a sort of sanctuary for all sorts of different people who loved to be there.

Many shared in the nursing care, and Janet and I and Zohra took the nights in turn. Zohra was Janet's home help. I wish I could tell all her story, but her disability makes her easily recognizable. Her first appearance many years before was quite dramatic. She was carried into Out-patients by her two brothers. She sat down in front of the doctor and said, 'I've come for my leg.' Farnham, who was new in the hospital then, replied that he knew nothing about her leg. He listened sympathetically to her story. About thirteen years previously another doctor had amputated her gangrenous leg and told her parents to bring her back when she was fully grown and he would fix her support. She was then three. She was now sixteen. For thirteen years she had waited in hope. It had been a difficult journey, and Farnham felt he could not disappoint her. She went to stay with Janet for a few days while the local carpenter constructed a wooden peg leg. She half-hopped and was half-carried home. She kept coming back and making herself more and more useful, and in the end it was arranged that she should stay. She became cleaner, cook, child minder, nurse and in many cases, teacher. At first her movements were greatly impeded by her disability. Then something happened. A friend of Hazel's, Olive Shaw from Lebanon, was sent home with cancer of the leg for immediate amputation. She thought that this was probably the end, but was told to her joy that there were no signs then of secondaries and she could go back to her beloved school in Beirut, where she worked for another two years. She was fitted out with a beautiful light, jointed, metal leg and quickly learned to walk more or less normally. Olive wanted to give a thank-offering to God for her recovery and it was at this point that she heard about Zohra and her peg leg. She wrote for Zohra's measurements and had a limb made which was a replica of her own. For some reason or other, Paul, Oliver and Claire unpacked it. They brought it up to the front door with great ceremony while Zohra screamed in amazement and delight in the kitchen. It was a great success. There was no activity she would not attempt. During their last years she became a devoted and skilful nurse to the Grannies.

I have noticed that in old age and senility the personality seems to crystallize. The basically self-centred become more so, and the loving and selfless become gentler and humbler in their weakness and easy to care for. Our Grannies definitely belonged to the second class. Granny Thompson was a strong, brave, loving woman who had been among the earliest women to qualify as doctors and had gone out as a medical missionary with the China Inland Mission. Her great claim to fame was that she had once sewn a half-severed head on again and the victim had survived. It was a story the children never got tired of hearing. Although completely crippled and locked by arthritis, she never complained. Sometimes she liked to assert herself and stage a small rebellion when she was presented with her daily bowl of bread and milk for breakfast. Granny Thompson grumbled and said, 'I shall complain to the management. Can't you give me anything else?' 'Of course, Granny. What would you like? Scrambled egg?' (Being toothless, the choice was small.) 'No.' 'What about some porridge?' Granny: 'No.' 'Or some nice bread and butter? Salad?', the shrewd blue eyes twinkled, then … 'Bread and milk.' She gave a little giggle, then closed her eyes.

The presence of God was very real in that quiet room, where the two old saints rested and waited to go home. Bored, rich, elderly English ladies, tired of the constant round of cocktail parties and the small social set, beginning to be slightly afraid of the future, would come and read aloud to them. The Grannies liked gentle Christian books, but they could not concentrate for long. It was a common sight to see the reader ploughing doggedly on while both Grannies sat propped up, their mouths open, snoring gently.

'Something happened to me in that room,' said a kind society lady after the Grannies died. 'I found a peace that I had not known before. I think I came to know God.'

Janet went back to England in 1974 to make a home for the six children, and the ensuing year was a dark one. Farnham developed typhoid fever very suddenly, and while he was still acutely ill, officials came up from the capital to say that the government was taking over the hospital, claiming the whole compound. All the buildings, including our own homes, were to be taken from us, and no compensation offered. We were given about three months to clear out, but there was one bright spot. They offered to employ all our Moroccan workers and expatriates who wanted to apply. There was anger and protest in the town, but nothing could be done. Farnham staggered back to Outpatients, and so many crowded in that the police had to come and control the hordes. At home both Bente, my dear helper from those years in the mountains, and Said, the little boy staying with me, contracted typhoid. Isolation was almost impossible, because Said absolutely refused to stay in bed. Whenever I sat down he appeared on the mat at my feet, burning and shivering with fever, but determined to stay put. The Grannies dozed peacefully and Zohra worked day and night.

Janet returned to help pack up the home and to move me, Zohra and the Grannies into a comfortable flat above a grocer's shop in the native quarter, as both were far too frail and confused to face being transplanted to England. Then came the sad day when Farnham and Janet finally left Morocco and people cried in the streets. The Grannies were simply lying there peacefully, waiting to go to Heaven. They posed no problem in life, but I did dread the day of their death. For Christian death in Morocco is a complicated affair. The burial must take place the same day, the grave digger and the Anglican clergyman must be found, the British Consul informed, weeping Moroccan Christians entertained, friends informed, and the service planned. Most of those close to me had left. This particular problem loomed very large in my mind. I seemed unable to trust that all would be well. Besides, a mother is a mother, and I dreaded the thought of her going as well as the fear of just not being able to cope. But I forgot that the mercy of the Lord is new every morning and 'precious in the sight of the LORD is the death of his saints.' Hazel came to stay for a fortnight on her way from England back to Lebanon. There was no visible change in the condition of the Grannies. My mother smiled sweetly and vaguely at Hazel. Perhaps she knew her, perhaps she didn't, but she always recognized and responded to love. It was very hot. We were able to leave them both with Zohra and spent a day together on the beach.

Zohra had done night duty, but she came in the early morning. 'Granny St John was breathing so fast,' she said. I gave her a penicillin injection, but there was nothing to be done. Hazel and I sat beside her, holding her hands. Apart from fast breathing, she was not in distress. At 9.30 she gave a little sigh and stopped breathing. She might simply have been fast asleep on that beautiful August morning, and we knew that she had passed over. That morning Jesus stood on the shore. Because she was so deeply loved by the expatriate community, they made room for her in the beautiful little cemetery surrounding the Anglican church instead of in the large foreigners' cemetery outside the town. Many came to the service, and throughout the sorrow and busyness of the day was that sense of amazement – I was not alone. God took her while Hazel was with me. Granny Thompson, whose bed had been surrounded by screens during the comings and goings, did not appear to notice that her old friend was no longer beside her. Locked in arthritis, she could not turn her head, and in the days following the funeral she seemed in particularly good form. When about a month later Janet wrote to say that the children were all back in school and college and she was coming out to look after her mother for a fortnight to give me a break, I wrote back telling her that Granny Thompson seemed so well and that we were all enjoying her.

Janet arrived and I went for a couple of days to rest at a retreat up in the mountains, the Cachette, a tiny house built mostly by Farnham and his friends and children on a piece of land left to him by a grateful patient. It was primitive, but so beautiful. In spring one looked down the mountainside on a golden cloud of mimosa blossom and in summer the coast lay blue and shimmering through curtains of green. Many happy family holidays and quiet retreats had been spent there, and I was enjoying the peace early in the morning of the second day when Janet arrived. 'I think you'd better come,' she said. 'I think Granny Thompson is going to heaven.' Granny Thompson was as usual quite definite about it. She had contracted pneumonia in the night. Her breathing was rapid and penicillin, which had always averted these crises before, was ineffectual. But up she gazed at the end of the bed and told us that she could see her husband and the three boys waiting for her. 'Can you see the Lord Jesus, Granny?' asked Janet. 'No, no,' came the whispered reply 'That's not allowed yet.' She lingered on for several days and we took it in turns to sit beside her and sing the old hymns she loved best. She was dozing quietly at 2 am one night when she suddenly simply stopped breathing. It was Janet's last day. Her flight was booked for the next morning, but she was there to help and make all the necessary funeral preparations. Granny Thompson was buried in the same grave as my mother at five o'clock that evening. It is just beside the entrance, and all who go into the church can read the inscription as they pass: 'The beloved of the Lord shall dwell in safety by him.'

There was a terrible sense of desolation as we cleared the beds away and made the room into a sitting room. Zohra, who had lost her job and the main purpose of her life, wept and wept, and I felt as though some great centre of peace and stability had suddenly been swept away. There was so much still to do, but I felt too tired, after all the night nursing, to start again. Yet I had not been alone. Our times had been so wonderfully in his hand.

Looking back over her life, nothing seems more wonderful than God's timing. It was only two or three weeks after Granny Thompson's death that the news came through, 'Clarendon has been burnt down.' Our aunt, the former head, who lived retired in a flat on the premises had been, most unusually, away for the night. But her home and all her property had been destroyed. My brother John, a GP in Coventry, and his wife, a nurse, had taken her in. I think I knew then that I would have to go home. John had fairly advanced Parkinson's disease and really needed help. Three of the seven children were still at school, and my sister-in-law had already taken in several elderly members of the family and nursed them one by one till they died. She could hardly be expected to start all over again. I said I would come over and see the situation at Christmas. But there was still Zohra's future to be settled, and many, many other dear friends to visit and say goodbye to.

Zohra found a job with kind English people and Granny Thompson, as an acknowledgement of years of loving, patient, devoted service, had left money in her will for Zohra to buy her own little house in the native quarter of the town. But the money had not come through when she came to me and said she had found the ideal house if the money could be advanced. But the owner wanted cash immediately.

Knowledgeable friends agreed that the house was all that she wanted and the price surprisingly reasonable. Only the cash was lacking. It seemed as if nothing could be done. I had to go out that morning, and I remember walking down the street thinking, 'If I was Hudson Taylor or Amy Carmichael, I could ask for this money to fall from heaven. But I am not like that. I could hardly expect him to do such a miracle for me.' Then the verse of a hymn came very clearly to my mind: 'O infinite Redeemer, I bring no other plea. Because Thou dost invite me, I cast myself on Thee.'

Not because of my worth or my unworthiness; the invitation is for all. 'Come unto me ... ' and the ground of our asking is simply Jesus. I told the Lord about the need and went home. When I arrived back, a printed envelope was lying on the table. It looked so dull that I did not even open it until after lunch. The Scripture Union had made a mistake, for which they apologized profusely later on. I had told them never to send my half-yearly royalties to Morocco, but to pay them into my bank in England. Some secretary had misunderstood and posted the cheque to me. The house was bought and later became a home for four young orphaned nephews and nieces adopted by Zohra. And always she testifies with bright face that God provides.

I went home at Christmas to see the situation first-hand. But I think I knew then that it was time to go home. I went back to pack up and say goodbye.

In a country where Christians stand together in a harsh, mocking world, with a continual threat of punishment, persecution or expulsion hanging over them, the links that bind us grow very strong. How could one just say 'Keep in touch'? Most of the older women had never learnt to write. Not that they were abandoned. Two or three of us would remain in secular jobs and would shepherd the little flock. But it was such a little flock. As the day drew near to leave, I struggled against waves of depression and regret. With so little to show for it, what had the years really achieved? I wish I had really studied the life and writings of Lilias Trotter at that time, as I did later when I wrote her biography *Until the Day Breaks*, published in 1990.

It was during this period that Wendy Moynagh came on a visit and gave me the material for the biography of her late husband Dr Kenneth Moynagh, much loved as a doctor in Rwanda and then working largely with students in London. We called the book *Man of Two Worlds*.

22

Lebanon

In 1976 I came back to England and have made it my base ever since. During the first four years, my aunt Miss Swain and I lived with my brother John, his wife and family in their beautiful home in Coventry. Auntie had lost her flat and all her possessions in the fire at Clarendon, where she had been living since her retirement, but had taken her losses very bravely. My sister-in-law Gwynne helped me to care for her, and I took turns in helping John in the surgery. His Parkinson's disease was rapidly getting worse and he could no longer write his prescriptions and certificates legibly. His patients loved him dearly and many sad stories were poured out in the short time available. I often deplored the lack of time to talk and listen to their problems and I dreamed of a surgery with a full-time counsellor available to any distressed patient, and in the background a voluntary team of Christian visitors and prayer partners – an unofficial arm of the Church. Perhaps there are others who share this dream and are even now bringing it to pass. I only know from my experience that some of those who come to a doctor's surgery are often in real need spiritually and wide open to what the gospel has to offer, if one only had the time to tell them.

It was a sad time watching John become progressively weaker and more weary, yet struggling bravely on. It was also a happy time, greatly enriched by the kindness and friendship of my sister-in-law and the nephews and nieces who still lived at home or who often visited – seven of them altogether.

The time passed quickly, but in September 1978 a family crisis arose which altered the pattern. My sister Hazel, who had gone to Beirut at twenty-two with the Lebanon Evangelical Mission (now MECO) after getting her degree and teaching certificate, had now survived the first three violent years of the civil war. But she had slipped on the road in West Beirut one Sunday morning and broken her femur. Two passing lads assured her they could drive and, there being no one else in sight and her car some fifty yards away, she hoped for the best and gave them the key. Fortunately all went well. They took her to the nearby home of her friends Colin and Anne Chapman, who got her to the American Hospital. But they were not going to attend to her until a large sum of money was produced by the mission. Most of the doctors were off duty and ill, and it was 9 pm before anyone could attend to her. However, the operation went well in the end and four substantial pins were inserted – still safely in place today. She had to stay in hospital only a week, surrounded by many visitors and much kindness. Then, after another week of convalescence she was back in her flat on the fifth floor of the school, eager to start the new term, on crutches quite happily for the next six months.

The flat above had had a direct hit. The water was seeping through and her books and the walls showed signs of passing bullets. But, cheerful as ever, she managed to phone me, and feeling quite sure that she would be all right and that I ought not to leave Auntie, she advised me not to come.

However, my sister-in-law assured me she could manage and as I walked across the Godiva Square in Coventry, I knew it was right to go. I went straight to a travel agent, who assured me that there were plenty of spare seats on the next flight to Beirut, as it was not a popular resort at that point. I left within two days and arrived at the Beirut airport late at night, without having been able to get through on the phone to say I was coming. By the dim light of a few lamps I could see heavily armed soldiers all around. There were guns everywhere, and the taxi man wanted £30 to drive me to the school, which I knew was quite near. When I wanted to know why, he pointed an imaginary gun at me and said, 'Pop, pop, pop.' Apparently the direct route was too dangerous. I eventually found a more reasonable taxi man, who deposited me at the school gates. They were locked and barred, and it took me a great deal of banging and shouting to attract the attention of Youssef, the gatekeeper. At first he was extremely suspicious but when he knew I was Hazel's sister, his delight knew no bounds. He had a high sense of drama. He insisted that he would go up first and say there was a visitor. Then, having aroused the curiosity of Hazel and the boarding staff with her, he would come down and produce me. It was a tremendous success, and Youssef went off chuckling, feeling no doubt that he had organized the whole visit.

Hazel had become head of the Lebanon Evangelical School and Training College in 1950. In 1972, when the political situation was very uncertain, it was thought best to have a national as head and a very capable fellow worker, Katy Tleel, took over. Hazel was then loaned by the mission to become head of a new school on the outskirts of Beirut, which was being started with the support of a group of national Christians. It seemed to be in an ideal area, where Christians, Muslims and Druse were keen to send their children, even though the school was known to be giving Christian teaching. It grew from a hundred and forty in 1973 to nearly five hundred in 1975. Then the war broke out, and it was in a very dangerous position, right in the middle of some of the most serious fighting. For four terms they managed to open for only very short periods. Two members of staff were killed by stray bullets, a child was murdered on the way to school, and another shot through the shoulder in the school bus. Many nights were spent on mattresses down in the basement. But by January 1977 things were quieter and school started again more normally, though with frequent disturbances and far worse fighting to come later on.

Hazel's war time adventures could fill a volume. Two I remember specially. One night in June 1976, when she had had to leave East Beirut, she was staying in the Blind School building in West Beirut, the American ambassador had been murdered in the street that week and a great deal of fighting was going on. She was alone that night on the third floor, sleeping, as very often, on the floor to avoid bullets through the window (it was a current joke in Beirut that the ideal home was one large passage with no windows and a small kitchen and bathroom). A car bomb went off in the street below and a neighbouring building was hit. It seemed as if things were all collapsing, with a deafening noise all around. She prayed for protection and then, to try and drown the uproar, she switched on the battery radio on the floor beside her (there was no electricity at that time). With the two-hour time difference she struck the BBC 8.30 hymn singing, and a voice rang out clear and strong in the dark, without any introduction: 'My peace I give unto you. Not as the world giveth, give I unto you. Let not your heart be troubled, neither let it be afraid.' It was the Sunday evening service from a little Welsh chapel where we had once worshipped on holiday, and it seemed exactly as if the Lord himself stood in the room. The words were calming and strengthening then and on many other occasions. She travelled out of Lebanon two days later over the mountains in the funeral cortège of the American Ambassador – the only chance of leaving for some time – and remained at home until New Year 1977, when a skeleton school reopened.

On another occasion, at the end of the school year in 1978, there was a party to which the top class had been invited to celebrate the birthday of a Druse girl who lived in another village. Things had been quieter on the whole, and some parents were willing for their teenagers to attend with several of the staff. Hazel had refused, as someone was shortly leaving for England and she wanted to send letters home.

She was sitting on the verandah hard at work when a voice spoke. 'You ought to be at that party.' She was startled, but argued to herself that it was impossible, as she had lent her car to another teacher and the house was some little distance away. But the voice seemed to speak again: 'You ought to be at that party.' The conviction was so strong that Hazel could not ignore it. She went to the flat above and knocked. The owner's daughter was in the bath, but she appeared quite soon and agreed to lend her car. Hazel was hailed enthusiastically and the party seemed a merry one. Why had she come? she wondered as she ate a bowl of trifle and chatted to a friend. Then suddenly the happy noise stopped dead. She looked up. Round the walls were several gunmen, one of them pulling out the telephone wires. Another had the terrified children covered. 'Muslims and Druse over to that side. Christians against the wall here.' One lad escaped under a bed and was found some time later. But the other six boys, white and silent, obeyed. It was a planned attack to capture two sixteen-year-old lads who had been out at night with the militia. They were seized and hurried outside along with the other boys to a waiting truck, and almost certain death, it seemed.

But not without protest. The hostess was furious – to enter her house and arrest her guests was an unspeakable breach of hospitality. She charged the truck, telling them what she thought of them, and Hazel, who now knew why she had been summoned, followed her. Together they forced an entrance, and the soldiers, bewildered and surprised by these determined women, were thrown off guard. The truck roared off towards the mountains with guns sticking out of the roof. Their superiors would know what to do. They were bundled out at the entrance of the small arsenal under the road – a kind of secret military headquarters. The boys were pushed into an inner room and the uninvited ladies slipped in behind. Even as she entered the room, Hazel's heart lifted, for sitting at the table was the father of one of her students. He was acutely embarrassed at the sight of her, because after all she was his daughter's headmistress, and he acknowledged her politely. They took the two older boys into another room. The ladies barged in too. Not all the might of the military with their guns could stop them. In fact, from the point of view of the soldiers, the situation was hopeless. The boys were questioned, threatened and released, because nobody had the temerity to execute them or even sentence them to death in front of those impossible ladies. Though sadly one of the two was shot and killed a short time after, for the moment all was well. They were bundled back into the truck, two enormous officers wanting a lift sat in on top of them, and they roared their way back to the house, where the parents of the boys and all their friends were now wailing and mourning, beating their breasts, having heard the news. When the boys tumbled out of the truck, the demonstrations of joy were as violent as their demonstrations of grief had been.

I stayed with Hazel for five weeks, doing odd jobs and attempting to drive her when necessary through the terrifying Beirut traffic, where on a double carriageway drivers might get impatient at the frequent military checks and road blocks and charge right across the barriers, hooting violently, with cars streaming towards them. Our conversation was frequently as follows: 'Hazel, quick, who has the right of way?' 'No one, Patricia. It's the one who gets there first. Hurry.' 'Hazel, we can't go up there. It's one way.' 'But it's where we want to go and the other road is blocked. Go on and see what happens.' Somehow we always got through unhindered, once with a soldier walking ahead of us to ensure safe passage. These trips to town scared me stiff, but there were other trips which were pure delight; trips up into the unspoilt Lebanese mountains, where the vineyards were turning crimson, where green, green grass and autumn crocuses were springing up with the first freshness of rain on the dry slopes. Here you could turn and look out beyond a ruined city to the misty blue of the Mediterranean; often at this time of year great double rainbows span the coast from Tyre in the south to Tripoli in the north. We climbed to the cedars, visited fascinating little mountain villages. It was a Paradise of a country and it seemed incredible that down below its own people were systematically and deliberately destroying their own glory.

Apart from the driving, my presence was not very necessary. Hazel had an excellent staff and she leapt around on her crutches like an animated kangaroo. But to me the visit was a sheer gain. There was a temporary lull in the fighting, and the courage and determination of the population to arise from the ruins and start life again was something moving and inspiring. Also I made the acquaintance of Faith Willard from the States, with whom our lives were to become so inextricably linked from then on till now. Faith some years previously had come as a young woman on a trip to Beirut and had been introduced to Hazel. It was a brief meeting and Hazel did not remember it, but Faith went back to the States to rethink her future. She was a highly qualified and highly skilful counsellor in a large state school. She had glimpsed another kind of life, and after a few years she wrote and applied to work on the staff of the school in Lebanon. Hazel read the glowing testimonials and credentials and decided against. It would be like imprisoning a golden eagle in a bird cage. She thanked her for her letter, but explained she did not really feel that she would fit in. Faith was puzzled. She was sure that God had spoken to her and it seemed strange that he had not also spoken to Hazel. She wrote again and received the same reply. Nothing daunted, Faith tried the third time, assuring Hazel that she had been called to the post. Hazel gave in, but wrote cautiously, pointing out the difficulties and uncertainties in education in a land at war. Faith telegraphed back, 'Hallelujah, I'm coming!'

Her coming was certainly a great blessing, both in the school and in the neighbourhood, where she started a Bible study attended by parents and friends. And it was her enthusiasm and desire to share God's Word which encouraged Hazel to join her and Heather, a younger teacher, on Saturdays after I left in giving out to the foreign troops stationed in Lebanon several thousand Gospels, supplied through the Bible Society. The three of them drove happily in the ancient VW from one end of the country to the other past frequent check points manned by Syrian, Yemeni or Saudi Arabian soldiers; the soldiers were always surprised, usually polite and often eager for something to read that would relieve the monotony on roads where few cars passed. Several times soldiers would ask for extra copies 'for my family in Damascus ... or Horns'. At intervals were large military camps with sentries at the entrance. The three would say they wanted to speak to the commanding officer, and the soldiers, taken aback at seeing three foreign women, two of them very attractive with long golden hair, the third an older lady on crutches, the badge of respectability, would allow them through. In a central tent the officers would be lounging around drinking coffee, and again, startled at seeing three foreign ladies, they would offer seats, order more coffee and start to talk. Not once did they refuse books themselves and usually out of politeness the Syrian officers would agree to some books being given out in the camp. There were no spectacular results to report, but God's promise holds: 'My Word shall not return to me empty, but will accomplish what I desire and achieve the purpose for which I sent it...'

Back home again, I wrote *Nothing Else Matters,* a story based on the true experiences of a Lebanese family who had come to live with Hazel after losing their home and all their possessions in the recent fighting.

23

Settling Down in England

In February 1980 Farnham, aged sixty-two, died. He had undergone heart surgery from which he was recovering. He succumbed to a strange, rare virus, probably injected through the blood transfusion. He was admitted back into hospital and lingered semi-conscious for some days. He seemed to remember those things far back in our childhood, and on the last night, as I sat beside him (we kept watch in turn), we sang the old Swiss hymns together that we had learnt in the little meeting room at Rossinière.

He had known before the operation that he was going to die, although no one else expected it, and he had left specific instructions for his funeral. Over the years that he had worked at Addenbrooke's Hospital as an eye consultant, he had become increasingly burdened for the large community there. He and the chaplain had started a weekly lunchtime prayer meeting in the chapel, and it grew rapidly. It was open to all, and it was good to see consultants, nurses, cleaners and porters kneeling side by side interceding for the hospital. And prayers were answered. During the time he was there, Gideon Bibles were placed by every bed and the chapel services started being relayed to the wards. Farnham wanted that work to go on. In the last letter to his wife, he asked that his funeral service might be held in the hospital chapel during the dinner hour, so that all might come, and to last only half an hour so that all might have time to eat. There were so many with whom he had talked and prayed, and all was done as he requested. His old friend Maurice Wood preached, and the chapel was packed out, the hospital staff standing in places four deep around the walls.

He had asked that the gospel should be clearly preached, and he wanted it to be a joyful occasion. 'No black hats and no black scarves,' he said. He was rather vague as to what women usually wore at a funeral.

It is strange how grief blurred into a kind of grey mist with certain incidents unforgettably clear. I remember wandering down into the chapel at 2 am and having that certainty that Farnham was going to be healed, and the nightingales singing in the lane that led to the hospital; the bitterness of that February afternoon as we stood and sang round the grave. I remember motoring home alone after the funeral and feeling that a large part of me had died, and thinking, I never really knew what grief was before. And on top of the personal grief was the grief of the widow and the six children. I found no comfort.

It was three years later when my brother John died that the comfort was given. On the first Sunday after his death from cancer in the hospice, I felt I could not face a church service. Hymns were too poignant. I went to the Crackley woods, where the August bracken was waist high and the light thinned by the thickness of the green foliage. And here very clearly God seemed to speak. 'I will not leave you comfortless: I will come to you.' It was so clear that I felt I could speak too, as in a conversation. 'How shall I recognize the special coming?' I asked. And there flashed into my mind the words of an old hymn that I had learnt in my childhood, but had only ever sung in Arabic. 'I shall know Him, I shall know Him, by the print of the nails in His hands.' And I realized that in suffering we stand on common ground with him. We share a mutual experience. St Paul even prayed for it: 'that I may know him and the fellowship of his sufferings'.

It was a good thing for me that I moved house the same month that Farnham died in 1980. It gave me a lot to think about. John had been diagnosed as having cancer and was weakening rapidly. And now I knew that he would soon have to give up his practice. This meant the whole family moving to a smaller house in the same district and Auntie and I finding our own accommodation. I had joined a friendly little evangelical church on a council estate and decided to go and live in the area. It was difficult to leave Auntie and go house-hunting, and I had prayed that somehow the right house would be chosen for me. The second one I went to see – a council house five minutes from the church – was exactly what I wanted, and with the money from a house left to me by a great-aunt, it was at a price I could afford.

But I had not bargained for the extras. I had never heard of key money (£200), nor had I reckoned on a leaking boiler, wiring that had not been checked for thirty years, and a central heating system that had to be installed again from scratch. By the time I had settled in, I was about £1,700 over what I had reckoned. It was February, and no royalty money would arrive until June.

I was in no danger of starving. My brothers would have helped me had I asked them. But I did pray about the matter, and perhaps because it was a time of great sadness, the answer was instant and direct. A day or two later I received a letter from a lawyer in the Lake District. He said he had been looking for me for a year, and could I prove my identity? On doing so a second letter arrived, saying that an old lady had died a year previously. She had liked something I had written and had left me a legacy of about £1,800. It eventually turned out to be £2,000.

Why had they searched for a year? My name was uncommon, the name of the publishing firm was printed in the book. I can only think that God held it back. 'My times are in thy hand', said David. Had it come to me earlier, I might have felt no need for it and used it for other purposes.

I loved my new home, and Auntie, who had never lived in a small house before, adapted well. It was partly furnished by a wonderful supply from the church, where the fellowship was warm and alive with lots of offers of help. Two of the church leaders even donned overalls and between them painted the whole of the inside of the house. The neighbours were kind and welcoming, and a number of them have become close friends.

People dropped in. Children knocked at the door. We had a new garage built to replace the rather ramshackle one in the back garden, and this became the snooker room, which has brought in many young people. The boys tend to arrive at the front door, say 'Snooker', and shoot through the back without a glance in our direction, although in the winter I seize them by their coat collars and make them wipe their feet. We like to be noticed, however, and were pleased out of all proportion when one young lad, after weeks of treating us like two pieces of furniture, stopped himself suddenly with a jerk as he careered through the kitchen door and shouted over his shoulder, 'I like coming here; it's a dead nice house.'

Soon after moving in, we had a rather solid conservatory built on to the back of the house, which serves as a playroom and also a guest room when needed. Friends and family often visit, as do friends from Lebanon and Morocco and elsewhere. So we began to know students at Warwick University, especially foreign ones, who are often lonely and wanting to visit an English home.

These were happy years, and growing old did not seem difficult. I found new sources and ideas for writing too. The enormous number of broken homes and bewildered children prompted me to write *Where the River Begins*. The prevalent interest in occultism among young teenagers prompted *The Victor*, a story based in Tyre in Lebanon in the time of Christ.

Hazel arrived from Lebanon in 1981, having reached retiring age. She came just as I had to go into hospital for a laminectomy on my cervical vertebra. I had been in a lot of pain for three weeks, and the night before the operation, as I packed for Auntie to move up to my sister-in-law's home, I was feeling at the end of my tether. Suddenly the rail in the wardrobe, where all Auntie's clothes were hanging, broke, depositing everything in a heap at the bottom of the cupboard. Try as I would to conceal it, Auntie saw I was unduly distressed. She could not really judge what was happening. I knew I would have to pick up the clothes, and stooping was acutely painful. I walked downstairs in very low spirits . . . a knock at the front door. Young Alan Parker from the church stood there, shy and slightly embarrassed. 'I was driving home,' he said. 'I was early leaving work. I suddenly had a feeling you might be needing help.' I just refrained from hugging him and hurried him upstairs. In about ten minutes the bar was mended and the clothes neatly hung.

Hazel arrived about two days after my operation. I was being visited, simultaneously, by a prince of the royal family of Ethiopia and our garage man. I would have been delighted to see either and talk about Ethiopian politics or cars and have a chat, but I could think of absolutely no subject of common interest. They sat one each side of me. My neck being in a thick collar, I could address one only by turning my back on the other, and I felt miserable. Suddenly Hazel appeared in the doorway, brimming with enthusiasm and solutions for all problems. She grasped the situation immediately, and took my guests off in turn for cups of tea downstairs, leaving me free to roll on my side and enjoy the other guest, foreshadowing things for the future. She has been solving our problems ever since with cheerful common sense and usually refuses to recognize that the problem exists. As she says, 'It's a great life if you don't weaken.'

I quite enjoyed my ten days in hospital, but felt anxious about my hands. They were so weak as to be almost paralyzed. I could not hold a pen or eat with a knife and fork, and no one seemed to know why or be able to tell me if it would pass. After I got home, in spite of physiotherapy there was little improvement, and I began to think more deeply about the subject of healing through prayer. I had not prayed to be miraculously healed of my neck pain. I believed that under God the surgeon would heal me. He did. As the days passed in the ward, I began to realize what a tragedy it would be if Christians were all healed and never went to hospital. People are so vulnerable in hospitals and willing to talk. And how good if there was a sick Christian in every ward. But my hands seemed different. They affected my nursing and my writing. And had the weakness persisted, Hazel would have had to give up her deputation programme and stay at home with Auntie.

I asked three of the elders of the church to come and lay hands on me and pray for healing. They came at midday on Sunday. Although nothing happened immediately, by evening I found I could hold a pen and write legibly, and next morning I opened the door. After about twenty-four hours my hands had regained their normal strength.

If me, then why not John, who was fast going downhill, his cancer apparently spreading? Everything was happening in the family. A planned wedding, an expected baby, a GCSE exam. And although he loved and trusted the Lord, he could not accept the thought of leaving them all. Could there by prayer and faith be healing for him? It seemed so needed.

We went that year as a family to the first Spring Harvest conference at Prestatyn. John was well enough to attend some of the meetings. The teaching was clear and definite. If we prayed 'God's will be done on earth as it is in Heaven', then we could pray with assurance for healing. For there is no cancer or disability in Heaven. Sickness is not God's will. John asked for prayer, and the leaders were caring and loving beyond all our expectations. In a conference specially geared to the young, where individual ministry was going on all day and all night, the whole team and several of their wives gathered to pray for John. His wife and daughter were also present, and as healing was claimed for him we left Spring Harvest full of hope and expectation.

John died within four months, but something happened. He entered into a peace and acceptance of God's will for him that was almost palpable. He often spent the day in our house as he grew weaker. Towards the end I helped Gwynne, my devoted sister-in-law, with some of the night nursing ... and always there was that new sense of the peace of God that passes understanding and silences questioning.

And I too ceased to question. Faith is not being sure that you are going to get well. Faith in the Gospels was a hand stretched out to make contact with Jesus, and then something always happened. Just as in the Gospels no two healings ever took place in quite the same way, so Christ reserves the right to touch where he in his love sees best. There are degrees of faith – little faith, faith as a grain of mustard seed, great faith – and the quality of that faith may well have affected the peace of mind of the petitioner, but it could not affect the Lord's response. Trembling Peter sinking in the waves, the frightened woman who touched the hem of his garment, were upheld and healed as certainly as the confident centurion. Answer to our prayer may come in our body, our mind, our spirit, our circumstances, or in blessing sometimes long delayed, or even on the other side of death, and usually in our sorrow we fail to think much about that amazing final healing.

It came home to me forcibly in Rwanda when I visited the island where the old lepers, too disabled and disfigured to go back to their villages, were cared for the rest of their lives. I was told that when a leper died, there was no thought of sorrow. The other lepers would dig his grave by the shore of the lake and prepare a feast. At sunset they would gather to eat and drink, and all that night they would dance and sing round the graves, celebrating and sharing the joy of the leper in his new resurrection body, free from pain and weakness and disfigurement. I remember thinking, 'This is the real, right response to Christian death.' But I am glad that Jesus wept. He knows that it is almost impossible at first to see through the mists of sorrow to the glory beyond. We just have to believe it is there.

John died in 1983, and nine months later in 1984, Auntie died. She was very weary and ready to go. She was stone deaf and could no longer read much. It was difficult to cheer her. During the last years of her life, her great concern was for the grandchildren of the emperor of Ethiopia, five dearly loved girls whose guardian she had been during the years they and other Ethiopians were at Clarendon. When the Revolution broke out they were all imprisoned without trial, together with their mother and other women of the royal family, in one small room. Miss Swain thought about them, prayed for them and worked tirelessly on their behalf, sending herself and encouraging others to send all the supplies and help possible through a neutral agency. Sadly she died before they were released after fourteen years in prison. But prayer for them was answered; in spite of all they have been through, their courage and unshaken faith in God have been a wonderful witness to his power to keep in all circumstances.

I wonder whether, from Heaven, Miss Swain was allowed to watch her memorial service in London and rejoice when hundreds of her old students gathered to give thanks for her life and one after another testified to her love and influence on their childhood and young womanhood. It was a beautiful service, a pageant of praise.

24
The Refugee Camp

I had nursed my aunt for eight years, and life seemed a bit empty at first, although our little church round the corner was flourishing and there were a number of enquirers and new converts to help to teach and train. But while I waited and prayed, wondering whether I should return to Morocco, the pictures of the Ethiopian famine began to appear on our television screens, and England was shaken. Over the past years we seem to have got used to pictures of war, famine and misery, and the public may be suffering from what has been called 'compassion fatigue'. But in 1984 nothing quite like that had been seen before. Even the children from the streets around were knocking at the door, asking what they could do for Ethiopia. We got a working group together and held a Christmas sale. It helped the children, if it did little to relieve the famine. But some found no help, and the question kept coming up, as each news time revealed fresh horrors: where was God in a situation like this? Did he care? Why? Why? Why? He could send rain if he wanted to, remarked one bewildered teenager.

I wanted an answer to that nagging question, a question asked thousands of years before: 'Is the Lord amongst them or not?' So when I was asked as a representative of Global Care, a Christian charity with which I was already involved, to visit the refugee camps on the Sudan/Ethiopia border, I was glad to go. Christian Outreach, a relief and development organization in Leamington Spa, had set up an emergency children's feeding centre and Global Care was a major funding partner. So in May 1985 I left England in the full tide of its late spring and its uprush of tender new life, and flew out to Khartoum with Ron Newby, the founder and director of Global Care. And there we travelled by jeep eastwards into the terrible drought desert to the camps on the Ethiopian border. I am not going to pretend that I enjoyed the month that I spent in the camp. In some ways it was a nightmare, but I will always be glad that I went. So many questions were answered, and life was the richer for the experience.

Firstly, there was the heat. I was allotted a bed in a fairly crowded mud-walled, thatched hut. But the closeness was unbearable, and I pushed mine into the yard. I woke about 4 am, when it was relatively cool, and waited for the sun, like some fierce beast, to spring up over the wall of the enclosure. By the time we had breakfasted and reached the camp, it was warming up to its usual temperature of 120 degrees. The stockades had no walls – only a slatted roof supported on posts, through which the sun filtered in patches. For several days, at about 3 pm, when we returned to our little compound, I was quite sure that I was going to die of heat. But by the end of the first week, one got used to it, and I decided to live. Actually, I think I was the only one of the group – the rest were in their twenties – who did not give in within the first month or two of arrival.

Then there was the grief. We would start for the camp at about 6.15, crossing the dam with its blessed strip of green, bumping across the desert in our overloaded Landrover. Sometimes carcasses of goats and camels lay rotting in the sand. They had strayed from the herd who still grazed round the dam and the muddy river, and they died of thirst. Sometimes we would look ahead and see strange mirages of trees and water. They shimmered away in the morning light as we drew near, and the first concrete view on the horizon was rows and rows of army tents. Thousands of them standing stark in the glare of the sun, and ever increasing, for we aimed to arrive before the cavalcade of trucks brought the daily toll of starving from the border, usually about one thousand four hundred new each day.

We were spared the worst horrors. We were in an overflow camp, and those who came had already been screened at the camp further south, where 80,000 people lived in shelters by a river that was beginning to dry up. But even so, some would not have survived the bumpy journey overnight, where some forty people stood in each lorry to go in convoys. Our first job was to welcome the travellers and help them alight.

First to leap out were the children, some of them tottering on stick-like legs, but radiant to have arrived.

They wrung our hands, smiling up at us, their pinched little faces aglow, eyes bright for a moment. Some had been journeying for weeks, on and on through the ravaged, scorching landscape, burying their friends along the way. But this was home. This was where they would stop and rest, the end of the journey. Though weak, joy overflowed.

The sick came next, lifted down carefully, and sometimes it was too late. A woman, pitifully covered, was carried away, her weeping husband and wide-eyed children following behind. Another had given birth in the truck, and often women were pushed to the front clasping almost moribund babies, who were rushed to the feeding centre – only often it was too late.

Then came the unpacking of cooking pots and filthy blankets, and families huddled together in the shade of the stockade. It was very quiet, for few had the strength or energy to talk. The children curled up on the rush mats and slept. Everyone was served with mugs of fortified milk and high-protein biscuits, while healthier babies were fed on a milky kind of porridge. Then the registering, the screening, the weighing and the measuring by the medicals began, family by family. It was late afternoon before they were issued with their rations and allotted a tent, and meanwhile the sun got hotter and hotter. Was the Lord among us or not? The Ethiopians are a noble race. They wore their rags with a touching dignity. During the whole of my month there, I never once heard a murmur of complaint or a word of impatience, and the same could be said of the overworked young team of nurses, doctors, dieticians and their hastily trained local helpers. Never once on duty did I hear them succumb to obvious weariness or irritability, although I did once find one crouched behind the biscuit cartons, weeping bitterly over the death of a baby.

I worked mostly in the babies' feeding centre, where the severely malnourished and dying were fed by spoon or nasal tubes. Their cold little bodies were wrapped in patchwork blankets, knitted by kind women's meetings in England. They added a gay touch of colour to the dust-coloured rags and blankets they arrived in. There were no nappies. Water was too severely rationed to do much in the way of washing clothing. But somehow nobody minded. They had arrived. It was the end of the journey. They often collapsed on the rush mats, leaving their babies to us, and slept and slept and slept.

I acquired an interpreter and sat with him in the entrance to the tents, asking questions and hearing amazing stories of hardship and survival. Long, long treks through drought territory; many little graves along the road, for it was the children who succumbed the soonest. They died of dehydration, of malnutrition and hunger, of snake bite and heat stroke, and even from the bombing and gunfire of government troops, for the civil war was at its height. But having reached a temporary haven, they seemed able to speak calmly and objectively about their experiences. Some were quite merry. Even in a refugee camp it is good to sit down and rest. Perhaps the worst factor at that point was the boredom. Apart from further and further forays into the shadeless, burning desert to search for firewood, the daily queue for the water ration and the weekly queue for food rations, there was nothing to do. Later, classes were organized for the children. Twice a day the women bored little holes in the dry earth and kindled their tiny fires to cook dried beans. In consequence, my arrival in the tent with the interpreter was an exciting event, attended by laughter and much shaking of hands.

The people were Coptic Christians and wore crosses round their necks, although no church had been organized at that point. But I heard through Ron Newby of Global Care of a thriving little refugee church in the town of Gadaref, some fifty miles to the west, where Arabic was spoken. So when I had a weekend off, I decided to visit. I begged a lift in a supply truck with a few others, and we jolted over the trackless desert for some miles before we joined the tarmac road, reaching there about midday.

Gadaref, a dusty, rather smelly little town, left sweltering in the heat, was important at that time, for it was the storage centre for all the overseas aid for the three great camps that lay on the Ethiopian/Sudanese border. The northern camp sheltered 120,000 refugees, the southern one 80,000. Ours was the overflow, containing to date 20,000. Dozens of skilled, dedicated young workers – medics, water engineers, mechanics, dieticians, sanitation experts etc, co-ordinators of all nationalities, representing dozens of charities, were continually passing through, and beds could be had at the residence of an English lady there who kept open house for all who came. So I presented myself and asked for lodging. I was shown a low, scorching room containing one small bed, opening off a verandah. It seemed unnecessarily spacious until I realized that all the other beds had been pulled out into the garden – and we just managed to squeeze my bed in between two others. I left my rucksack on top of it and went to explore. I had been given the address of an Arabic pastor, a lonely Christian in that busy little Muslim town. He was an old, tired man, and we sat on his verandah and he told his story. For years he had faithfully ministered to a congregation of about eight – his young family and two or three others. A young Ethiopian refugee had come to him and asked if he could bring some of his fellow countrymen to the church and translate the service into Tigri. The pastor was pleased, and on the first Sunday about ten had come. The following Sunday twenty came, on the next, fifty. Now the little building overflowed. He advised me to come early next morning if I wanted to get a seat. It was wonderful to sleep in that green, green garden that night with the sweet scent of flowers. I stretched out on a mattress with an Irish policeman and a Welsh pastor at either side of me. Nobody minded. It was too hot to be fussy.

I reached the little church building in good time for the service, but even so, had not a lad got up and offered me his seat, I would hardly have got one. The place was crowded to the door with men, women and children, standing packed in the central aisle or on the steps of the platform. Their faces were bright and eager, and they were singing and clapping. They literally shone. Gone was the patient apathy. These people were expectant, and when a tall, handsome-looking Ethiopian mounted the platform to translate for the Arabic pastor, they leaned forward and listened with rapt attention, as those who tasted the bread of life. They were not hungry physically – the camp was an old one and was now receiving regular rations and they were partially amalgamated with the town. But they were all far from home and very poor, and had little hope for the future. From whence then the light and the brightness?

The young man, Melaku, invited me to visit him at the back of the church that afternoon. He was a well-educated young man who spoke English fluently, and he told his story clearly and without bitterness. He had not left Ethiopia because of the famine, for he lived in the south, which was relatively unaffected. He had left to save his life.

At the time of the revolution he had been a boy of about fifteen, and the communist teaching had thrilled him. Here was a wonderful new road of freedom and opportunity for the young, a chance to break free of all the old restrictions of culture and religion. He threw himself into it with all his energy and enthusiasm, and at first it seemed to him and his dazzled comrades that they owned the world.

But gradually, when it was too late to turn back, they began to realize that things were not what they had seemed. His father's farm was taken from him, and people who questioned began to disappear. They were free to tread that one road, but no other. They were trapped in it. Melaku and many others like him began to be afraid.

But his friend appeared not to be afraid. In fact he kept breaking into song, and Melaku, who loved music, asked him what he was singing. The boy replied softly, 'Come with me on Sunday morning, and you will hear.' Melaku accepted the invitation. He went with his friend to a small evangelical church, shortly to be closed. For the first time in his life he heard the gospel read in his own native language, and to use his own words, 'I fell in love with Jesus.' He acquired a New Testament and pored over it, weeping over the story of the cross, glorying in the truth of the resurrection. A wonderful new life seemed to be opening ahead of him, a release from the trap.

But one of the community leaders of the new communist regime noticed the difference in the boy and immediately discovered what was happening. Melaku was sent for and told that in future the meeting for young comrades would be held every Sunday morning. He was required to attend.

It was then that Melaku began to realize what being a Christian was going to cost him, now and in the years ahead. He was only sixteen, but he made his choice. He knew that he could never turn back from the claims of that tremendous love, and he continued to put Christ before every other commitment and to speak of him to all who would listen. In the next five years he was imprisoned three times and was beaten, shut away and humiliated, made to run many miles in blazing heat. But each time, miraculously, he was released. And each time when he was released young people came creeping to him under cover of darkness. He taught them the secret of his strength and endurance. Sometimes they met in a house, sometimes on the hillside, never twice in the same location, until one evening his friend came to him and said, quite simply, 'Tonight we must both get away. Tomorrow they are going to shoot us.'

There was no time to lose. They collected a little food and the necessary documents and identity cards to ensure their freedom across the border, and set off running through the night. They were strong and athletic and they ran for seventeen hours before they crossed over the border to the safety of eastern Sudan. But they had to swim across two rivers, and their papers were washed away. Nameless and officially stateless, they were put straight into a refugee camp.

But Melaku knew that if only he could get to the Sudanese capital of Khartoum, his old friends from the now closed church would recognize him and help him. In Khartoum he would find fellowship, an identity and a future. He made contact with a camp official, who believed his story and agreed for him to travel up to the capital in a police car. They set out and drove all day, stopping for the night at Gedaref.

Melaku slept deeply and awoke to find himself once more a nameless refugee. The police had gone off without him. He was not dismayed. Khartoum lay within a day's journey. Besides, at Gedaref there was work for a strong, able young man such as he, unloading the endless stream of trucks bearing food and medical supplies to the camps along the eastern border. He would wait a few days.

But it was during these few days that he met the Egyptian pastor and realized the great new mission field that lay right there in front of him. And so, for the sake of his Master, who had become a man, Melaku became a refugee. And as that evening I stood at the back of that overflowing church with its crowded aisles and its joyous singing, praising congregation, I knew that I had found the final answer to my question.

We would have changed their circumstances, but we would not have changed them. God's solution is sometimes different. He does not always lift people out of the situation. He himself comes into the situation, as Christ the eternal man once entered this world and in a sense came to stay. He does not pluck them out of the darkness. He becomes the light in the darkness, the peace in the midst of the conflict, the spirit's riches in the midst of poverty and loss and physical degradation. Right there in the desert, he gives 'beauty for ashes, the oil of joy for mourning, the garment of praise for the spirit of heaviness'. When the long, crowded service was over – I have never been more thankful for an electric fan – people lingered, breaking up into little groups round some individual who lacked their obvious joy. Some sang softly, some spoke or prayed earnestly, and I went up to Melaku and asked him what they were doing. He looked surprised at my question. He had imagined that this was the custom in every evangelical church. 'Why, those in the centre only came in new today,' he replied. 'They do not yet know Jesus. Those who know are telling them. Then they will find Jesus too.' I watched fascinated, as I suspected that a newcomer would not be allowed out till he did. Suddenly, as I watched, the light began to shine on some of those dark faces and I felt I had the answer to my question. Surely the Lord was amongst them even now.

I came home and wrote *I Needed a Neighbour*, published by Scripture Union in 1987.

25

Global Care

In 1979 I was invited by the youth leader, Ron Newby, to speak to the Young People's Fellowship at our church in Coventry. I told them about a small orphanage in Morocco set up by two young women missionaries. A girl had knocked on their door one night and thrust what seemed a bundle of rags into the arms of one of them and run off into the darkness. Inside the rags was a tiny baby girl who was the first of many other children who came in the same way. In those days if an unmarried girl had a baby, the lives of both could be at risk from their families and neighbours. The two ladies then felt the call of God to make the children their life's work and in a wonderful way acquired a farmhouse in the mountains where they brought up many children over the years. From the hospital in Tangier we were sometimes able to send them babies who had been abandoned.

The Young People's Fellowship group responded to what they had heard by organizing a sponsored walk to raise funds for the orphanage. When the young people later scattered to various colleges, most presumably forgot the sponsored event, but the leader, Ron Newby, did not forget. Some time later he went out to visit the orphanage and continued to send funds and to keep links. Perhaps this foreshadowed his vision, which was fulfilled later, of founding Global Care as a Christian charity with its compelling slogan: 'You can't change the whole world but you can make a world of difference to some children in need.'

In 1983 (two years before I went out to the camp in the Sudan) Ron Newby, who at that time was also director of social work of a large national children's organization in the Midlands region of England, was at the Christian conference called Spring Harvest. He was impressed by two men from Uganda whom he met there, and invited David Wakumire and his brother to his home in Coventry, and brought them down to visit us. They told us of the awful conditions in their country after the Idi Amin massacres, which left thousands of children orphaned, especially in the Luwero district. David had started to help these children in a small way and, realizing Ron's extensive professional childcare experience, urged him to come over and visit Uganda.

In November 1983 Ron was seconded by his employers to visit Uganda. Arriving there he was invited to meet the head of the government's Voluntary Social Services, a woman who was desperate at the way things had got out of hand, with countless numbers of orphans and needy children. She and Ron had agreed to go and visit the most dangerous part of the country, Luwero, where civil war and massacre were rife. Hearing what was planned, the official driver of the government vehicle refused to go. So Ron and the party drove themselves.

After a long drive through deserted countryside, they came into an area where they discovered a large derelict property with its windows boarded up. Two soldiers were digging a grave at the back of the premises for three small children to be buried that morning. Inside in the dark, squatting on the floor were about two hundred children, snuffling, coughing, sick and too weak to cry, their only food a daily meal of boiled beans from a great cauldron outside. They were suffering from measles, dysentery, conjunctivitis and many other ailments, with no one to keep them clean. Ron asked who they were and was told they had been picked up in the bush, fleeing from soldiers who had raided their village in pursuit of rebels and had killed their parents.

'Will you please take some children,' the officials begged, and Ron finally chose twelve who seemed as though they might recover and who, he had been assured, apparently had no living relatives. He packed them into the back of the vehicle and brought them to Mbale in eastern Uganda. There he appointed Christian workers, rented a house, and a children's temporary shelter 'The Rock' was started.

Recognizing that institutional life was not natural to Ugandan culture, David Wakumire, backed by persuasive visits from Ron, took on the establishing and organizing of a child sponsorship programme. This involved supporting a widowed mother or the placing of a destitute child with a Christian family to act as guardians, preferably with the child's own relatives if they could be traced, and paying for school fees, some essential clothing and, if necessary, food and medical needs. There are at present about five hundred children so sponsored by supporters of Global Care in Britain and by SEHU, a partner group in Holland.

The children are carefully monitored by David and his team and they mostly live within a radius of twenty to thirty miles from Mbale, eastern Uganda, the centre of the work. The scheme now includes a vocational training centre too, with courses in tailoring, secretarial studies, agriculture and other relevant studies. Every summer Christian camps are planned for all the children in two large groups, a time of happy holiday and Christian teaching, and in 1993 a discipleship course was added for older teenagers and young people.

My active involvement with Global Care has given me the opportunity of meeting and sometimes hosting many wonderful Christians from overseas with whom we work in partnership, like Edith, David Wakumire's wife. In addition to running her own home with a large extended family of orphaned children, Edith works with an AIDS counselling and support project which she has established to bring help and comfort to countless numbers of families affected by the rampant spread of AIDS.

In 1983 Global Care was officially founded and registered as a charity by Ron Newby, who became also its first chief executive. I was asked to serve as the charity's president, and as one of the trustees I began then to be closely involved in this exciting and rapidly expanding work, focusing on the special and individual needs of children suffering in a world of massive and overwhelming problems.

In 1984 Ron Newby again visited Uganda and helped create the Christian Childcare Project in Mbale. A simple newsletter was produced from the end of his kitchen table and so began what is today an international children's charity working extensively for suffering children in some of the poorest and most troubled parts of the globe.

Then came the horrendous Ethiopian famine in 1984. The stark reality of a dry stone wall at a relief camp, dividing those selected to live from those destined to die, was shown on British TV and then around the world. With so little food available, those who were to die watched in mute resignation; their neighbours ate, while they starved to death. Deeply moved by these pictures, both Ron and I were not surprised when Global Care's supporters began phoning to ask, 'What can we do to help?'

Soon the kitchen table was swamped with contributions and Global Care was able to pay for the first £10,000 worth of emergency food and vital medical supplies to be airlifted to help a partner relief organization at camps in eastern Sudan, bordering Ethiopia. During Easter 1985 I travelled with Ron Newby to visit these camps, and my stay in one of them has been described in a previous chapter.

In 1986 we decided to expand Global Care's work and expertise to help other Christian organizations and missions like Friends of Bangladesh with their 'Home of Joy' for orphaned and abandoned children in Khulna, Bangladesh, and in India where some ex-Operation Mobilisation workers had helped establish a children's home near Badlapur for babies given up by their young mothers enslaved in prostitution in the red light district of Bombay. We also began to help a small number of children in Lebanon who were injured or affected by the fighting in Beirut.

In 1988 Global Care first started financially supporting work, too, in war-torn Mozambique. Many thousands had fled as refugees, some badly mutilated by soldiers' knives, to the northern Transvaal area of South Africa. Later, working again in active partnership with Operation Mobilisation personnel from South Africa, we were able to assist a major relief and development programme among displaced people at Xilembene and Palmeira in Mozambique, where hundreds of small children were fed daily at the emergency feeding centres. Development programmes also included crop growing schemes which were organized by local church groups. Now with the sixteen-year-old struggle in Mozambique abating and peace agreements being signed, much needs to be done to re-build this former communist state. Opportunities for Christian witness abound in the country at present, and even a number of government and rebel soldiers have found Christ, been baptized and joined newly planted churches.

In 1992 similar feeding centres were set up for children in the drought-stricken areas of Zimbabwe and local Christians supported in establishing a children's care centre.

During 1990 I was again seriously affected by the recurring horror of seeing on the TV screen the appalling neglect of children in Romania. When at the end of 1989 the Ceauşescu regime came to an end in Romania, it was found that many thousands of children were locked away and forgotten in orphanages and in institutions intended primarily for mentally defective patients. This was the result of Ceauşescu's policy of forcing women to have unwanted pregnancies to increase the nation's future work force and to produce children they could not afford to feed. With my active involvement and prayer support, Ron Newby with his small team of volunteers ventured out to organize some of the very first convoys of aid relief to Romania. Our little home and those of some of our neighbours were frequently used as collection depots for clothing and food! Ron was able to gain the confidence of top government officials who registered Global Care as a foreign charity to pioneer a model of 'family type' care for children who needed to be taken out of large depersonalized institutions, some of which were in the most deplorable condition.

In the beautiful Transylvanian town of Tirgu Mures in Romania, Global Care established its 'Homes of Hope' project. In September 1992 I was thrilled to join a small group from Global Care travelling out to Romania, as I'd been asked to officiate at the opening ceremony of the Homes of Hope, staffed by dedicated Romanian Christians. This lovely, spacious property with its garden is situated on the edge of the town and has truly. become 'home', a Christian family home, at first to twelve little children who have moved from a large institution into two self-contained ground and first floor apartments to form two new families of six each, with other children to be added. loan Pasca, the Romanian project leader, and his Christian staff team were actively at work caring for the children in their new surroundings. Children at the Homes of Hope who were formerly branded by the officials as 'ineducable' are now attending ordinary day schools.

Back in April 1991 nothing could have adequately prepared us in Global Care for the massive task ahead when we launched, together with an Operation Mobilisation team in Turkey, a relief aid programme to the Kurdish refugees who were fleeing the ruthless onslaught of Saddam Hussein.

Ron Newby had just returned from Morocco when the plight of the Kurdish people had broken in th news. Over Sunday lunch Ron, my sister Hazel and I talked of what might be done. The idea of responding to such need seemed formidable, yet we realized that while 'we can't do everything, we mustn't do nothing'.

Within days a relief aid operation was under way from Global Care. Tens of thousands of blankets and tons of food and medical supplies and tents were donated and taken several thousand miles by trucks and by shipping containers to the Kurdish refugees high in the mountains of Turkey and Iraq. The way people responded to the tragedy with both money and voluntary help was magnificent. Little children donated their pocket money.

Schools and churches throughout Britain rallied with support, and storage at our Coventry base had to be extended to include the use of an aircraft hangar at our local airport. Numerous volunteers worked around the clock, and one man who walked off the street and into the offices to help with packing came to faith in Christ through the testimony of the team.

In the early nineties, as Albania came out of its almost total isolation from the rest of the world, Global Care was again asked to help with the very great needs of children in that land, and one special child, blinded and badly disfigured by terrible burns, was brought to England for surgery and given a completely new lease of life.

Most years since I left Morocco I have been back for some weeks to see folk I know there and usually I've been able to visit the orphanage Global Care helps to support. In recent years I have also been able to introduce to Global Care a number of very needy children from families I know and the charity have been able to assist them.

Over the past ten years Global Care has developed beyond what we ever imagined. We thank God for the way he has blessed the work as we seek to give both physical and spiritual help and make a world of difference to countless numbers of children.

And Ron's kitchen table? Well, it is now in daily use at the Homes of Hope in Romania for children who not very long ago had no concept of 'kitchen table' or 'family meal'. That seems appropriate. Global Care now has its own International Office here in Coventry and continues to respond with practical Christian care to the needs of suffering children anywhere around the globe.

Postscript

Since this was written, work has focused particularly on the very many children orphaned or separated from their parents in the terrible fighting in Rwanda.

The Patricia St John Memorial Fund. At the Thanksgiving Service on November 6th 1993 the fund was set up to continue to bring help through Global Care to children in need in many different countries.

Contributions to the fund can be sent to Global Care, 2 Dugdale Road, Coventry, CV6 1PB, info@globalcare.org. Registered Charity No. 326488.

26

Home on the Estate

Much has happened during the last few years. They have been some of the richest and most fulfilled years of my life, but one cannot easily write about the present. Those involved are very much alive and close at hand, and with such a host of living friends in the church and in the neighbourhood, whom does one mention and whom does one leave out?

Hazel and I love living here in Canley and find our council house and small garden a great joy. One of the best things about our home is that we are only five minutes' walk from Canley Evangelical Church where I have worshipped for the last fifteen years. It is a church which has more and more seen itself as serving the community as well as faithfully sharing God's Word. The building was enlarged in 1984 and almost every day there are activities for different age groups including day care facilities for the elderly. At Ladies' Hour on Wednesday afternoons, well over a hundred, some widowed or lonely, find a warm welcome and many are visited in their homes. We gain a lot, too, through our weekly house groups in different homes when we study God's Word in an informal setting and pray for each other as individuals and families. It is such a blessing to share in the outreach of the church in these different ways, as well as in the young people's work, and to be able to introduce with confidence new folk to this loving and welcoming fellowship. Since 1990 numbers have so increased at the Sunday morning family service that the possibility of having two services is now being discussed. It is so good, too, that we can work and pray in warm friendship with our neighbours at the Anglican church nearby and have a joint Saturday evening service with them each month.

We are fortunate in having a lot of guests in our home, some from near at hand, others from different parts of the world. Being near Warwick University, we get to know students, specially some from overseas, and a number of them also come to the church. Since 1984 we have had lodgers, the first a social worker, Hazel Jacques, who overlapped for six weeks with John White, an MSc student; they fell in love almost at once and are now married and missionaries in Lebanon. Then we had for two years a Bangladeshi PhD student, followed by a succession of Chinese postgraduate students, mostly for a year each, a new man always ready to come in the day after the last one leaves. All of them have become good friends, adding much pleasure to our lives.

We enjoy, too, the young people and children from the estate who often drop in. My first guests were a group of seven or eight lads aged between fifteen and eighteen whom I met soon after arriving in Canley. They were sitting on the steps of the fish and chip shop one Sunday evening when I was passing on my way to church. They hailed me, singing the Queen Mother's song, 'Grandma, we love you', and I replied, 'And I love you.' 'May we visit you?' they asked. 'Yes,' I said, 'at eight o'clock, after church.'

On my return, rather to my surprise, the whole group were waiting on my doorstep. I was alone with my aunt then, and had to go upstairs to see to her. So I welcomed them in, showed them where to make tea and said I would be down soon. They behaved beautifully, and we finished up the evening with a story and a prayer. Each week for several months they came, until for various reasons they scattered, and never once were they any trouble; if I was delayed upstairs, they would call up, 'Miss, Miss, we're waiting for your story and your little prayer.'

Younger children came to play snooker in the old garage in the back garden or other games in the small conservatory play room and we were able to start a boys' club and a girls' craft class, both of which finally outgrew the premises and are now held at the church on different evenings with very efficient younger leadership. A group of children who have become Christians, mostly at the summer camps or holiday clubs, still meet here for Bible study each week, led now by our church youth worker.

Individual children and a few older folk come for Bible study on their own, and one boy who came regularly each week for some years was a special joy. He came alone for some time and then sometimes brought two or three friends along too. Invited to Sunday School when he was eight years old, he replied, 'I'm sorry to disappoint you, but I am *not* coming to Sunday School!' A day or two later he reappeared at the door with a large children's Bible and said, 'I've had a good idea; you shall teach me alone each Sunday morning when you come back from church.' He was unusually bright and interested and wanted to go right through the Bible. The Ten Commandments specially interested him and one winter evening he rushed in exclaiming, 'Just had a narrow escape; slipped on the ice and bumped my head. Almost took the name of my God in vain, but just managed to turn it into Gosh!'

Our sisters-in-law and nephews and nieces and 'greats', now fifty-three in number with two more on the way, contribute much to our happiness and frequently call on us. Farnham's six, as doctors and teachers, have followed in their father's footsteps and are scattered all over the world. Their letters in successive years from China, Central Asia, Abu Dhabi, Morocco, Sweden and Canada keep us in touch; and on their visits home they bring their mostly large families to stay and the children sleep on mattresses on the floor. A special delight every few years is seeing Dan, Farnham's third son, and his wife Sue, now with four little girls (and a baby boy just added). After eleven years in China they have recently moved to Alma Ata in Khazakstan, working with Operation Mobilisation, Dan as leader of their teams in Central Asia.

Our only remaining brother, Oliver, who has three very successful sons, lives in a beautiful converted barn not far away, where we enjoy visiting. He retired after years as chief scientist with the Civil Aviation Authority and now with his wife Eileen is fully involved in all aspects of village life and in the organizing of various musical activities.

Another big part of life has been the summer camps in the USA. Farnham's youngest son, still a medical student, was being married in Canada in 1985. We longed to go to the wedding but felt the expense was not really justified. Just then a letter came from Hazel's great friend from her Lebanon days, Faith Willard, who runs the seven-week summer 'Camp Good News' each year for some one hundred and eighty children and teenagers from all over the States and some from overseas. Her brother Peter Willard has similar camps in Maine. Faith wrote that if we would come and take the Bible studies for the counsellors and other workers in the preparation weeks at the two camps and stay on for some other talks, and just be there, they would pay our return air fares. The times we were needed at the camps fitted in exactly with the date of the wedding, and we accepted with alacrity.

The two camp sites consist of some main buildings and a number of log cabins set in woods, one beside a lake and the other by a wide river, both very beautiful indeed. The friendships we made there were something quite special, as was the opportunity of seeing, or hearing of, numbers of young people coming to Christ and committing their lives to him. There is a lovely mixture in both camps of older, very responsible workers, some of whom became

Christians at camp themselves when Faith's father was in charge and who have come back year after year, and a number of enthusiastic and keen Christian university students who act as counsellors, each responsible for six or seven campers. The kitchen, too, is always a specially nice place to work, with a very international team of men and women, professional people, housewives and students. I have returned for five summers and Hazel for seven, and we have learned to love these Americans dearly. The age gap seems less felt than in England, and the counsellors especially accept us more as one of themselves and discuss many matters with refreshing frankness. Our singleness fascinates them, and they have a way of accosting us suddenly with such questions as, 'Say, ma'am, how come you never married?', or 'Say, ma'am, how d'you figure out being single?' (that really makes us think!). In both camps there is great emphasis on helping those in need, and car washes on Saturdays are a special way of helping to raise funds for projects in Bangladesh.

At the end of our time in camp in 1985, David and Donna's beautiful wedding took place at the Prairie Bible Institute where Donna's father worked. Then came the thrill of nearly a week in the Canadian Rockies with David's in-laws, who welcomed Janet and Martyn and Hazel and me as if we were really their own family; and we have loved their return visits to us. The wedding of Oliver, Farnham's second son, in Sweden was an equally lovely occasion, as were other weddings in England too numerous to mention.

The work of Global Care, described in a previous chapter, has occupied a lot of my time and thought. For every child rescued, fed, taught and loved, we thank God, and we count it the greatest privilege to be involved and long to share the needs and opportunities with others.

Perhaps the most significant thing about these last years has been the gradual but growing realization that the apparently almost fruitless years of toiling and praying in Muslim lands are beginning to yield a harvest. The news reaches us of a new hunger there for God's Word, and a new burden of prayer in the hearts of God's people. We cannot publish what we hear. We can only rejoice over these small green shoots. I spent some time reading the books and diaries of Lilias Trotter, veteran pioneer missionary in North Africa, and eager that they should be remembered I wrote her biography, *Until the Day Breaks,* published by STL. Surely much of what is happening today is due to the love and prayers and patience of those like Lilias Trotter who trusted God to bring a harvest, even though there were so few results apparent. I have seen the beginning of that harvest on my visits back to Morocco, usually for a month or so each year. I see many old friends and some who are interested in doing the Bible correspondence courses, as well as my nephew Paul, who for years has worked there, a surgeon like his father; he, too, has five sons and one daughter. Every night the message of the gospel is being broadcast across the country, thousands are listening and many are writing in for Bible correspondence courses. And here and there someone listens and knows,

'This is the truth, this is the word of God.' Sometimes he or she listens alone, and sometimes to the lonely help is sent in strange ways.

I remember a day, a few years ago, when on a visit to Morocco I was staying alone in a small fanatically Muslim city and I went out on the balcony early. The sun had risen behind the mountain, bathing the red tiled roofs of the houses in light and colour. I prayed that on that very morning I would find one person at least who wanted to hear about Jesus and his gospel, and then I set off to climb to the top of the town.

I did not know where or why I was going, but I came to a little public garden on the hillside, a place where tourists like to sit. But the tourist season was over and the place was deserted except for a man in uniform, guarding the entrance.

I like to avoid policemen on my solitary walks so I turned down the path to the right – but he had seen me and called to me. I went back, wondering if I was to be questioned, but he was merely bored and wanted a tourist to talk to. He was delighted to find I spoke Arabic, and we spent some time chatting pleasantly. When I rose to go, it was nearly time for another guard to relieve him.

It was then that God seemed to speak very clearly in my heart, 'Give that man a Gospel.' I reacted immediately, 'Lord, if I give him one he may well report me at the police station and they may send me out of the town. I still have visits to make.'

But the Voice was implacable. 'Give him a Gospel.' So I drew out a Gospel of John and holding it firmly between my finger and thumb I said, 'Have you ever seen one like this?' He gazed at it in silence for a moment and then gave a great shout. '1013 Marseilles,' he exulted, and almost tried to seize it from my hand.

It was the box number of the Radio School of the Bible, and when I told him I had actually been there he looked at me as if I was a being from another world. Excitedly he poured out his story. He had been listening to the gospel broadcast on the radio for about two years and, like many others nowadays, he had simply known that this was the truth and he must follow it up. He had written once to Marseilles and for the last two years, slowly and laboriously, he had been working through the lessons on Luke. He had never seen a Gospel of John, nor met another Christian.

He insisted that I go home to lunch with him. I followed him at a discreet distance and was royally welcomed by his wife and his brother-in-law who was up from the desert in the south. He had never seen a Gospel and insisted that I give him a supply to take home with him, and these I fetched for him from the hotel later in the afternoon. But first we had a long talk all together and I was able afterwards to put my friend, the guard, in touch with an older Moroccan Christian in another town who promised to visit him one day.

A younger man whom I always look forward to seeing when I visit my old haunts is the one who lived for two years in my home as a boy. He has no fixed address so we can never correspond, but somehow he always seems to know when I arrive and within a day or so will turn up, rather disreputable but very welcoming and affectionate, usually at breakfast time. It was in connection with him as a child that I felt, more than at any other time, that a real miracle happened. He came to me at nine years old after living for some time on the streets. His father had married again and the stepmother had no place for him. At nine years old he was on his own, living by his wits, a clever but very attractive little thief, eager to be loved and accepted by someone, who at that point happened to be me. He was certainly not easy. I got him, with difficulty, into one school after another, but he was never tolerated for more than a few days, or else he ran off of his own accord. I often wondered how we could put up with him ourselves any longer, but how glad I am now that we did.

On one occasion a guest came over from Gibraltar to spend the day with us in Tangier. She had her handbag beside her, but somehow when she came to leave, an English £20 note was missing. My heart sank as I realized at once that my small friend, who by that time was nowhere to be found, must have taken it. There was nothing for it but to replace the money, which at that point was not at all easy.

When he finally reappeared I insisted that he tell me what he had done with the money and he admitted he had taken it to a money changer. Knowing nothing of its value, he had received in Moroccan money the equivalent of two English pounds. I went with him to the money changer, who not unnaturally professed to know nothing whatever of the deal. There seemed nothing more to be done, at least for the moment, but two days later as I was driving through the town a man on a motorbike swerved in front of me and called out, 'Follow me.' For some reason I felt compelled to do so and found myself outside an empty hut along the beach. The man, whom I had never seen before, beckoned me in and without a word handed me the equivalent of £18 in Moroccan money, and then in a flash, he disappeared. An angel on a motorbike!

And now, as life draws on towards evening and one looks back over the years, what conclusions or assessment can one draw? At first, standing alone, it is easy to see nothing but the failures, the mistakes, the might-have-beens and to ask what, if anything, has been achieved. But then Christ comes and stands beside us and says, 'Look with me.' He reminds us of that amazing, unique verse in the book of Joel, 'I will restore the years that the locust has eaten,' and we realize that he can do something that no earthly farmer can do. The earthly farmer can look at his blighted crop one year, recognize the loss, and determine to do better next year. But Christ says, 'I will restore the years that the locust has eaten, I will bring a glorious harvest out of this very blighted crop – the blessed harvest of self-confidence turned to the trust of a broken and a contrite heart, and a deeper, more thankful love – for to whom much is forgiven, the same loves much.'

I have often wondered why Jesus said to Peter, 'I have prayed for you that your faith fail not.' Why didn't he say,

'I have prayed for you that you will not deny me', and the tragedy would have been averted? I think the reason was that Pentecost was very near, when the Spirit of Jesus would seek access into Peter's heart, and before he could receive that Spirit, his own boastful pride and self-confidence needed to be shattered. He needed to learn his own weakness, he needed to weep bitterly, but not to despair. At the moment when his faith might fail him, his Master was there, praying for him. And when we look away from ourselves to those hands that have held us, lifted us and guided us over the years, we see nothing but a track of undeserved mercy and unfailing, forgiving love.

I think David, shepherd and king, illustrates this most clearly. His life that began so brightly was spoilt by a period of sin – of murder, adultery and lying. Could any harvest be gathered from such a blighted crop? Certainly he had to pay for his sin in the years ahead, but he said, 'Into your hands I commit my spirit', and nothing placed unreservedly into those wounded hands can turn out ultimately evil. Now that time has put the whole story into perspective, what is left as a permanent and indelible memorial of those dark years? Just the 51st Psalm, the prayer by which millions of sinners have turned back to the Saviour. In his hands, bathed by those wounds, the evil was transmuted to his glory. And that is so often his way. When he purposes to build, he seeks for a ruin. When he plans to plant a garden, he starts in the desert.

THE ALCHEMIST

My Master an elixir hath that turns
All base and worthless substances to gold.
From rubble stones He fashions palaces
Most beautiful and stately to behold.
He garners with a craftsman's skilful care
All that we break and weeping cast away.
His eyes see uncut opals in the rock
And shapely vessels in our trampled clay.
The sum of life's lost opportunities,
The broken friendships, and the wasted years,
These are His raw materials;
His hands rest on the fragments, weld them with His tears.
A patient Alchemist! – He bides His time,
Broods while the south winds breathe, the north winds blow,
And weary self, at enmity with self,
Works out its own destruction, bitter slow.
Then when our dreams have dwindled into smoke,
Our gallant highways petered out in mire,
Our airy castles crumbled into dust,
Leaving us stripped of all save fierce desire,
He comes, with feet deliberate and slow,
Who counts a contrite heart His sacrifice.
(No other bidders rise to stake their claims,
He only on our ruins sets a price.)

And stooping very low engraves with care
His Name, indelible, upon our dust;
And from the ashes of our self-despair
Kindles a flame of hope and humble trust.
He seeks no second site on which to build,
But on the old foundation, stone by stone,
Cementing sad experience with grace,
Fashions a stronger temple of His own.

Epilogue

August 14th - November 6th 1993

Although in the autumn of 1992 Patricia was twice in hospital for a week or so with heart trouble, and knew that her life here might end at any time, she still lived it to the full and in a letter written the day before she died she said, 'I am feeling so much better these days, I think I may be here for a long time yet.' Her plans for the following week included Bible studies with individuals and with a group, the giving of invitations to boys and girls for the holiday club at the church with which she was going to help, and a picnic with some local children, driving them in her car to a pleasure park across the city.

August 14th and 15th were specially happy days with a family reunion on the Saturday for the wedding of our niece Rosy, John's youngest daughter. On the Sunday we had a number of guests in our home, including an older man who told quite spontaneously during tea how he had come to know the Lord through talking with Patricia, something she had not known about before. At the evening service she read verses about Moses wanting to see God's glory; how we see something of that glory now in Christ, and how one day we shall see him in all the fullness of his glory. Her last words on Sunday night were, 'Hasn't it been a *lovely* weekend!' And then, in her sleep we believe, the Lord took her.

Even as we waited for the ambulance, along with the deep sense of loss, there was gladness that there had been no long and painful illness, but that she had walked, as it were, straight into fullness of joy in God's presence. Her life and her going seemed very like that of Enoch, about whom she had written more than forty years ago:

Now Enoch walked with God,
Walked in a fellowship so close and sweet
That all the clamour of the crowded street,
The angry tumult of the busy mart,
Could not disturb his tranquil, yielded heart.
He walked with God.

So far he walked with God
That earthly loss and gain were left behind
And earthly anchors had no power to bind;
He left the harbour and put out to sea,
Bound for the deeps of love's eternity,
Where souls meet God.

So close he walked with God,
He looked with God, and with that opened sight
He saw all shadows swallowed up in light.
He looked on men with God's compassionate eyes
And ministered to their infirmities

And blessed their need.

So long he walked with God

So imitate their talk – he could not say

When earthly twilight changed to Heaven's day.

Only his Master spoke, 'Earth's paths are rough

And you and I have travelled far enough.

Come home with me.'

Much loving help was given and we felt that prayer was wonderfully answered both for the very crowded funeral service at our own church in Canley and for the Thanksgiving Service on November 6th at All Souls', Langham Place in London, with more than four hundred of her family and friends from school days onwards. Different ones told of Patricia as they had known her as a schoolgirl, a young missionary, a writer, a member of the family and of the church. Then David Wakumire of Uganda spoke of what her friendship had meant to him personally and of the help she had given through the work of Global Care to many African young people. In his closing address, Simon Barrington-Ward, Bishop of Coventry, spoke of the impact Patricia's writing had had on himself and on his children and used incidents from her books to illustrate his theme of forgiveness, needed in these days as never before.

There were hundreds of letters after her death, many also telling of the influence her books had had on the writers and their children. Letters from Central Europe told of the blessing translations of Patricia's books had been when there was little or no other Christian literature available for children under the communist regime.

Others said how more recently translations of her books have been used in Russia as well as in other countries – and her films are also being shown.

Some remembered her sense of humour and joy in life, a joy she was quick to share with others. As one of her nephews said, 'A cup of tea and a sandwich with Auntie could be a celebration.' She loved to give treats to children, and one day shortly before her death she took a small boy to the woods and hid Easter eggs for him to find. When he had several in hand he looked up with shining eyes and asked, 'Do you think the Patricia bird will lay another egg?' Life with Patricia was never dull.

A doctor, well known in the town, sent a card with a picture of an open door. On the back was written, 'In memory of Patricia, whose ever "open door" led so many of us to Christ's peace and love.' In different ways so many have expressed the thought that in her they have seen something new and meaningful to them of the love and life of Jesus. Patricia would no doubt have been surprised, though we know that deep down that is what she would most have wanted.

But perhaps it was her prayer life that was the most acceptable to God. Early in the morning, after lunch and often during the night when she could not sleep, she prayed for many situations, needs and individual people. She rejoiced in answers that came swiftly and in others after long waiting; some, we believe, are still to come.

The Pace Setter

(One of the many people who was inspired by the example of Patricia has written these verses in memory of her.)

You made it look so easy, running on ahead,
Our boots are clogged with clay,
Our backs are bowed with heavy loads,
Provisions for the way.
Our eyes look furtively behind,
We want to know
Who's catching up on us,
Who's coping well,
Who's fallen by the way.
We've done our exercises,
Earned good marks in all our training days,
Watched video c – discussed a dozen ways
The right techniques to find.
You simply ran – and left us far behind.
Now you are lost to view,
And we so very far behind

Are heavy with the weight of our great loss.

Looking at you had helped us keep on course,

Now we feel lost, afraid – confused.

A mist has fallen on us – we are cold.

'O Master of the Games –

Why did you take from us our best Olympic Gold?'

As the mist clears – I see another Runner,

Not so very far away.

He turns to answer me:

'Her work is done – she was a setter of the pace.

Now look to Me and looking run your race.'

Anonymous – by request